Christus Vincit

Christus Vincit

CHRIST'S TRIUMPH
Over the Darkness of the Age

BISHOP ATHANASIUS SCHNEIDER
in conversation with DIANE MONTAGNA

Angelico Press

First published in the USA
by Angelico Press 2019
Copyright © 2019 Bishop Athanasius Schneider and Diane Montagna

All rights reserved:
No part of this book may be reproduced or transmitted,
in any form or by any means, without permission

For information, address:
Angelico Press, Ltd.
169 Monitor St.
Brooklyn, NY 11222
www.angelicopress.com

ISBN 978-1-62138-489-2 pbk
ISBN 978-1-62138-490-8 cloth
ISBN 978-1-62138-491-5 ebook

Book and cover design
by Michael Schrauzer
Cover image: "Salvator Mundi,"
by Quentin Metsys
(Wikimedia Commons)

To the Immaculate Heart of Mary,
Mother of God and Mother of the Church

To all the little ones of the Militant Church of our days, who as bishops, priests, religious, fathers and mothers of families, young people and children, have in the past decades been marginalized, humiliated, and punished for the sole reason of their unshakeable fidelity to the integrity of the faith and the liturgy of the Holy Mass.

God chose what is foolish in the world to shame the wise; God chose what is weak in the world to shame the strong; God chose what is low and despised in the world, even things that are not, to bring to nothing things that are, so that no human being might boast in the presence of God.

1 Corinthians 1:27–29

CONTENTS

INTRODUCTION xi

  I The Tribulation of Those Days 1

    1 Good Soil 3

    2 God Calls 13

    3 Athanasius 29

  II The Sun Shall Be Darkened 49

    4 Secularism and the New Dictatorship 51

    5 Islam and the Dechristianization of Europe 71

    6 Religious Indifferentism 85

  III The Moon Shall Not Give Her Light 105

    7 Loss of the Supernatural 107

    8 Vatican II 117

    9 Papal Power 137

    10 The Society of St. Pius X 147

    11 The Fourth Great Crisis 153

    12 Doctrinal Confusion 165

    13 Beyond the West 193

  IV The Stars Shall Fall from Heaven 217

    14 The Eucharist and Holy Communion 219

    15 "Reform of the Reform" 235

    16 Reform of the Clergy 261

    17 Advice for Families and Laity 279

    18 The Holy Angels 285

    19 Fatima and the "Third Secret" 299

    20 *Christus Vincit* 305

APPENDIX: Declaration of Truths 313

INTRODUCTION

For a number of years now, the interventions of Bishop Athanasius Schneider on the controversies raging in the Church have provided clarity and hope for beleaguered adherents of traditional Catholic teaching. Never before, however, has Bishop Schneider stepped back from the occasional intervention to unfold at length his own witness to "that faith given once and for all to the saints" (Jude 3) and conveyed to him by the martyrs of the Communist persecution. This book is offered as a *vade mecum* for the perplexed in these difficult times.

Christus Vincit ("Christ conquers") is the first book-length interview with Athanasius Schneider, auxiliary bishop of St. Mary in Astana, Kazakhstan. Born Antonius Schneider on April 7, 1961, in Tokmok, Kyrgyzstan (USSR), Bishop Schneider's early years were spent in the Soviet underground church, before emigrating with his family to Germany. In 1982, he entered in Austria the Canons Regular of the Holy Cross, originally founded in Coimbra. He was ordained to the priesthood on March 25, 1990. Appointed to the episcopate by Pope Benedict XVI, in June 2006, at the age of 45, he was consecrated a bishop in St. Peter's Basilica. Bishop Schneider speaks German, Russian, Portuguese, Spanish, English, Italian, and French, and reads Latin and Greek.

The bishop's ancestors were Germans who migrated from Alsace to Odessa on the Black Sea Coast of the Ukraine. At the close of the Second World War, the victorious Stalin deported the Schneider family to the Krasnokamsk gulag in the Ural Mountains. Maria Schneider, the bishop's mother, played a key role in the underground church and sheltered Blessed Oleksiy Zarytskyj, a Ukrainian priest who was martyred by the Soviet regime in 1963.

Like his fourth-century patron, St. Athanasius the Great, Bishop Schneider says things that others won't, fearlessly following St. Paul's advice: "Preach the word, be urgent in season and out of season, convince, rebuke, and exhort, be unfailing in patience and in teaching" (2 Tim 4:2). Many have been impressed by his conviction, zeal, and clarity, and his total dedication to his vocation as a Successor of the Apostles.

The aim of this volume is to allow the reader to get to know Bishop Schneider better, and to convey how he views the world, the Church, and the perennial tension between the two.

The text is established on the basis of three main interviews. The first took place over the course of several days in January 2018 in Munich, where Bishop Schneider was visiting his mother, who is in the care of a community of religious sisters. The second conversation took place in May 2018 in Rome. The third took place in March 2019, also in Rome, after the *ad limina visit* of the bishops of Central Asia.[1] Bishop Schneider then carefully reviewed the manuscript and refined and amended his reflections.

It is hard not to be struck by the bishop's love for the Eucharistic Lord, his confidence in Christ's triumph through those he calls the "little ones," and his own willingness to imitate the Good Shepherd in laying down his own life, whether by daily sacrifice or the final extremity, for the flock of Christ.

The title *Christus Vincit* was Bishop Schneider's own choice. He was drawn to this Latin phrase especially because of the hope and encouragement it gives to the faithful. It also emerged during our conversation that, for him, it captures Christ's use of "the foolish things of this world to confound the wise" (1 Cor 1:27). The subtitle, *Christ's Triumph over the Darkness of the Age*, was inspired by the verse in the Prologue of St. John's Gospel: "The light shines in the darkness, and the darkness has not overcome it" (Jn 1:5). As will become clear, this verse captures the arc of the narrative and the spirit of hope that imbues the text.

The book is divided into four parts, each with a title taken from chapter 24, verse 29 of St. Matthew's Gospel. In his inaugural encyclical *E Supremi*, St. Pius X remarked that so serious was the gathering storm of error at the beginning of the twentieth century that he would not be surprised to hear that the Antichrist was already on this earth. The same pope would go on to describe Modernism as the synthesis of all heresies and the herald of the end time. The Church Fathers do not fail to give

---

1 An *ad limina* visit, or more fully *ad limina apostolorum*, means the obligation, on the part of residential diocesan bishops and other prelates with territorial jurisdiction, to visit the thresholds (*limina*), i.e., tombs of the Apostles, Saints Peter and Paul, and of meeting the pope to report on the state of their dioceses. It is a formal trip usually made together by all bishops from a single region or Catholic bishops' conference to discuss with the Pope issues specific to their region.

us a spiritual interpretation of the famous words of Our Lord: "Immediately after the tribulation of those days the sun will be darkened, and the moon will not give its light, and the stars will fall from heaven, and the powers of the heavens will be shaken" (Mt 24:29). The tribulation, St. Augustine tells us, will precede the great falling away. "These things shall be 'after the tribulation of those days,' not because they shall happen when the whole persecution is overpast, but because the tribulation shall be first, that the falling away may come after" (*Ep.* 199, 39).

The "Sun," Christ, will be obscured in the hearts of men, and the "Moon," the Church, will no longer win men's hearts by her beauty. "In that ungoverned fury of wicked persecutors, the Church shall not be seen." The "stars," members of the Church who seemed reliable touchstones of orthodoxy, will fall from the true faith and the moral life. "Many, who seemed to be shining in God's grace, shall give way to their persecutors, and shall fall, and even the stoutest believers shall be shaken," St. Augustine tells us. And yet, like the fall of the rebel angels from heaven, it is a sign of the coming triumph of Christ (Lk 10:18).

Whether Our Lord's words do refer to our days or not, their resonances in the experience of Bishop Athanasius Schneider and so many others are undeniable, and his insights into the apocalyptic challenges facing Christ's flock in these days count as essential reading for those truly alive to the signs of the times.

Finally, I wish to offer my heartfelt thanks to all those who in any way helped with this book. God knows who they are and, in His love, will surely reward them. Over the course of this work, I have repeatedly been reminded of God the Father's words to St. Catherine of Siena in the spiritual classic, *The Dialogue of Divine Providence*: "Daughter, I could easily have created men possessed of all that they should need both for body and soul, but I wish that one should have need of the other, and that they should be My ministers to administer the graces and the gifts that they have received from Me."

Diane Montagna
September 3, 2019
Feasts of St. Pius X and St. Gregory the Great

I

The Tribulation of Those Days

I

Good Soil

Your Excellency, you are the auxiliary bishop of Kazakhstan and yet you have a German name, which points to a very interesting family history—one that encompasses the persecution and tribulation these two countries experienced. You, too, have personally suffered from the effects of this persecution. Please tell us about your family history.

It is a story that dates back centuries. I belong to those Germans who are called the Germans of Russia (*Russlanddeutsche*), who were farmers in the Russian Empire in two large settlements of German people; they had been invited by the Tsars. They were farmers who cultivated the land. The first group was the so-called Volga Germans, who had come already in the second part of the eighteenth century, especially under the Empress Catherine the Great, who was German and invited them to settle on the Volga River. The second group, the so-called Black Sea Germans, came later in 1809–10 and settled on the shore of the Black Sea. I belong to this latter group. They came from southwest Germany and my ancestors specifically—I know them all by name going back two hundred years—came from Alsace-Lorraine. This area was German-speaking but sometimes belonged to France, sometimes to Germany. My ancestors on both sides came from villages in northern Alsace, north of Strasbourg.

How did you learn all the names of your ancestors?

There was a book published about sixty years ago by a German historian, who was also born in Russia. It contained all the names of those people, where they came from, where they were settled, and so on. I know my grandmothers, and they knew their grandmothers. In this historical book, I learned the family names of those who had immigrated, and so I was able to make the connection. They were all Alsatian Germans on both sides of my family, and they established German villages there with German names. My mother's village close to Odessa, for

3

example, was called Elsaß—and then there are villages with the names Straßburg, Karlsruhe, Mannheim, and so on. The German culture was transplanted there and those German farmers—thanks be to God—were deeply Catholic. Their faith was simple but very deep; they passed on the faith to us. In these German villages they built beautiful churches with all the necessary furnishings. They also had their own German priests and spoke only their German dialects in the villages. A diocese was even erected by the pope in the nineteenth century for these Germans—Tiraspol was the name—and it was for all the Germans in South Ukraine and on the Volga River. The bishop resided in a town called Saratov on the Volga River, and there was a cathedral and seminary there until the time of the Communists, so they had their own clergy.

Their bishop was also German, chosen from among their own people?

Yes—from among their own people. The last bishop, Aloysius Kessler, died an exile in Germany after the Communists expelled him in 1922. When Communism began, there were over two hundred German priests from this diocese. What's beautiful is that no one apostatized. Not one. Almost all of the two hundred priests from the diocese, with the exception of a few priests, were killed or imprisoned. So, there was a very strong and very deep Catholicism in those German villages. I knew my grandmothers, and I am so thankful to God that they and my parents transmitted the Catholic faith to me. They lived there until the Second World War. The Communists imprisoned the priests in the 1920s and 1930s and closed the churches. Many of the beautiful churches were destroyed or converted into dance-halls and stables or were used for other similar purposes. The horrible years were in Stalin's time from 1936 to 1938, which are called the Dark Years, the terror years, though Stalin cynically called these years the time of purification. It was a purgation, a "cleansing," Stalin said. The Communists killed primarily priests, wealthy people, and intellectuals, all of whom were seen as potential enemies. There was a genocide, and what's incredible is that history is almost silent about this. In these two years, Stalin killed millions upon millions of innocent people—his own people, not foreigners. It is a proven historical fact.

Stalin's military carried out this genocide against his own people?

Yes. My grandfather from my father's side was also a victim because he owned land; it was reason enough for him to make their list.

Was he exiled? Killed?

He was killed. He was a young man, twenty-seven years old — Sebastian
Schneider — and my grandmother was made a widow at twenty-five, with
two little children. My father was seven and his brother was two years old.
The Communists came in the night, with a vehicle already filled with men
waiting to be shot, and they took him away. The men were then brought
to a central place and killed there. So, he was taken in the night and my
grandmother was running after him to protect him. When he was already
on the truck, he said to my grandmother, whose name was Perpetua, in
his simple German dialect: "Perpetua, remain as you are!" (*Perpetua, bleib
wie du bist!*). My grandmother interpreted this as him saying not to marry
again — to remain as she is. She instantly understood his words in this way.

St. Paul tells widows "it is better to remain as you are" (cf. 1 Cor 7:8).

Yes, "as you are." That is what he said to her. But in her later years,
grandmother said to me that he wanted to tell her that she had to remain
the faithful Catholic that she was. She became a widow at twenty-five
years old and lived seventy-four years as a widow.

Like the prophetess Anna (cf. Lk 2:36)...

She lived to ninety-nine and died on her birthday in Germany, where
she lived with my uncle, my father's younger brother. And I buried her.
She was still alive when I became bishop and she was still very sharp.
Rarely in my life have I seen someone who prayed so much. It was incredible. She prayed almost day and night.

*How did you perceive that? Was it because she had the Rosary constantly
in her hands?*

Yes, the Rosary. She had a thick old prayer book that she prayed with,
and she would tell us: "Today I woke up at four o'clock in the morning
and just started to pray." We all knew that she woke up very early. She
would pray at least three hours in the morning. Then she did her work,
and then she stopped and prayed an hour. Then in the afternoon, and
in the evening, she prayed three hours.

A life of domestic monasticism...

Yes! We saw this. With her books, she prayed in a simple way: litanies,
novenas, all the rosaries, and so on. And so *she lived always in the presence*

of God. When I was a child, she always gave me a blessing as grandmothers do for their grandchildren, making a small cross on my forehead. After my episcopal consecration in 2006, I visited her. She saw me for the first time as a bishop and asked me to give her the episcopal blessing. I blessed her and then I said, "Now, grandmother, you have to bless me." She was sitting (she couldn't walk well). I knelt down before her and then she spoke a word, the likes of which she had never said before — this was not her style, as she was a very simple woman with only two or three years of schooling. When I knelt down, she became very solemn and made a cross, not like how she had done when I was a child, but a really big cross over me like a priest, very solemnly, and she said, "*Mit Gott und für Gott sende ich dich in die Welt.*" "With God and for God, I send you into the world." I wrote this in my Breviary. I consider it so precious, this blessing — it's a great and special gift of God to have received this blessing from my grandmother, who lived seventy-four years as a widow.

Returning to the story of your grandfather and his apprehension by the Communists, did the townspeople like your grandmother know that their husbands, fathers, and sons were being taken away to be executed?

Yes, of course. A couple of weeks later, the police came to check her house. She had holy pictures everywhere on the walls, which was forbidden during this time of "purging" — when people had to live according to the new Communist lifestyle. The police entered and asked her: "Why do you have these pictures? You know it is not permitted. You have to take down these pictures." She did not obey the order, so the policeman went up to the wall and wanted himself to rip them off the wall. At that moment, she shouted at the policeman in a loud voice: "You did not put that picture up on the wall and you do not have the right to take it down!" The policeman was shocked, taken aback. At that moment, he did not touch the image and quietly left the house. In this time of terror everyone was afraid. It was a miracle, I think, because God protects the widows and their little ones. Furthermore, it was not common for my grandmother to shout, because she was by nature a timid person, and she never spoke loudly. Never in my life did I hear her shout loudly, she was very mild.

It sounds like the casting out of a demon.

Yes. Then, some years later, she had to work in the "kolkhoz" system — which was a Communist abbreviation for "collective economy" in the village, where nothing belongs to you, and you have to work in the fields — and she was expected to work on Sunday. She refused, even though her husband was killed and she herself was a target of the tyrannical authorities. The chief commanded her: "You have to work on Sundays in this kolkhoz!" Whereupon she answered: "You can kill me because I will not work on Sundays." And then they left her in peace. I consider this the second miracle. This is an example of the soil from which I was born.

What about the other side of your family?

My grandmother on my mother's side was also a very pious woman. My grandfather from my mother's side was killed by a bomb in his house during the Second World War. My mother's parents were farmers and had seven children. My grandfather went to the stable where the cows were. He always went with his little son, the brother of my mother, but this time he said, "I'll go alone." He felt something. "I'll go alone, and you stay here," he said. So he went out to the stable, and then the German military flew a plane overhead and dropped a bomb on the stable and he was killed instantly. My grandmother and all her children were watching. It was very traumatic for them. She was alone with seven children on the farm. It was very small — because it was kolkhoz — and the people said that the children would die because at the time there was no food. But God helped, and they all survived.

During the Second World War, the German army occupied this part of Ukraine. When they drew back, they evacuated all of these Germans to East Germany, close to Berlin — about three-hundred thousand people.

How were they transported back?

First by horse-drawn carriages or on foot to Romania, and then by train to Berlin. Then, when the Russian Army occupied Berlin — they were not in Berlin but settled close to Berlin — they arrested all of these Germans from Russia and brought them back for forced labor in railway trains used for cattle transport. They were relocated to several places.

Transported like those who were taken away to concentration camps?

Exactly. It was the same form of transportation. One part went to Siberia; one part went to Kazakhstan; one part to the Ural Mountains. My mother and father went to the Ural Mountains.

And your grandmothers?

They were together with the whole family. They were taken there.

How old was your mother at the time?

She was almost fourteen and my father was sixteen: they were teenagers. Twenty percent of the people died on the way — of hunger, disease, and the cold. My father's train (he was not in the same train with my mother, they hadn't met yet) was brought directly into the forest. In the Ural Mountains there are very wide rivers and they were brought directly to the forest by tugboats. There, they had to cut trees, large trees, by hand. People died of this work. It was inhuman work.

How cold was it?

Oftentimes in the winter it was forty degrees below zero Celsius.

How did they survive?

Many people died! They froze to death. It's a miracle that my family survived. They were brought there into the forest, and during the day some people always died because they had very little food and had to work the entire day. The extraordinarily hard work exhausted many persons. They would fall in the snow and then they froze to death.

No one knew whether he would return in the evening alive. The exiles were all Germans. Some were Catholic, others Lutheran. When they were walking in the morning in the snow to their work, the German Catholics would begin to pray the Rosary in a loud voice — and the Lutherans joined them. The Lutherans joined because in the presence of death, even Lutherans invoke Our Lady. As for my mother, she was brought to the German ghetto in a town where they had to remain and were under control. There was no free movement. They had to live in barracks, entire families, and they had no beds and so had to sleep on the floor.

Did the whole family have to work? Or just the men?

The women also. My mother had to work when she turned sixteen. Everyone had to work once they were sixteen, even the girls.

Cutting down trees in the Ural Mountains?

She was in the city along the river and her task was to take big tree trunks from the river with a rope — which was heavy work for a man — and she had to do this at sixteen years old. Sometimes the water was frozen, and she had to carry these trees through the snow, working outside in temperatures sometimes thirty to forty degrees below zero, having had only three pieces of bread to eat for the entire day, no more. In the morning, her mother made her these pieces of bread with butter and nothing else. She had these in her pockets and during work the bread froze! They had only thirty minutes of a break all day and she would have to warm up the bread with her breath in order to eat it. They had so little food. There were seven children, she was in the middle, and there were three younger children. And she also had to take care of them.

Would there have been any priests in that area?

Unfortunately, they had to go ten years, more or less, with no priests. But the families transmitted the faith, and every day they prayed. For example, in Lent, on Fridays in the evening after this hard work, neighboring families came together and prayed the Stations of the Cross in a room. Even after an exhausting day, they prayed the Stations of the Cross in Lent. And then priests came secretly. In particular, there was a Ukrainian priest in exile in Karaganda, Blessed Fr. Oleksiy (Alexij) Zarytskyj, who travelled a distance of two thousand kilometers to the Ural Mountains.

Why was he in Karaganda?

It was a gulag in Kazakhstan, one of the most infamous concentration camps in the Soviet Union. He was there in the gulag and then was freed and put under a kind of house arrest. He was not allowed to move beyond the city limits but nevertheless he escaped and traveled to see Catholics, knowing that if he were found, he would be put back in the gulag. He came to my parents in the Ural Mountains, secretly. He was such a holy man. My father and my mother both always talked to us about Blessed Father Oleksiy Zarytskyj. Both of them said that they had never in their lives met such a holy priest. He really gave himself totally. At night he heard confessions, because they were ten years without a priest. He would celebrate Mass and give Holy Communion and so on. Sometimes he would go two days without eating, because people came continuously — thousands of Germans who were Catholics. They came secretly to confess.

Was he ever caught?

Once, Father Oleksiy began to celebrate the Holy Mass and suddenly a voice cried out, "The police are coming!" My mother, who was attending the Mass, said to the priest, "Father, I can hide you; let's flee!" My mother led the priest into a house outside the German ghetto and hid him in a room, also bringing him something to eat, and said: "Father, now you can finally eat and rest a bit; and when it gets dark, we will flee to a nearby city." Father Oleksiy was sad, because, though all had made their confessions, they could not receive Holy Communion; the Holy Mass, which had just begun, had been interrupted by the police raid. My mother said: "Father, all the faithful will make a Spiritual Communion with great faith and much devotion, and we hope that you will be able to return to give us Holy Communion."

When evening came, preparations were made for his escape. My mother left my eldest brother, Josef, who was two years old, and my eldest sister, Maria, who was just six months, with my grandmother. They called on Pulcheria Koch, my father's aunt. The two women took Father Oleksiy and led him twelve kilometers through the forest, in the snow and cold, in 30 degrees below zero weather. When they arrived at the little train station, they bought a ticket for Father Oleksiy and sat with him in the waiting room; the train was not due for an hour. Suddenly, the door opened. A policeman entered and spoke directly to Father Oleksiy: "Where are you heading?" The priest was not able to respond, out of fear — not for his own life, but for the life and fate of my mother. My mother responded to the policeman: "This is our friend, and we are accompanying him. Look, here is his ticket," and she handed the ticket over to the policeman. The policeman, looking at the ticket, told the priest: "Please do not enter the last car, because it will be dislodged from the rest of the train at the next station. Have a good trip!" The policeman exited the waiting room. Father Oleksiy looked at my mother and said, "God has sent us an angel! I will never forget what you have done for me. If God will permit it, I will return to give all of you Holy Communion, and in my every Mass I will pray for you and your children."

So your parents were married before they met Fr. Oleksiy. How did your parents meet?

It's an interesting story. They married in 1954. My maternal grandmother — who had five daughters and two sons — said, "My daughters, don't be worried about your future husbands. God has already deter-mined a husband for each one of you. You have only to pray." My grandmother Melania Trautmann told her sons and daughters that they would not find their future spouses at dancing parties. She did not consider it appropriate for a Catholic to look for a future spouse at dancing parties, so the children obeyed. My parents met during the time they had to work in the Ural Mountains. And so, Joseph and Mary — my father is Joseph and my mother is Mary — married on May 31, the last day of the month of Our Lady, in 1954. My parents first met Blessed Fr. Oleksiy one year later. He often came to my parents and was their confessor.

Who celebrated the marriage of your parents?

They were married according to Church law. When there is no priest for one month, people can still marry.

It requires their mutual consent . . .

Yes, and witnesses. They said it was very beautiful. There was an older lady who took a book, and they had to pronounce their marriage vows as in Church, before two witnesses. My parents pronounced their marriage vows exactly as was written in the prayer book in German. So they did not have to be married again.

In 1960, they moved to Kyrgyzstan, where there is better weather and climate. I was born there on April 7, 1961. We were four children — my older brother, Joseph; then came Maria, my sister; and then my sister, Erica, and I am the youngest. Then Blessed Fr. Oleksiy came to Kyr-gyzstan, secretly, and he found our house and celebrated a secret Mass. I was one year old.

Who baptized you?

Now, this is a very nice story. I was already baptized and was one year old when Blessed Fr. Oleksiy came to celebrate Mass at our home. He celebrated the Mass secretly, and my mother put me in the cradle to the side of where Father was celebrating. I became an altar boy at one year old! There were no priests in Kyrgyzstan, and only very rarely would a priest come secretly. My mother could not leave me without baptism — it was impossible for her. So, one week after my birth, she baptized me herself because she knew her catechism well, and she knew that it was possible.

Your family was very well formed in the faith.

As I said earlier, they read the catechism even during forced labor. They were always repeating the basic contents of their good old German catechism and they had written down the most important Catholic truths.

To baptize me, my mother took a prayer book, in which the baptismal formula was written, and water. I was one week old, and my father was present. She spoke the words as she poured the water over me, and when she finished, she looked up at my father and asked, "Did I do this correctly?" And my father said, "I don't know." And then she said, "Well, I have to repeat it." And she repeated the entire ceremony. Again, she poured the water over me, pronouncing the words, and then she felt reassured that it had been done properly. I was baptized Antonius, after St. Anthony of Padua. Six months later, a Jesuit priest, Fr. Antonius Šeškevičius, came from Lithuania and told all the German mothers to bring the babies who had not been baptized by a priest because he wanted to make sure we were baptized. My mother brought me to him and I was "baptized" for the third time. So, I have no doubt about the validity of my baptism!

2

God Calls

You were the youngest child. I imagine you were very loved...

I think so, yes. Well, it is the grace of God, I think, because I was the last one and I never in my life had psychological problems. I believe this is because I received so much love from both parents in a very harmonious marriage — this is what preserves a child from serious psychological problems later in life — and, then, of course, everyone in the family had a strong Catholic faith. I grew up in a very harmonious home. My father didn't even smoke! And he was very dedicated to us.

And he loved your mother very much...

Yes, very much. He was so good.

Your sister has said that you all felt as children that "the heart of our parents was in the Eucharist." [1]

Both my parents gave us children an example of a life according to the Catholic faith. I can say that the heart of my parents was in the Eucharist. They taught us a deep love and veneration towards the Holy Eucharist. Even into their old age they insisted on receiving Holy Communion always kneeling. When my father was no longer able to kneel because of knee problems, he regretted that he was constrained to receive Holy Communion standing.

You were raised in good soil...

Exactly. Earlier I spoke of my grandmothers, both of whom provided that good soil. There is something very interesting about my great-grandparents: my maternal great-grandmother was considered the most pious woman in the village; her name was Gertrude Volk. All spoke well of her. She was the most pious woman of the village, really pious.

1   Edward Pentin, "How Bishop Athanasius Schneider Became a Leading Voice for Catholic Truth," *National Catholic Register*, January 17, 2018.

What does "pious" mean for you?

For me, to be "pious" is to live the faith very deeply, consciously, faithfully, with an intense practice of your faith. In the Bible, the word is "just." She went to Mass every day, she lived according to the commandments of God, she was kind, she was *just*. She was the most pious and observant person in the village. At the same time — because my parents were from different villages, and they met only in the camps in the Ural Mountains — in my father's village, his grandfather Joseph Schneider was the most pious man in the village. Really.

God worked in a special way through your family.

Yes, yes. Another example: my great-grandfather Joseph Schneider and my grandfather Bernhard Trautmann always served Mass for the priests despite the danger, because that was already during the time of persecution. It was the Latin Mass.

What are your fondest memories from your childhood?

One of my fondest memories from childhood were our family prayers on Sundays.

How old were you at the time? And what do you remember?

I was eight years old in Kyrgyzstan and I remember it very well. On Sundays, we closed all the doors, drew the curtains, and knelt down — my parents with the four children — and we sanctified the day of the Lord because there was no priest, no Mass. We had to sanctify the day of the Lord, so in the morning we prayed the Rosary, a litany, prayers, and then we made our Spiritual Communion, to unite ourselves spiritually with the Mass which was being celebrated in some place at that time, at which we could not assist except in spirit. And we would invite the Lord to visit us and we made the Act of Contrition. It was our Sunday worship as a family, in the house, in the domestic church. Then, sometimes, a priest secretly came, and it was always a very deep and silent joy.

Would he come to your home?

The priests came to different houses: to my uncle's and to others. We went to my uncle and then assisted at Mass and it was all very quiet. I remember that, when I was a child, when the priest was there, we all had to speak in a low voice. I was a child of eight years old, I could not

have known what the catacombs were, but now I realize it really was a
catacomb atmosphere.

A boy of eight is able to take all of that in . . .

It's all right before my eyes, these Masses: the secret Mass, with the
priest, a very silent solemnity. We confessed, we assisted at Holy Mass, and
then the priest had to flee. We lived by the fruits of this Mass until the
next time a priest came. And this gave us the strength to remain faithful
to the Catholic faith in the midst of atheist Communist propaganda.

How often would a priest come?

It depended. Sometimes every six months, sometimes once a year. It
always depended on the priests. They were sometimes in prison, sometimes under house arrest, so it was a very hard time. But this was, for
me, one of the deepest experiences in my life. Sunday worship in the
family and the Spiritual Communions. There were some years when we
went without Holy Communion. And today, the so-called divorced and
remarried, who are living objectively against the commandment of God,
against the indissolubility of marriage . . . priests and bishops have asked
for them to receive Communion. It would be better for those couples
if they lived without Communion, acknowledging their situation with
humility. But this is only a side note on another theme.

What else comes to mind about your childhood?

Christmas very often comes to mind. Christmas was a day of work
and school, so we had to celebrate at nighttime on Christmas Eve. As
there were a lot of German Catholics in our town in Kyrgyzstan, my
parents always organized the prayers, the meeting to celebrate Christmas
Eve, though it was forbidden.

How would this be organized? Was your family ever caught?

On Christmas Eve all the Germans came to our house. I remember
as a child, our house was full — some were even standing outside — and
we were singing all the beautiful Christmas songs, all in German. The
one which I most loved as a seven or eight-year-old child, and sang the
next day, was *Adeste fideles* in German — "*Kommt, lasset uns anbeten*"
("O Come, All Ye Faithful"). I would sing this. It was this song that
impressed me the most.

How did we manage this? It was formally forbidden to organize meetings, but our best friend, a Russian named Anatoly, who was one of the chief policemen of the city, lived across the street from our house. He had no children and we, the four children, were fortunate because he loved us so much. We considered him our uncle, and he was a good friend of my father. He would come over to the house, and they played chess together. (We never played cards in my family. It was forbidden! My parents considered it inappropriate for a Catholic to play cards, as did my grandparents. We had chess and checkers and other beautiful games.)

One evening, my father said to Anatoly, "You know, we are Catholics, we have Christmas this night, and we have to pray together." Anatoly said to him, "It is forbidden, but I will guarantee that tonight no policeman will come. I will guarantee it for you." And so, he protected us. In this way, we could celebrate Christmas Eve in quiet and calm.

Then, in 1969, we moved from Kyrgyzstan to Estonia. I was eight years old.

Why Estonia?

My parents' aim in going to Estonia was to immigrate more easily to Germany. My father had experienced the Communist regime and he did not like the regime, and not only because they killed his father. He therefore said to us children, "You are Germans and Catholics. I do not want you to grow up to become Communists." We spoke only German at home. In the street and in school, of course, we spoke Russian. But my parents never spoke Russian with us, even though they knew the Russian language because they had to work.

So, my father wanted to immigrate to Germany to maintain a German identity for us, and the Catholic faith, so that we would not lose the faith when we grew up. It was his chief concern. Therefore, he wanted to escape and distance us from the Communists. Estonia was more Western — at least it was closer to the Western border of the Soviet Union. He had heard that the local authorities there were more open to allowing Germans to emigrate to Germany.

So we moved to Estonia. The first thing my parents did was to begin looking for a Catholic church. They heard that 100 kilometers away, in the town Tartu, in the center of Estonia, there was a Catholic church. We lived in the south of Estonia on the border with Latvia.

What was the town called?

Our town was called Valga; it was on the border. There were twin cities: Valga and Valka — Valka is Latvian and Valga is the Estonian town. During Soviet times it was practically one city, but the people spoke different languages: Latvian and Estonian. But Russian was of course the common language.

My parents went to look for the Catholic church; they were searching almost the entire day and finally found it. It was an old Catholic church in the Gothic style, which the government had allowed to remain open, and there was a priest there. They came home and said to us, "Oh, children, we are so happy! We have a church so close to us. Only 100 kilometers!" I remember this. "So close to us. Only 100 kilometers!" We were all so happy.

How would your family travel to church on Sundays?

We always went by train. We would leave in the morning at six o'clock, when it was dark. In those times, we were not yet all adults, and it was not permitted for minors to go to Church.

This is surprising: minors were not allowed to go to Mass?

They were not allowed, and the boys were not allowed to serve Mass. We went in the morning by train while it was still dark, and then we came back at night, once evening had fallen and again it was dark. This is also one of the most beautiful memories of my life, these Sunday Mass trips. I remember them so well.

Did other families have such a long distance to travel?

We had the longest distance to travel. All the other faithful who came to Mass were close to the city. It was such a beautiful Gothic church. It was completely traditional, and the liturgical reform had not yet been implemented, even though it was 1969 or 1970 so — after the Second Vatican Council. And there was a holy priest, a Capuchin priest from Latvia, Fr. Janis Pavlovskis. He had spent seven years during the Stalinist time in the Karaganda gulag in Kazakhstan. When he was released, he went first to Latvia and then to Estonia.

Your Excellency, before we go on: you have mentioned the Karaganda gulag both in reference to Blessed Fr. Oleksiy Zarytskyj and now in regard to

Fr. Janis Pavlovskis. In 1973, the Russian writer and historian Aleksandr Solzhenitsyn published his three-volume work, The Gulag Archipelago, *in which he chronicled the horrors prisoners faced in the Karaganda forced labor camps. It is said that Hitler looked to Stalin's Karaganda gulag as a model for his own concentration camps. Can you tell us what prisoners faced in the Karaganda gulag under the Soviet Communist regime? How many people died there? How many priests?*

The Karaganda gulag with the portmanteau "Karlag" was part of the "Gulag." The "Gulag," an abbreviation for "Glávnoye Upravléniye Ispravítelno-trudovykh Lageréy" (Russian for: "Chief Administration of Corrective Labor Camps"), was the government agency in charge of the Soviet forced labor camp system that was set up under Vladimir Lenin and reached its peak during Joseph Stalin's rule from the 1930s to the 1950s. It was called the "Slave State." The Karaganda gulag covered an area roughly equivalent to today's France. In the twenty-eight years of its existence (1931–1959), over one million people passed through the Karlag. The first to be subjected to repression were priests, religious ministers, intellectuals, nobility, officers, and peasants. They were labelled "enemies of the people" ("public enemies"). They were transported in cattle trucks from all over the Soviet Union to Kazakhstan. There, what awaited them was grueling hard labor, torture, famine, and death.

Several hundred priests and religious died in the Karlag. Today, in the center of this former hell, in the village of Dolinka, near the city of Karaganda, stands the Museum of the Memory of Victims of Political Repression. In 1997, in order to perpetuate the memory of the victims, the first President of Kazakhstan, Nursultan Nazarbayev, officially established May 31 as the annual Day of Remembrance for the Victims of Political Repression. Events dedicated to this day are held every year in Kazakhstan. On this day the government asks representatives of the main religions to lead prayers for the souls of the victims of the Karlag. The older people who experienced and still remember the terrible times of repression say that the soil around Karaganda is soaked with the tears and blood of countless innocent persons. Once the late Russian Orthodox Patriarch of Moscow, Alexij, when visiting Karaganda, said that the area of Karaganda can symbolically be described as an "anti-mension"—a kind of "corporal" in the Byzantine Rite, in which are sewn the relics of martyrs.

And already in your early years, you met two priests who were imprisoned in Karaganda?

Yes, Blessed Fr. Oleksiy Zarytskyj was the first. He died in 1963 in the Gulag. The parish priest in Estonia, in Tartu, Fr. Janis Pavlovskis, who had also been imprisoned there, was a holy man. He radiated holiness. He was silent, discreet, very educated, very kind. Not a cold detachment but a very noble detachment, with real goodness. And so he very much impressed me, his face and his calm. He heard my first confession when I was 10 years old and gave me my First Holy Communion. My mother prepared me for First Holy Communion, she was my catechist. She gave me good preparation.

What do you remember about your First Holy Communion?

My First Holy Communion was so beautiful. The preparation was so good. For my first confession, the holy priest showed me how I had to confess, where I had to go, where I had to kneel down. He said, "this is a confessional"; "here I will sit"; "you will go here, you will kneel there," with so much kindness. I was a child, and one has to show children these things very concretely.

When I received my First Holy Communion, there was a group of children, and the priest arranged everything in a very beautiful way. With a candle in hand, we went through the Communion rail to the high altar, to the highest step, and there we received Holy Communion from the high altar, kneeling, as the deacon kneels on the top step: there I received my First Holy Communion. It was so beautiful for me — and unforgettable.

My mother and the priest gave us a beautiful instruction. They said, "You will receive your Savior and God in this little Host. And He is living there." And this I remember: "He is living. Be careful, He is living, and this is your Lord!" Since then, it has always been so for me: He is living there! I thought, when I received the Lord, *He is living and He is entering into me*. For me, the Host is so holy because there is my God, as both my mother and the priest had told me.

On Sundays, once the Mass was over, how would your family spend the rest of the day?

Since we had to wait until night for the train, the priest said to my parents: "Because you are the farthest away, come to my room and spend your time there, so as not to sit in the railway station." So we went there after Mass. There was a little path between the church and the house, not so far, just a little path, and in this house the priest had only one room. No apartment (there were other people living in the house), only one room, a little one. In this room, our time was spent after Mass. We could make tea, a drink, eat something, and sit, read, and talk. Then we would slowly make our way to the railway station.

While we were in the room of this holy priest, he was in church speaking with people or visiting someone and we could be alone as a family.

What do you remember about this little room?

What impressed me when I came into this room as a boy was that it was full of books. He was a very educated and learned man. He wrote a Catholic catechism in Russian, a very good and traditional one, and a very good book on the history of the Church. He had books, books, books. It impressed me. And then, there was a book I remember which impressed me so much. He said to us children, "You can look at it. This is a book from Rome, with pictures." There was a picture of the catacombs. I asked him, "What is this?" "They are the catacombs," he said. And I asked, "What are catacombs?" He responded, "They were hiding places, where the first Christians had to hide when there were persecutions, and sometimes they were killed in these places." This phrase impressed me, and I cherished it in my soul.

Can you say more...

When he said this to me and my siblings, it impressed me with the feeling of admiration for people who are killed because of their faith. For me, it was very sublime. Something noble. I felt this in my soul as a boy.

Did you know at this point any of your own family's history and what they had suffered?

No, but the information about the catacombs impressed me.

Do you have any particularly vivid memories from this time?

I will tell you a rare episode, which is in my living memory and is still so fresh. I was ten years old. I think it was after my First Holy Communion in Tartu and usually we went after Mass along this little path to the house where the priest was living, and since I was the youngest I went with my mother. As children do, we were asking many questions out of curiosity.

I had the idea to ask my mother how one can become a priest, only out of curiosity. In that moment I had neither the plan nor the intention of becoming a priest. I asked because Fr. Pavlovskis impressed me and I wondered how one can become a priest. Then my mother stopped and said to me, "In order to become a priest, it is necessary that God calls." She said nothing more. These words are so fresh in my memory.

I can go to Estonia and find the exact spot on the path where I asked my mother how one can become a priest. In fact, in 2016, I was in Tartu and I celebrated the traditional Mass in that church, at the high altar, where I had received my First Holy Communion.[2] When I went out after Holy Mass, the first thing I did was to go to the point of the path where I spoke with my mother about the priestly vocation. I stopped there and thanked God for my vocation to the priesthood. When my mother said to me, "it is necessary that God calls," I could not understand these words, I was ten years old. "What does this mean, that God calls?," I thought to myself. I remember that during that conversation with my mother I looked up to heaven, and in my childish mind I was thinking that a call would now come to my ears, to call me, since my mother said to me "it is necessary that God calls." And there came no voice from heaven. Therefore, it was so strange for me; I could not understand these words.

Were you sad?

No, I just could not understand. It was for me incomprehensible that no voice came from heaven. Never again would I ask anyone how to become a priest — but I became a priest. And I never spoke with my mother or my father about the priesthood. But this answer was always so fresh in my memory. "It is necessary that God calls."

Your family then emigrated to Germany. How old were you at the time?

When we settled in Germany, I was twelve and a half years old. As we left for Germany, Fr. Pavlovskis blessed us and then he said to us these words, which I will never forget: "When you go to Germany, be careful.

---

2 In 1977, Fr. Pavloskis went to Kazakhstan and built a chapel there and took care of the Catholics in the city of Taras in southern Kazakhstan. In 1991 he went to Riga, in Latvia, and was the parish priest at the Church of St. Albert. He died in Riga in 2000. When Estonia became independent in 1991, Catholic missionary priests came from abroad and unfortunately put a table for celebration *versus populum* in that church. — *AS*

There are some churches where Communion is given in the hand." When we heard this, we looked at one another, and my mother and father said spontaneously, "Horrible!" Really, we could not imagine how the Holy of Holies, the Living God, could be taken in the hand. That was for me inconceivable, really. He said to us, "Please, don't go to these churches." And we promised to do as he instructed.

What happened when you arrived in Germany?

When we came to Germany, to a little Catholic town in southwest Germany, there were three churches there. We went to the first church and we did not go to Communion because we had just come from a long trip. We could not go to Communion; we had to prepare ourselves with confession. In Estonia, we observed the custom of going to confession every month, even when we had not fallen into mortal sin, because we felt it was necessary to confess every month to receive Holy Communion worthily.

So, on the first Sunday after our arrival in Germany we did not receive Holy Communion, and we could observe the scene of the distribution of Communion. It was horrible for us: almost all of the people received Communion in the hand. And it was given quickly, with people standing in a line, like in a cafeteria.

What year would this have been?

The end of 1973. When we arrived home after Mass, I told my mother "Oh, Mamma, today Mass was like getting candies in school." Because I remembered once in school when we received candies: we had to stand in a line and they gave us candies in the hand. And so that was the parallel I made. My mother said, "We will never go to this church again."

The next Sunday, at the next church, it was the same as at the first church. And at the third church, it was the same situation. When we came home, my mother was so sad. She looked at us, and was crying, and said, "Oh my children, I don't understand, I cannot understand! How can people treat Our Lord in this way? How are people able to treat Our Lord in this way..." This experience motivated me to write my book *Dominus Est* on Holy Communion — this painful, unforgettable situation when we came to Germany and my mother was crying over the situation of the distribution of Holy Communion in the hand.

As a boy, you maintained a great reverence for the Holy Mass and the Blessed Sacrament. When did you receive your vocation to the priesthood?

I started to serve Mass (because in the Soviet Union, children could not serve Mass) and after the first Mass, I felt in my soul that I had to become a priest. I cannot describe this. I felt this in my soul, and then I started to remember the words of my mother: "It is necessary that God calls." Since then, I have never had a doubt about my vocation. Never. The conviction was so deep. I was so convinced in my soul that I had no need to speak with anyone about the priesthood. I could not imagine anything other than being a priest. It was so clear for me and in some way also it was so personal.

What was your education like in Germany once your family settled there?

I spent the next two years in a boarding school with religious priests.

What priests were they?

The Pallottine Fathers. They were quite liberal.

And so why were you there?

Because I came from a Russian school. And the German government offered the boys who came from the Soviet Union the possibility of attending a kind of preparatory school for two years, to make it easier to enter a German school.

You had to study for these two years then in order to prepare to enter the "Gymnasium"?

Yes, because it was a different kind of school system. I also had to improve my German, because I spoke German, but in dialect. I had to speak correctly, in literary German (*Hochdeutsch*), so this preparation helped me.

Did you have to live there?

Yes, for almost two years.

How old were you?

Thirteen and fourteen. I was there for two years with other boys who all came from Communist countries: Poland, Romania or the Soviet Union. The priests didn't wear the cassock or their religious habit.

This was a shock for me. I was very straightforward and asked a priest, "Father, why aren't you wearing the cassock?" And he answered, "You, little chap, should not instruct me!"

And their manner of celebrating Mass?

The Mass was celebrated in a manner I had never known. "Why do you celebrate the Mass in this way? In the Soviet Union, we had a very solemn and pious Mass," I would ask the priests. And they made some jokes. I spoke without any anxiety. A child says what he is thinking. I was convinced that I had to be a priest, and I went to Holy Mass every day — the only one in the school who did so, because we had to go to Mass only once a week at school: Sunday and once during the week. I went every morning because there were sisters who went to Mass at seven o'clock, before breakfast and before school, and I served that Mass. And so, the Pallottine priests already understood that I intended to become a priest.

At that time, I felt not only that I would become a priest, but that I had to become a religious priest. At boarding school, I began to read many biographies of the saints. And first I read the life of St. Francis of Assisi. To consecrate yourself radically to God, this impressed me so much that I was convinced I had to become a religious priest.

What came after the two years of boarding school?

There was a Gymnasium run by the Pallottine Fathers in another town. It was a boarding school for boys, and they wanted me to enter that school. But it was too liberal. I was fourteen years old at that time and I said to them, "No, I will not go here." And so, I went home to live with my parents. Even when I went to school, I would go to Mass every day before school. From the time I was thirteen, I could not imagine starting the day without Mass. Every day I participated in the Mass. When I was in the Gymnasium, I even started to go, when possible, twice a day. In the morning and the evening. It was for me, at this age, a necessity to participate often at Holy Mass. I felt this necessity in my soul. I also spent time in Eucharistic adoration.

Where did you go to Eucharistic adoration?

There was a church near our parish with an evening Mass twice a week, and after the Mass there was one hour of Exposition of the

Blessed Sacrament: silent adoration. It was the most beautiful time for me. I would remain in the back of the church, in the last row, hidden, with the Blessed Sacrament exposed for one hour, and it was so beautiful for me.

What do you remember about that time of adoration as an adolescent?

It was for me simply peace in the Presence of the Lord. I believed Jesus was there. That was enough for me: I believed Jesus was there and so I had this kind of peace and silence. I loved the silence so much at this time. And I prayed my Rosary, among other prayers.

Do you have an earliest experience of Our Lady's presence in your life?

As a child, I simply loved Our Lady, the pictures mother gave me, and so it was natural. When I was thirteen or fourteen, I started to live a deeper and more intense spiritual life, and I began to love Our Lady more deeply and consciously. I could not point to any special, extraordinary event in my life. It was so normal for me to love Our Lady. Since my childhood, she has always been present but not in an extraordinary way.

How did your desire to become a religious priest grow?

When I was fifteen or sixteen, I watched a film about the Carthusians and how they lived. I remember it very well, and I was so enthusiastic that I desired to go to the Carthusians. It was for me the deepest desire to be completely dedicated to the Lord, and then I asked my Lord, "Where can I become a good priest?" The official structures of the German Church at that time were liberal, as were the religious congregations. From the soil where I grew up, from my parents, my grandparents, from that holy confessor and martyr-priest, I had the instinct in my soul against Modernism and Liberalism in the Church. So I asked the Lord to show me the way.

And how did He answer you?

We had a neighbor lady, who sometimes brought us religious magazines and journals, and there was a flyer from the Canons Regular in Austria, with pictures and photos, and their daily schedule. They were in cassocks, in the habit. The flyer featured photos of Exposition of the Blessed Sacrament in a very beautiful monstrance; the canons had a traditional *horarium*, very exact, and a description of the style of life, which was traditional and strict, with Adoration of the Blessed Sacrament, devotion to Our Lady, to the holy angels, to the Holy Cross, and so on. There was an address, and I kept this, and said to myself, "When I finish the Gymnasium, I will enter there." It was already decided. I was fifteen years old when I decided this.

Some months later — perhaps six months later — I had finished my custom of serving at my parish in the morning as an altar boy on a Sunday, and I was in church at another parish to assist at a second Mass out of devotion. That was for me a "necessity." At the second Mass, I was almost in the last row and I knelt for the entire Mass, only contemplating. I was not responding, I simply wanted to be at Mass.

There was a man behind me and it must have been strange for him to see a boy kneeling for the entire Mass and not responding; he observed me from behind. When Mass was finished, I stayed for a little while and he waited for me outside until I came out. When I came out, he approached me, introduced himself, and said, "Do you want to make a spiritual retreat with good priests?" And I said, "Okay. If they are good priests, yes." Then he gave me his phone number and I told him that I had to ask my parents, and my parents permitted it. Then he organized a bus ride. I traveled to a retreat house, it was a hundred kilometers away, to make a three-day silent retreat. There was a full bus of people, and we arrived at this retreat house, and the Mass there was celebrated *ad Deum* — toward the Lord. It was exactly 1976, at the end of October, three days before the Feast of All Saints. The Mass was celebrated *ad Deum*, but in German. There was a Communion rail, and the Canon was in Latin, but the rest in German. I was present at this Mass and it was so beautiful for me. It was what I always desired.

The priest who preached the retreat was always in his cassock. I asked him, "Where do you come from?" He said, "Well, I come from Austria, from the Canons Regular." And I said, "I have a flyer about you!" It was the second confirmation of a vocation, the second sign from the Lord. So, when I finished my time as the Gymnasium I entered the Canons Regular of the Holy Cross in Austria.

The Canons . . . can you say more about this order?

It was originally the Canons of Coimbra, Portugal, to which St. Anthony belonged before becoming a Franciscan. He was a Coimbra canon and was ordained a priest there. But this Order of the Holy Cross was suppressed by the Masonic government of Portugal in the nineteenth century. Then, in the 1970s, several Portuguese and Austrian priests revived the Order with the permission of the Holy See, and therefore they have this connection to Portugal.

When did you tell your parents about your decision to enter the Canons Regular?

Well, after I had participated in this first retreat, my parents also regularly participated twice a year in the retreats preached by the Canons Regular from Austria. My whole family participated. My parents came to love these priests very much. In the summertime, I visited their monastery in Austria and would spend several weeks there. When I was close to finishing the Gymnasium, I told my parents I was interested in entering there, but I am sure my parents had already intuited this. We had not spoken about it. The idea that I would enter the canons was quite natural for my parents.

3

Athanasius

Where did you make your novitiate?

I made my novitiate in Portugal, from 1982 to 1983. Then, in 1983, a bishop came from Brazil, Bishop Manuel Pestana, from the diocese of Anápolis. He asked our Order to help him train priests in his diocese, to run the seminary. We had another monastery in Brazil, close to São Paolo, and he knew the priests there and held our Order in high esteem. He had come specifically to Rome to visit us and to ask the Order's General Council to open a new house in his diocese and to run the seminary, and even to open a theological faculty. Then he came to visit us in Portugal. Bishop Manuel Pestana was a holy and humble man. He died in 2011.

I imagine you would have begun your studies in 1983. Where did the Order send you?

I was in Rome in 1983. The Order sent us to study at the Angelicum. I started in October 1983 with philosophy.

What do you recall about Bishop Manuel's visit to Rome in 1983?

Bishop Manuel was a very short man — like a boy — so short and round, but a holy man. And a brilliant thinker. I have never in my life met a man who was so cultivated and at the same time so simple. When you saw him, he was like a parish priest from the country. The simplicity in his behavior was coupled with such dignity. As a Brazilian he was very warm and cordial but was highly educated and cultured. He had a private library that contained around 20,000 volumes. He had a completely traditional mindset. I mean this is the true Catholic sense. His diocese had been destroyed by Liberation Theology before he arrived there. It was a complete spiritual ruin. There was no seminary. Confessions were abolished and there was only general absolution. No exposition of the Blessed Sacrament. Only Liberation Theology, sociology, and so on. That is why he asked us to come and help him to restore Catholic priestly formation. And so it was decided. I was in the first group, which was sent from Rome to Brazil in March of 1984.

So you were still a student then ...

Yes! But the superiors said that, as they were starting a theology faculty, they had to have students, so they sent their own students there. Brazilians also came. In this way, we had a faculty of professors and students to start something. The bishop was so happy. So, we went to Brazil and I studied there; I continued philosophy and theology.

Were you happy to go to Brazil?

Yes, I was. Young people like adventures. I was a young man and I liked adventures and it was for me a good experience. In my group there were twelve of us all together. Even the bishop taught us. His hobby was teaching; he liked it very much. He taught in the seminary, so he was my professor too. He had lots of work to do as a bishop in his diocese, but he also found time to teach. Bishop Manuel ordained me to the priesthood. I count it as one of the great graces of my life to have had Bishop Manuel Pestana as my teacher and as the bishop who ordained me.

Tell me about the day you were ordained.

It was the 25th of March — the Annunciation — in 1990. Bishop Manuel Pestana ordained me in Brazil, in the church of our monastery in Anápolis. He was a holy man — a very mild man but a warrior. A journalist from a São Paolo newspaper called him: "The Athanasius of Brazil." He always wore the cassock. No one ever saw him without the cassock. Even when he was traveling all over the world, he always wore his cassock. And this was an example for me. I imitate him also in this way.

What went through your mind as the bishop laid hands on you and you were ordained a priest?

When Bishop Manuel Pestana laid his hands on me, I felt in my soul that from this moment I entered a new spiritual reality of being forever united with Christ. I felt that Christ took me up into His priesthood. It is difficult to describe with words, but God gave me the grace to spiritually experience in that moment the truth of the indelible mark of priestly ordination.

And after ordination, what went through your mind as you celebrated your first Mass?

During the offering of my first Holy Mass, which was in Latin, I was profoundly touched by the words of the consecration "*Hoc est enim Corpus Meum*" ("For this is My Body"). The second grace-filled moment during that Holy Mass was the doxology, with the words "*Per Ipsum et cum Ipso et in Ipso est Tibi Deo Patri omnipotenti in unitate Spiritus Sancti omnis honor et gloria*" ("Through Him and with Him and in Him, is to Thee, God the Father almighty, in the unity of the Holy Spirit, all glory and honor"). I perceived that the most beautiful and most sublime meaning and aim of Christ's redeeming sacrifice on the Cross is the honor and glory of God the Most Holy Trinity, and that the whole meaning and aim of the life of every creature, and particularly of the life of a priest, must be the honor and glory of God the Most Holy Trinity. And then one of my favorite lines from the Psalms came to my mind: "*Non nobis, Domine, non nobis, sed nomini Tuo da gloriam*" ("Not to us, O Lord, not to us, but to Thy name give the glory").

Did you choose the name Athanasius as a religious? Or was it chosen for you?

In our Congregation, in my time, at profession we changed our name. The superior in those days would tell the group—I think there were eight of us—that we could suggest to the superior three names and the superior would choose one of these. I answered, "I have no suggestion. I can propose nothing to you. I leave it up to you to choose what you want." Then I added, "Though I love my baptismal name, Antonius. But if you want, you can choose another name." And then when the moment came for my profession, he said to me, "You will be called Athanasius." I never in my life imagined this name, Athanasius.

You knew who St. Athanasius was of course?

I was familiar with him as a saint because I had read the *Lives of the Saints* in a general way, though I had not yet studied the Fathers and Church history specifically. I also knew him from the Breviary.

What went through your mind when you heard yourself called Athanasius?

I don't know, but I started to read more about him, because he was my new patron. I started to read his works and the history of his time.

Tell me more about your experience as a young religious in Brazil.

I was very happy to be in Brazil, working closely with the poor people in this diocese. It is not correct when liberals say to us, "Oh, you are only dealing with doctrine and so on, and you are forgetting the real people and the poor." It is unjust, and it is untrue. I lived in Brazil, in this diocese, and we cared very much for the poor, for real persons. We went to mission stations and celebrated Mass there for the people. My time in Brazil was a real missionary experience. We came to mission stations in our cassocks and the people loved this. We helped them materially, and then we taught them the catechism and prayers and the Rosary, and they loved this too.

Did you celebrate Mass for them?

I was a seminarian and a deacon then. But after my priestly ordination, I was sent to another monastery in São Paolo, close to Aparecida, and in those days we had five little villages around the monastery and were in charge of their pastoral care. In the first year of priesthood, I was in charge of five little rural communities close to the monastery — maybe ten kilometers or so from the monastery — in completely rural areas. There were no roads, only paths, and sometimes I had to ride on horseback to bring the Blessed Sacrament to the sick, to the poor people, or when it was raining as there was no possibility of going by car.

The first years of my priestly life were one of the most beautiful times in my life. These humble, rural, simple, pious Catholics who were there and whom I could help. And I was living in a monastery, which I loved very much, and where we had perpetual adoration.

Adoration was perpetual?

Yes, in this monastery in Brazil. The novitiate was there as well, and I was the spiritual father, the confessor, of the novitiate. On the weekend — and during the week, sometimes in the evening — I celebrated Mass in these rural communities.

After one year of ministry there, my superior from Rome called me. "Are you happy in Brazil?" he asked me. "Yes, I'm very happy," I answered. He said, "Well, we've decided that you must leave Brazil and come to Rome to do a doctorate, because we need teachers for our theological faculty in Brazil. I will give you three days to think about it." Three days. I said to him, "Father, I don't need three days to think. I made a vow of obedience. I'll go immediately."

Soon after, I went to Rome and then I thought to myself, "Now what shall I be studying?" The superior said to me "You will study Patrology." They decided; I did not decide. I did not have to choose anything. They chose for me.

What did you think of the decision?

Well, of course, I loved the Fathers very much. I did my doctorate at the Patristic Institute Augustinianum.

Were you a good student?

Throughout my life I never had difficulties in school. It is a gift of God. My mother was always good in school and I got this gift maybe from my mother. My father had more practical gifts.

But you got that gift, too, didn't you?

I got a practical sense for reality from my father. My mother also had a very practical sense. My parents had grown up as the children of farmers.

When I was almost finished with the licentiate — I had only the baccalaureate before my ordination to the priesthood — I was elected General Councilor of the Order. I was 32. By the time I was elected, I was no longer excited to be in Rome. Rome was too noisy for me. But my superior said, "Of course, you will finish your mandate and then you will return to Brazil."

Did you miss Brazil?

I longed for Brazil. I loved Brazil very much. The superior said, "You are studying to be a professor there on our faculty — but on the weekend you will do pastoral work." I thought I would return to Brazil, teach in the seminary as a member of the faculty, and on weekends go to the villages and do pastoral work. And during the week live a monastic life. Beautiful. I could not imagine a more beautiful life.

What was the topic of your doctoral dissertation?

"The Shepherd of Hermas: Ecclesiology and Penance." The topic was the connection between the Church and the forgiveness of sins. It is a practical topic and has a deep theological sense.

Before I finished the doctorate, a priest came from Kazakhstan. I had never been to Kazakhstan, even though I had lived in Kyrgyzstan.

Someone wanted to introduce this priest to me. He said, "Do you still speak Russian?" I said "Yes; I have not forgotten Russian." "Please come to Kazakhstan to help us with the priestly formation there. We have just established a seminary in Karaganda, so we need professors," he said. "I am a religious priest. I cannot decide," I replied. "You have to address my superior."

Then the bishop of Karaganda wrote to my superior and the superior said, "Yes, I will allow it. But only for six weeks. No more. Because I need him in Rome; he's a Councilor, and later he must go to Brazil." So, I went to Karaganda in 1999 for the first time, for six weeks.

Then suddenly I realized that Blessed Fr. Oleksiy Zarytskyj—who blessed me when I was one year old when he celebrated Mass at our home, and whom my mother had saved—died in Karaganda. And Father Pavlovskis, who gave me First Communion, was also imprisoned in this town. And Providence had sent me there to form priests. I was very moved by this sign of Divine Providence.

When I went back in 2001, the bishop of Karaganda said, "We need Father Athanasius permanently to be the spiritual father for the seminarians." He was in Rome, and he said to me, "Father, please come." And I said, "Your Excellency, I want to do this, but I am a religious, I cannot decide by myself." He replied, "When I write to your superior, he will answer me, 'only for six weeks,' and I need you permanently." Then he said, "But tomorrow I will have an audience with the pope—John Paul II. I will ask the pope tomorrow if he will intervene so that you may be freed for me, for Kazakhstan." I said to him, "Yes, you can do this, you are a bishop." And he did.

He is Polish and so he spoke to the pope in their native language. After some days, the pope's secretary phoned my superior general and said, "The Holy Father has received a request from the bishop of Karaganda that you free Fr. Athanasius to go permanently to Kazakhstan." My superior agreed and sent me there, permanently, with another priest from my Order.

Had you ever met Pope John Paul II before your time in Rome?

Yes, I had. It was a nice experience. When I was nineteen years old, I was finishing the Gymnasium, and Pope John Paul II made his first apostolic visit to Germany in November 1980. He visited Fulda, close to Frankfurt, when we lived in south Germany.

Because I was in school, I had to ask the director to give me leave because it was a school day, a work day. He asked me why I needed the day off from school. I told him it was because I would go to meet the pope. My other classmates heard this and said to me, "Oh, you will meet the pope?" I said, "Yes, I will meet the pope."

I was the main altar boy in my parish and there was another young man who was from the Soviet Union; he also entered my Order later on. He was sent with me to Kazakhstan. Father Victor is his name.

The parish priest said to Victor and me, "The pope will be in Fulda, let's go there and maybe we will meet him because he will meet the priests and seminarians. Even though you are not yet seminarians, you are my older altar boys and I can give you a cassock and surplice and declare you to be a kind of seminarian."

We went to the Cathedral of Fulda for the Mass. We didn't find a place to sit so we were in the back, on the side. It was filled with priests and seminarians. We were dressed in the cassock and surplice. I was nineteen and Victor was eighteen — very young "seminarians" — and our parish priest was there with us. I read in the program beforehand that, after the Mass, the pope would meet the German bishops in the seminary building. It was adjacent to the cathedral, and one could reach it directly from the cathedral through the sacristy. We had arrived several hours earlier, so I saw this from the outside. When the Mass was ended, we looked at each other. "But we have not met the pope," we said. "He was there, and now he's going to the seminary." I said, "How can we go back home, not having met the pope?" I said to the parish priest, "Let's go to the seminary. We have to meet the pope!" So we went there, through the crowd of priests. As we were dressed in cassock and surplice no one stopped us, because they likely thought that we belonged to the seminary staff or were part of the liturgical service. We went to the sacristy. Inside, no one stopped us because there was a large throng, with a lot of priests and bishops.

I wasn't familiar with the building because I had never been there, but from outside I saw it had three floors. I said, "Very quickly! We have to meet the pope." And I went ahead with the parish priest behind me, following me, and we were practically running through the sacristy. Then I opened a door, and we found ourselves in the building, but I didn't know which floor the pope was on. I said, "Quickly, we have to go!" And so we climbed the staircase. I stopped on the second floor — I had the intuition he was on the second floor, not the third, not the first, but the second floor — and so I stopped and opened the first door. There was a long corridor and at the end of the corridor, I saw some red zucchettos and I said, "If there are red zucchettos, the pope cannot be too far away."

We went down this corridor and there were several closed doors, and in one of the rooms was the pope. At the end of the corridor, there was a big auditorium. The entire Bishops' Conference of Germany was waiting for the pope, for the meeting. In front of the door some cardinals were standing and speaking. We went down the corridor and straight past the door where the pope was, not knowing that he was in there. We approached the cardinals — I remember Cardinal Casaroli and Cardinal König were there, and another bishop, whom I don't remember — and they were chatting cordially. They saw us but didn't react. Perhaps they thought we were some of the secretaries, because there were so many bishops. "Stay here," I said to my parish priest and to Victor, "We will not go away. The pope will pass through here, because the aula is there, and he will enter." I did not know that we had passed the door of the room where the pope was. And then, suddenly, this same door opens, and Pope John Paul II comes out and walks in our direction because he had to go to the hall. We saw the pope approaching down the corridor with his secretary and bodyguard, so I ran towards him. Then the bodyguard gave me a sign, some meters before, not to go any further. Then I shouted loudly in Russian, "Most Holy Father!" The pope stopped when he heard Russian and signaled to me to come to him, and then the bodyguard could not stop me because the pope was motioning to me, inviting me to come. I went to him and gave him my hand and spoke Russian with him, saying, "Most Holy Father, I came from the Soviet Union, please bless all the faithful in the Soviet Union." And then I knelt down, and he asked me, "Are you from Kazakhstan?" I said: "No, Holy Father, but I will ask you to bless all the faithful in the Soviet Union." Why he asked me about Kazakhstan, I would come to know only later on. It was because one of the priests of his diocese, from Krakow, when he was cardinal archbishop of Krakow, was working in Kazakhstan secretly. He was beatified in 2016, Blessed Władysław Bukowiński, and he was very close to Cardinal Wojtyła. That is why he spontaneously asked about Kazakhstan.

The pope blessed me very solemnly in Russian and all the cardinals heard this, and the bodyguard acted very reverently to me. I stood up to walk, and as he approached the aula he gave his hand to my parish priest and to Victor. The pope went inside the hall, and the doors were closed. There was no one in the corridor anymore but we three alone. Then we said, "Well, now we have to rush to the railway station in order not to miss our train!" So, we went to the railway station, got on the train, and returned home.

When I returned to school, the first thing the entire class asked me was, "Did you meet the pope?" And I said, "Yes, I met him." This was my first meeting with the pope.

What was the next meeting?

The second time was when Pope John Paul II intervened through his secretary to send me to Kazakhstan, permanently, in 2001. I met him again when he came to Kazakhstan later the same year. I arrived in the beginning of September, and he came for an apostolic visit at the end of the same month. He met all the priests from Kazakhstan in the cathedral of Astana [Nur-Sultan], where I am now auxiliary bishop. So, I went up to him again and said to him, "Holy Father, you sent me here."

Prior to that, I had twice concelebrated morning Mass with the Holy Father, in his private chapel. I was at his side twice. His secretary had me perform the *lavabo* of the pope, twice. So, I had met Pope John Paul II several times.

It is said that he spent a lot of time after Mass in silent prayer.

Before Mass also, yes. I had the impression that he was a deep, spiritual man, united with God.

After being sent by Pope John Paul II to Karaganda, what were the first years like as a priest?

When I was there in Karaganda, I was the spiritual father of the seminary. I was also the chancellor of the diocesan curia, the director of the Catholic newspaper, and a parish priest. In these first years before my episcopate, I had never worked so much as a priest.

It sounds very intense.

I enjoyed it, but it was really challenging. It was a great burden. It was all pastoral work. I went to the Steppe communities. I founded three new parishes. I started to build chapels for the people, and to organize catechesis. Then there was formation of the seminarians, helping the bishop in the curia, and so on.

And then you were appointed a bishop.

In late March 2006, when I was in Karaganda, the nuncio called me from Astana asking me to come to the nunciature. He wanted to speak with me, so I asked him, "Why do you want to speak with me?" He said, "This I cannot say over the phone. You have to come." I was in charge of the seminary academic program, which the nuncio had asked me to develop and to request approval for from Rome through the nunciature. Therefore, I thought he would discuss the program of studies with me.

I went to him and he asked me whether I wanted to have a coffee and I agreed. As I was drinking the coffee, he said to me, "The Holy Father, Pope Benedict XVI, has appointed you a bishop." I said to the nuncio, "The pope appointed me bishop and I knew nothing of it before?" "You did not need to know anything beforehand," the nuncio responded. Then I asked him, "Did you ask the priests who live with me their opinion?" "Yes, I asked them." "Did you ask the other bishops?" "Yes, I asked them." Then I was silent. I made no response. Then the nuncio said this: "You have to know that your appointment was a personal choice of Pope Benedict XVI. I have to say this to you." The moment I heard these words, I was convinced that this appointment was the will of God for me. I was convinced. But I was not happy. A kind of sadness came upon my soul. I am not melancholic, but at this moment a kind of sorrow came to my soul. I sensed such a heavy burden coming upon me. I felt that I would lose my freedom. This was the feeling: "I will be less free than a priest is."

Even though you were already working a great deal.

That was another sort of burden. The burden of a priest was sometimes also a physical burden — I had been physically tired from so much work and driving to my little parishes in the Steppes — but this episcopal appointment brought another burden — a spiritual burden.

I had not formally said "yes." The nuncio only said to me, "Please sign this sheet of paper, that you accept." I confess, I did not even read what was written there. I signed the letter without reading what was written.

What did the letter say?

I don't know! But I suppose it was the acceptance letter that a nuncio normally has to send to Rome. But with my voice I had not said "yes." I was in silence. Interiorly I said "yes," of course. I said to myself in my heart, "This is the will of God."

Then the nuncio said, "You have the freedom to choose the date of your consecration, the place, and the three consecrators. When you have decided, tell me." Then I went home and decided the date, and that it would be held there in Karaganda, because Karaganda was important to me: Blessed Fr. Oleksiy and my parish priest from Estonia, Fr. Pavlovskis, had both been imprisoned there.

Some days later, the nuncio phoned me and asked whether I had already decided. "Yes," I answered. The nuncio said to me, "The Secretary of State, Cardinal Angelo Sodano, said he would like himself to ordain you bishop, together with the new bishop of Kyrgyzstan, in St. Peter's Basilica in Rome. You are free, but it would be a joy for the cardinal." I said, "If it would be a joy for the cardinal, then I agree." And so, I chose neither the date, nor the place, nor the consecrators for my consecration. Others had chosen this for me.

Why did Cardinal Sodano want to consecrate you a bishop?

Because he liked Kazakhstan very much; I think this was the reason. He had already been to Kazakhstan twice. There were two bishops whom he wanted to ordain from this region: myself, from Kazakhstan, and the new bishop from Kyrgyzstan. It was strange; I was born in Kyrgyzstan but was consecrated for Karaganda. The other bishop was born in Karaganda but was consecrated for Kyrgyzstan. He was also from a German family. And so, we both were consecrated in St. Peter's Basilica on June 2, 2006.

Thus, it was not my decision. It is better in life that God decides. I see this in my life more and more.

You said you felt a burden come upon your soul when you were appointed a bishop. What came to mind once you were consecrated?

After I was consecrated a bishop, there came into my memory the prayer which my parents wrote for me as a memorial for my priestly ordination in 1990. Since then, I have kept this prayer in my Breviary as a precious gift from my parents. The prayer reads: "Lord Jesus, give me love, a strong and ardent love for you and, for your sake, for all men and for all that is good. Give me fortitude, so that I may consider the whole world insignificant, if it will seek to separate me from you. Give me joy in my priesthood, for which you have chosen me. May I faithfully observe your commandments and give me the grace to do great things in my priesthood with deep humility and a pure intention."

Your mother had saved and hidden priests. What did she say when you were appointed a bishop?

After my episcopal nomination, a priest who was a family friend came to my mother and congratulated her on the episcopal appointment of her son. To which she replied, "This does not mean very much for me. What is important is that my son remains faithful to Jesus." Each time I phoned my mother, even after I became a bishop, her last words to me were these: "You remain faithful to Jesus. Everything else is unimportant!" This simple wisdom of a Catholic mother far surpasses the sterile intellectualism of the new Pharisees and scribes, who are represented by the liberal and neo-Modernist clerical clan in the life and the structures of the Church in our days.

What is your episcopal motto?

Kyrie eleison. When the nuncio told me that I had to choose an episcopal motto and I went back home it was immediately clear for me, "Kyrie eleison." These words were immediately in my mind. I thought, "Kyrie eleison" is not only a prayer to ask forgiveness; it is also a prayer of praise of the Lord. He is the *Kyrios*, the Lord. Thus, for me, it was a prayer of praise and a prayer for mercy. I thought, "What all of us and the entire world most need is mercy, to pray for forgiveness to the Lord. This helps; this will save the world."

Additionally, *Kyrie eleison* is a Greek expression, from the East. I was appointed bishop in the East. Through this Greek prayer there is a connection between the Greek and the Latin Church.

I understand that, as auxiliary bishop in Karaganda, you played a key role in building the Cathedral of Our Lady of Fatima, the largest Catholic church in central Asia. What was the inspiration for the cathedral? And what can you tell us about your experience in building it?

When I came to Karaganda in 1999, I saw that the Karaganda Cathedral was a small building on the outskirts of the city that was built during the time of the persecution of the Church. I recognized the pastoral necessity of building a new cathedral that would be closer to the central districts of the city, offering a dignified and easily recognizable exterior image of a typical Catholic cathedral. I believed the new cathedral should also be a memorial to the victims of the "Karlag" and a place of atonement for the great crimes against Jesus Christ and the dignity of man committed on the soil of Karaganda by a godless and totalitarian regime. The new cathedral also stands as a visible sign of the confession of the Catholic faith and as a tool of evangelization — an "evangelization through the stones," an "evangelization through beauty," and an "evangelization through culture," as it were.

Named for Our Lady of Fatima, the cathedral's title has great significance for this region. The special meaning which the message of Fatima holds concerning Russia is well known. The name "Russia" in the Fatima message represents the political system of a militant godless materialism. Bearing in mind that people from more than one hundred different ethnic groups, who all suffered at the time of the Communist regime, live in Kazakhstan, a second title was then added: "Mother of All Nations." It could be said that the motives for the construction of the Karaganda Cathedral were twofold: to preach the true Catholic faith through architectural and sacred beauty, and to have a place of remembrance and atonement for the victims of the "Karlag." These motives are deeply pastoral.

The cathedral is located in a very nice and central part of the city. It is a beautiful neo-Gothic building made of white sandstone with two large towers. Inside, the church has a carved, gold-plated high altar and side altars in the classic Gothic style. They were made by artists from south Tyrol. The undercroft is a gothic-designed crypt, with two monumental sculptural groups in the side wings. One sculptural group represents the mysteries of the Nativity in different scenes, and the other the mysteries of the Passion of Christ; we also had an audio system installed with texts and music related to each scene. On the gable above the main façade is a large white marble statue representing Our Lady with her Immaculate Heart, the same design as the statue on the façade of the Basilica in Fatima.

I imagine the cathedral draws considerable attention.

Yes, I have a nice story about that. Two local ladies from Muslim families passed by the cathedral, and the one woman asked her companion, "What is this building here?" Her friend answered, "This is a Catholic mosque." Our Lady of Fatima has already attracted many people through this beautiful church, including non-Christians. And that is one of the main goals of a Catholic church building, to bring people to Christ.

Looking back on your years as auxiliary bishop of Karaganda, in addition to building the cathedral, what were your main duties? And what was the most important lesson you learned during that time?

My main task, as is usual for any auxiliary bishop, was to assist the diocesan bishop of Karaganda — who at that time was Bishop Jan Paweł Lenga — in the exercise of the pastoral office of the diocese entrusted to his care. My ordinary episcopal ministry included visiting parishes, mission stations, and religious convents, holding meetings with priests and religious sisters, and helping organize diocesan pastoral assemblies and spiritual retreats for the priests. On a practical level, I was also helping the diocesan bishop in the work and administration of the chancery. The diocese had a minimum of administrative structures. Apart from the diocesan bishop and the auxiliary bishop, there was only one priest and one religious sister working in the chancery. There was minimal bureaucracy. And this was so beneficial and healthy, because we really had time for the work of direct evangelization.

Additionally, I was also the President of the Diocesan Liturgical Commission and the chief editor of the monthly Catholic newspaper "Credo," the only Catholic magazine in Kazakhstan. I was also teaching Patristics and Liturgy at the inter-diocesan major seminary located in Karaganda.

To my great joy, the diocesan bishop told me after my episcopal ordination that, if I wanted, I could continue to take care of the three little missionary parishes that were entrusted to me as a priest. One of the deepest joys in that time as an auxiliary bishop were the moments when I was travelling on the bumpy roads of the endless Steppes to visit the very small communities, who with a deep faith were longing to see a priest. On one occasion, I celebrated Midnight Mass on Christmas in the smallest and furthest community of the diocese. On that night, the temperature outside was minus 40 degrees Celsius. After the Midnight Mass, I shared a meal with the entire community; at the table I was surrounded by the smallest children on one side, and by the oldest grandmothers, the "babushkas," on the other. In that moment, I realized more than ever before in my life the truth that God builds up His Church with pure, little, and simple souls. This was one of the most beautiful Christmas feasts in my life.

As auxiliary bishop of Karaganda you also wrote Dominus Est, *in which you explore the proper interior disposition and exterior gestures for receiving the Lord in the Eucharist. Is the liturgical practice of receiving Holy Communion only on the tongue, which you defend in that book, common in the Karaganda diocese?*

Thanks be to God, in Kazakhstan the faithful always received Holy Communion kneeling and on the tongue. Our faithful could never imagine receiving Holy Communion standing, let alone in the hand. They had an almost instinctive desire, of course illuminated and nourished by faith, to approach Our Lord at the moment of Holy Communion also with exterior gestures of deep reverence and sacredness.

Unfortunately, priests from other countries were coming to us who started to teach the people to receive Holy Communion standing. They used intellectual arguments which are not the least bit convincing to the common sense and deep faith of the people. Such arguments included, for example, that Holy Communion has to be received while people are moving in a line as in a "procession"; this is, in fact, an imprecise and tendentious argument. When foreigners visited Kazakhstan, they asked that Holy Communion be given to them in the hand. This scandalized our good simple Catholics.

Therefore, as president of the Liturgical Commission of the Conference of the Catholic Bishops of Kazakhstan, I prepared a draft for a general decree, immediately after my episcopal ordination in 2006. The decree contained norms stipulating that in the entire territory of Kazakhstan in all Catholic churches, chapels, and religious communities, Holy Communion has to be received by the faithful while kneeling (except of course for health reasons) and on the tongue; that receiving Communion in the hand is prohibited even for Catholics from abroad. These norms were approved by the bishops' conference, and in 2007 they received the recognition from the Holy See. This was for me one of the first and greatest joys of my episcopal ministry. These norms were then implemented in the Catholic Church throughout Kazakhstan. It is for the greater glory, defense, and love of Our Eucharistic Lord, really and substantially present under the sacred Eucharistic species. It can only be a deep joy for the soul of a priest and bishop when Our Lord is visibly more honored, defended, and loved.

You were then transferred to Astana?

Yes. Pope Benedict XVI had appointed me to Karaganda because the local archbishop wanted an auxiliary. In 2011, when I had already been the auxiliary bishop in Karaganda for five years, I was appointed auxiliary bishop of Astana. It was a good time for me, the five years in Karaganda. I was able to help the archbishop, and he was grateful for this. Then, when he retired, the Holy See said, "The archbishop of Astana has asked for an auxiliary; let us give you to him." Actually, I did not ask the nuncio for the reasons for my transferal. For me it is not important: in every place you have the Lord, and this is most important. In every place, we have the Holy Mass and the Blessed Sacrament. This is sufficient for me. As a priest and a bishop, you can work wherever the Church puts you. Therefore, it is not important which place or title I have. It is completely indifferent to me. I left Karaganda in 2011 and I have already been in Astana for eight years. I am happy. I can do good work there, and sometimes I can travel and give talks and conferences around the world, and spiritually help priests and the faithful who invite me. I accept invitations only upon written permission of the diocesan bishop of the place where I am going and with the consent of my own archbishop.

Have you ever been refused?

Yes.

Can you say where?

In the United States, in Germany, and in Austria.

Can you be more specific?

I cannot say. The reason why I was denied permission was that I am allegedly against Pope Francis. It is exactly the opposite. I never in my life have prayed for a person so much as I pray for Pope Francis.

In one diocese in Germany, I was not allowed to celebrate a Pontifical Mass. This was quite bizarre. The rector of the shrine invited me to celebrate a Pontifical Mass and give a talk. I told the rector that I could accept only if he showed me the written permission of his bishop. He wrote to the diocese, asking if Bishop Schneider could celebrate a Pontifical Mass at the shrine. The Vicar General of the diocese answered, "No, the diocese cannot give permission to Bishop Schneider to celebrate a Pontifical Mass because his presence causes division and tension." He continued, "Dear Fr. Rector, in the future please invite to the shrine only bishops who are strong in faith."

Strong in faith . . .

Indeed. Strong in which faith? Perhaps the Protestant faith of this Vicar General? Surely not in the Catholic faith. In any case, it was bizarre.

Many people wonder why someone of your learning and experience is still an auxiliary bishop. How do you respond to those — including some critics — who ask why you have not been appointed as bishop of a diocese?

I think that the sacred priestly and, even more so, the episcopal ministry, should not be understood and measured by the typical worldly category of a professional career. In the eyes of God, what degree of the hierarchy one occupies is not essential. What is decisive is how faithful you are to the Catholic faith, and how much supernatural love you have in carrying out your duties wherever Divine Providence has put you. It is a surer and more grace-filled path to allow yourself to be guided by Divine Providence than to choose yourself.

Your Excellency, turning to a more personal aspect of your life as a bishop, what is your daily prayer life like?

The most important part of the day for me is Holy Mass. It is the most important work. I consider it to be really a work, and this is the most important work: to celebrate the Holy Mass well, attentively, and with love. This is the most important thing. I have already done all my work once I've celebrated the Mass. The meaning of my day, of my life, is the Mass. With, of course, thanksgiving after Mass. And then the Breviary. I like the Breviary very much. I pray the old Breviary, which is longer than the new one. It contains all 150 Psalms in their totality.[1] The Breviary for me is rest.

1 The Liturgy of the Hours promulgated by Pope Paul VI in 1970 removed three psalms altogether, limited three others to certain seasons, and removed over 60 individual verses, including some that have been prayed since apostolic times.

Then, the third part of each day is dedicated to making time for adoration of the Blessed Sacrament. I have done this since my youth. In my congregation, we are supposed to spend one hour in Eucharistic adoration, more or less. It is desirable to do this. I try to do this every day. This is most important to me: the life of prayer.

When you read the Scriptures, what language do you read them in?

Usually I take the Vulgate, the old Vulgate, which is my normal text. Sometimes I read the New Testament in Greek. I have the bilingual edition, so when I meditate on or read the Scriptures, I read it always either in Latin or in Greek.

Are you comfortable speaking in Latin?

I have not had the occasion to speak Latin. But I had good training in Latin in the Gymnasium in Germany. I had seven years of Latin, five lessons per week. Then, of course, I used it in my studies, so I am quite acquainted with Latin. I like Latin. I also studied Greek for Patrology. I have also studied Hebrew, but not as much. I can read the letters, but I only took a short introductory course in exegesis and have not had the opportunity to study Hebrew more intensely.

Do you still teach at the Karaganda seminary?

Yes, I am still teaching there periodically. I go there for three or four days and give lessons in Patrology and Liturgy. This is also a joy for me because I learn something in every lesson, even though I have been teaching ever since obtaining the licentiate in 1993. I learn something new and deeper every time, even in a lecture already given many times.

Do you have any hobbies?

As a young man, when I was 15, I wanted to become a Carthusian monk, but it was not what Divine Providence willed. So even before I entered the monastery I lived like a monk. In my younger years, I played the piano, but I would not say it was a hobby. I cannot say that I have a hobby. Sometimes in my younger years I liked very much to bicycle and to swim. In Brazil I swam a lot during the years of my formation. On the property of our monastery, inside the cloister, we had a beautiful lake. It was a huge piece of land and the area was exclusively for our use. So, every day I swam there, running when I was a young seminarian, and swimming. I did it for my health and for recreation.

And do you have a favorite composer?

Yes, I like Mozart. He is one of the most harmonious composers in my opinion. Schubert is also beautiful. As for singing, I like Palestrina very much and the classical polyphonic composers.

Your Excellency, a final question about your life before we move on. Your family history involved great faith and, at times, great suffering; and the years of your own childhood were spent in the Soviet underground church. Where were you when the Berlin Wall fell?

In 1989, I was a deacon in Anápolis in Brazil.

What was your reaction?

It was for me very surprising and of course a joy. I had a deep joy that, finally, this atheistic system had collapsed. However, I could not have imagined that the breakdown of this atheistic system would usher in a worse situation in Europe, which is now before us: the dictatorship of gender ideology. This is really a dictatorship. It is actually the same method as in Communist times.

II

The Sun Shall Be Darkened

4

Secularism and the New Dictatorship

Your Excellency, secularism seems to be on the rise throughout the world and, as you say, a new dictatorship is emerging. What are the underlying causes of secularism in your view, and why is it that moral relativism seems to be spreading so fast in the West?

The deepest root of this movement of secularism in Europe — which began to construct a world without God, and to live as if God did not exist — is anthropocentrism. Secularism seeks to ban Jesus Christ from public life. Secularism is connected with relativism because when man says, "I determine what is true," then it can be true in this generation, and when the next generation comes, there can be another truth. Thus, it is always changing. This is relativism. Relativism is intimately connected with secularism and anthropocentrism. Relativism is a flight from reality.

What is behind this movement?

Ultimately Satan is behind it. There was a tendency in this direction before the so-called century of the Enlightenment. I believe it began in the fifteenth century with Humanism. This was also called the Renaissance. Its aim was to put man at the center, that man should be the measure of truth. It was not yet well articulated in the fifteenth century, but this tendency had already begun — the unhealthy autonomy of man towards God, towards the supernatural world.

Why the Renaissance?

Renaissance means rebirth. Rebirth of what? Of a pagan society. At first, they meant only a rebirth in art, but it happened in their mentality too. To praise pure naturalism — paganism is naturalism, not supernaturalism — and so to put pure nature at the center and thus weaken the supernatural bonds with God, with the Incarnate God Jesus Christ, who is supernatural. All of this was reflected in art.

In some ways, the art of this time was very carnal, not spiritual. Sensual art is for me not worthy of man. We are more than an animal. To paint the human person almost exclusively in his naturalistic, anatomic perspective is unworthy of him. Man is more than this. We must also portray man as a spiritual being, with a supernatural dimension.

Secularism started with anthropocentrism, and the catalyst that helped this movement to grow and spread was the Protestant so-called Reformation (begun by Luther in 1517). In the religious sphere, man declared himself the center, and this is subjectivism. It was, in some way, a tendency to pride that was expressed very clearly in Luther and then in the Enlightenment. Then came the movement of Deism, which began in the seventeenth century in England. It was not yet formally Freemasonry, but it was born in the Protestant environment.

Could you say more about the connection you see between secularism and Protestantism?

Secularism, in my view, is the necessary consequence of Protestantism. It is the *subjectivism* in virtue of which man decides what is true, and the subject, or the private man, is the authority who determines the true meaning of revelation. This led to faith — objective faith — being weakened. For Luther, faith was subjective. *Sola fide:* for him, faith is a subjective conviction without submission to the objective content of divine revelation as transmitted by the constant tradition of the Church. Today, even in the Catholic Church, we are in danger of neglecting the *objective content* of Truth and Revelation, under the pretext that one is expressing one's subjective conviction that "I believe in Christ; Christ is my Savior," or under the pretext of "the development of doctrine." To proclaim Christ without stressing the objective content of the immutable truths of divine revelation and the divine commandments ultimately signifies a new subjective religion of emotionalism, similar to many Protestant denominations. In this attitude we find, in my opinion, one of the deepest roots of the crisis in the Catholic Church in our days.

You mentioned Deism. Can you explain the foundations of this movement?

Deism was a cultural and philosophical-phenomenon, especially in England, which held the theory that God is inaccessible, that we can know only that God exists and nothing more. For the Deist, it is impossible to know anything about God — completely impossible.

There is no communication, then, between God and His creatures.

According to this view, God created man and the whole universe and gave creation — man and the universe — complete and absolute independence in everything, and just let it run by itself without any direct influence, without any divine and supernatural action. Any direct divine revelation is therefore excluded in this view. There is no possibility of revelation. This opened the door to Freemasonry, the main dogma of which is Deism: that there is complete and absolute independence and freedom of human beings toward God, or the Creator, or whatever you name this god. Since God is totally unknowable, you can name him whatever you want. You can name him Allah, or Christ — even though Freemasons do not accept Christ — you can call him Creator, Buddha, you can even call him Satan, or the Great Architect of the World. This movement goes back to secularism and anthropocentrism.

And where are we today?

Now we have reached a peak of secularism, of this complete independence of man, of this enormous anthropocentrism where everyone decides for himself what is true and what is good or evil. Such secularism brings us a horrible and cruel society. We are witnessing this — it is cruel. And what is the result? Egoism. Secularism leads to egoism. We have now reached a peak of egoism — and egoism is cruel: only I and no one else.

It is Hell.

It is Hell. "Only I." Ultimately this means, "When someone else is impeding or hindering what I want to do, I will kill him, I will destroy him." And so, they began to kill the innocents in their mother's womb because these babies are hindering them from achieving what they believe is their self-realization through pleasures, a false freedom, and worldly success. Then they eliminate sick people; then the handicapped, for instance those with Down syndrome, and so on. This is the path of the new dictatorship, patterned after the Nazi dictatorship in Germany and the Communist dictatorship in the Soviet Union. This is a process which leads ultimately to an exasperated egoism, to a cruel and inhuman society.

From its roots to the point where we are now, this trajectory has led to gender ideology, in which man decides what nature is, instead of God the Word "through whom all things were made" (cf. Jn 1:3).

Exactly. This leads to the peak, to the logical consequence of the independence of man, this anthropocentrism. At least the Deists accepted nature as it is, they accepted that God created it, and that one has to respect the natural laws, at least to some extent. But as a consequence, especially with the rise of Freemasonry, Gnostic thinking entered in, and this is ultimately Satanic thinking, where man puts himself in the place of the Creator. Man wants to become God, eliminating God the Creator and eliminating God the Savior, Jesus Christ. In this vacuum, man puts himself in the place of and declares himself to be God, the Creator, though not formally, to show that "I am equal to God, I am able to create something." This is demonstrated in so-called gender ideology. But this leads to insanity. So, society has arrived at a mad, insane way of thinking that is tainted with blasphemy, because gender ideology and homosexuality are an enormous blasphemy and a rebellion against the wisdom and majesty of God the Creator.

Would you say that a good definition of insanity is detachment from reality?

Yes, exactly. This is a detachment from reality because they say that we decide what reality is, what creation is, what man is, and so on. They seize on what is in some way the most mysterious part of creation, human sexuality. It is a very mysterious and holy area, given by God for participating in the transmission of new life, and life is a mystery. This is the means to continue mankind, to transmit life — God gives life, but the parents transmit life as co-participants. Secularists want to appropriate this domain to themselves. They say, "We, and no longer God, say who is male and who is female." This is blasphemy, rebellion, and insanity at the same time.

Man also wants to decide who creates life and how life is created...

They started with *in vitro* fertilization. This was the first step. They want to demonstrate even visibly that we determine who man is: not God, not the Creator — we do. In so many nations, by law there can now be a valid and legal marriage between persons of the same sex, which is clearly madness and contradicts all reality, all evidence. We have arrived at this point, and it is all a movement which grew out of anthropocentrism and the elimination of God from society. Therefore, we have arrived at a new pagan society, in some ways worse than pagan societies of the past. At least pagans in Roman and Greek society still accepted reality. But now our society has tried to change the evidence.

And technology affords man many more possibilities for cruelty and for indoctrinating the young . . .

Exactly. Anthropocentrism is intolerant — it doesn't tolerate others. This is a very dangerous movement. In the Church, we have to be witnesses against this new pagan society, against this new atheism. We have to bring light and a clear witness. Unfortunately, the crisis within the Church is having the opposite effect. Instead of being a witness to the truth, to reality, the Church is being infected by the spirit of anthropocentrism, gender ideology, and the legitimization of homosexuality.

You mentioned the role of Freemasonry in the rise of secularism. Have you studied it?

A bit. There are a number of solid scholarly studies on Freemasonry, such as Henri Delassus, *La Conjuration Antichrétienne*, with its remarkable subtitle *Le Temple Maçonnique voulant s'élever sur les ruines de l'Eglise catholique*;[1] Walton Hannah, *Darkness Visible: A Christian Appraisal of Freemasonry*; Paolo M. Siano, *La Massoneria tra esoterismo, ritualità e simbolismo*; and Alberto Bárcena, *Iglesia y masonería. Las dos ciudades.*

Can you say more about the place Freemasonry occupies in the secularist movement?

Freemasonry is a movement which has philosophical connections with English Deism. As I said before, according to Deism, God has nothing to do with us, so we are completely free. This was in some way the mental premise for traditional Freemasons as we know them. At the same time, Freemasonry is a kind of religion — we cannot forget this. At the heart of Freemasonry is a religion, a cult, a worship.

Is it Satanism?

Alas, ultimately it is close to Satanism. Not every Freemasonic group is Satanic, but the roots are Satanic and lead to Satanism in the highest degrees of Freemasonry.

Freemasonry is ultimately a Gnostic religion. Gnosticism was flourishing at the time of Our Lord Jesus Christ, precisely in the first and second centuries in the Greco-Roman world. This movement is characterized by the belief in imaginary intellectual entities, divorced from the evidence of

---

1   "The Masonic Temple in Its Intent to Rise on the Ruins of the Catholic Church."

concrete reality and denying a true, supernatural, and historically based divine revelation. Gnostic mythology was a purely man-made creation and was destined for an esoteric elite, not for all people. The Gnostic system offered an answer to the two basic questions asked by every human being: Where does evil come from? That is, why does evil exist? And how can I be saved? Gnosticism presented these two basic questions and concerns — the question of evil and the question of salvation — in a fascinating religious system.

Gnosticism's solution was simplistic. It says that evil exists in us and outside of us; that we observe evil in nature and in natural catastrophes, for example, in diseases, and so on. Gnostics draw the conclusion that every created visible nature, our body and sexuality for example, must be evil. They say that the creator of visible things is evil, the evil god. And so, they postulate an eternal and metaphysical principle of evil.

But on the other side, there is also the good. According to Gnostics, since the visible things we observe are evil, there has to be a principle of good, which must therefore be invisible. All that is invisible is good, they say, while all that is visible is a sign or indicator of evil. Gnostics ask: how do we know that God is the Creator? We know it from the Bible, they say. In the Bible it is written that God created man and the entire visible universe; and that God created man and woman, two biological sexes, and God said, "This is very good." The Gnostics therefore declared that the God of the Bible is the evil one, and that all that is written in the Bible as being good is actually evil and is not good. For the Gnostics, the human body and the two biological sexes are especially an evil. So, the Gnostics perverted the meaning of divine revelation in the Bible and turned it into the opposite. They perverted the obvious sense of the biblical affirmations. For example, when God gave the Ten Commandments, He said: "you shall not commit adultery." They say that this is a lie, that this comes from the evil god, and that the true sense is actually that it is good to commit adultery. When God says, "you shall not lie," the Gnostics say, no, you can lie when it is good for you. "You shall not murder": the Gnostics say that to murder can be good, because the evil god in the Bible gave the prohibition against murder. Thus, we see how diabolic Gnostic ideology is.

According to Gnosticism there are the two coeternal principles of good and evil and they constitute a metaphysical dualism. The good god is in your mind, is invisible. The better a thinker you are, and the more beautifully you come up with theories, the closer you are to the good god. *Gnosis* means "knowledge" in Greek. The more knowledge you have in your mind and the more secrets you know, the better. This elite circle of the Gnostic groups claimed to have access to knowledge of the good god, yet not through revelation in the Bible. Ultimately for Gnostics the one whom the Bible calls the "devil" is the good god.

These main elements of the Gnostic system are the basic principles of the religion of Freemasonry. The Freemasons took the main part of their thinking from historical Gnosticism.

But you also said that Freemasonry involves worship.

No religious group can exist without a cult, without worship. Freemasonry took their cult, their worship, from esoteric groups, especially from the Jewish, esoteric Kabbalah groups. Thus, the entire symbolism and terminology of Freemasonry is religiously Jewish and philosophically Gnostic. They took their symbolism and terminology from the Old Testament, and so they imitate parts of Judaism, but it is Gnostic because *gnosis* says that the Old Testament we read is from the evil god. Therefore, they borrow the same terminology from the Old Testament — the building of the temple, and so on — but they say: "We are building a new temple, not the visible carnal one, which is from the evil god. We the Freemasons are the spiritual and free and independent masons, we are completely free from God, from the God of the Bible." We have to ask: "From whom are the Freemasons free?" They declare themselves free from the true God. They say: "Our god is the Great Architect of the world, this unknown good god, whom we do not know, but we are his instruments and we are building up a new temple of humanity." The Freemasons do this through the use of symbolism and worship, and especially with an intellectual program that must be implemented and reflected throughout the whole of human society.

In the new temple of the Freemasons, man will be placed at the center and will be declared god. But in his Letter to the Thessalonians, St. Paul said of the Antichrist: "He opposes and exalts himself against every so-called god or object of worship, so that he takes his seat in the temple of God, proclaiming himself to be God" (2 Thess 2:4). This is the Antichrist.

In building up this new temple of humanity, the Freemasons consider themselves to be the elect ones. This is the complete opposite of divine revelation in the Bible, and especially the Gospel. Freemasonry's goal is to demonstrate that, in the end, man is god, that man is the one who determines what is good and what is evil. Abortion, gender ideology, and the systematic and demagogic manipulation of the truth in the mass media, for example, correspond to the basic theoretical principles of Freemasonry, in so far as they are Gnostic. As we said before, Gnostics believe that the prohibition against murder and lying and the creation of the two biological sexes are evil, and that the contrary of them is good. So, abortion, lying, and homosexuality (androgynism, as it was called in Gnosticism) are good, according to the Masonic ideology and policy.

They are somehow influencing the masses to unknowingly build the Masonic "temple"?

All of these elements, which contradict human reason and the revelation of the true God — whom Freemasonry considers the evil god — are for them the ideological stones for building the so-called new temple of humanity. In building the new temple of humanity, the first step is to eliminate Christianity, since Christianity is essentially supernatural, theocentric, and Christocentric, and not essentially natural and anthropocentric. In Christianity, Christ, His Word and His truth, is at the center. To eliminate Christianity is the first and last goal of Freemasonry — to eliminate Christ as God, as the Incarnate God and Savior. Freemasons would tolerate a purely human Christ, as a good teacher on the same level with Muhammad and Buddha, for example.

Today it is very dangerous to speak only about God and not about Christ as the true God. Humanistic and Masonic ideology seek to erect this new temple, and they call this the "progress of humanity." In this process of progress, man is put at the center, not Christ. Next, natural marriage and family have to be eliminated and their sense perverted, because according to the Gnostics and Freemasons the evil god, as they say, created marriage between one man and one woman. It was Freemasonry which introduced divorce legislation in Europe.[2]

2   Already the Pharisees, based on a norm conceded by Moses, promoted divorce. And later it was Martin Luther who theoretically and practically introduced the legitimacy of divorce on the religious level in Western Christianity. The Eastern Greek Church introduced divorce in practice already in the time of the Emperor Justinian in the sixth century based on the so-called principle of *oikonomia*, a new invented worldly principle, which, relating to the absolute prohibition of divorce, was alien to the teaching of Jesus Christ, the Apostles, and the vast majority of the Fathers of the Church. — *AS*

How do you know this?

It has been documented. The Freemasons themselves declare this and are proud that they initiated divorce and abortion legislation, for example.

You have seen these documents?

There are studies and books in which this is all documented. The Freemasons themselves have issued statements and declarations, for example, in the supplement of the French Newspaper *Le Figaro* from July 20–21, 2012. To eliminate the family, you start with divorce. Then there is "free love," feminism, contraception, and so on. According to this logic, you become the lord of life.

By using contraception, in some sense a couple is putting God at their service rather than placing themselves at His service in the transmission of life, putting Him at the center of their life and love. When we want a baby, God has to be at our service, and when we don't, we use contraception.

Exactly. This is anthropocentrism. Again, man is at the center—not God. Anthropocentrism is the heart of Freemasonry and their work of building the new temple of humanity and penetrating all social realities. However, Freemasonry's chief aim is to penetrate the Church from the inside. Freemasons tried to eliminate the Church during the French Revolution, in a cruel and barbaric way. However, they saw that this produced a stronger Church through martyrdom. Some argue that Freemasons had a hand in the formation of the Soviet Union, and their role in preparing the Bolshevik Revolution in 1917 is acknowledged by some historians who have studied this question.[3]

When did Freemasonry begin?

It officially began in London, in 1717. The statutes of the Masonic Lodge in London were written by a Protestant pastor named James Anderson. Freemasonry gained political power through and after the French Revolution, and its lodges prepared the various revolutions in the nineteenth century. Today Freemasonry openly acknowledges the French Revolution as its work. In the chamber of Deputies in Paris, during the

---

3 B.T. Norton, "Russian Political Masonry, 1917, and Historians," *International Review of Social History*, 28.2 (1983): 240–58. According to the *New York Journal-American* of February 3, 1949, Jacob Schiff, senior partner in Kuhn, Leob & Co., "sank about 20,000,000 dollars for the final triumph of Bolshevism in Russia."

session on July 1, 1904, the Marquis de Rosanbo stated: "Freemasonry has worked in a hidden but constant manner to prepare the Revolution.... We are then in complete agreement on the point that Freemasonry was the only author of the Revolution, and the applause which I receive from the Left, and to which I am little accustomed, proves, gentlemen, that you acknowledge with me that it was Masonry which made the French Revolution." To which Mr. Jumel answered: "We do more than acknowledge it, we proclaim it."[4]

Vladimir Lenin, for example, was also a member of a Freemasonic lodge.[5] The Prime Minister of Russia, Kerensky, was also a known member of the Russian Freemasonic Orient; he had the Tsar deposed and established a civil government. It was the Russian Freemasons who deposed the Tsar in 1917. The first civil government, from February to the October Revolution, was substantially a Masonic government. The Freemason Kerensky prepared the way for Lenin.

How did Lenin come on the scene?

He was already a member of a number of terrorist groups and aligned with the Communists. However, he received his entire logistical support from the Masonic government in Russia itself, from Kerensky, and from the Freemasons in Europe, especially in Germany. The German government brought him in a private railway car to St. Petersburg to start the Revolution. The Freemasons wanted to carry out an experiment with the chaotic Communists through the establishment of a completely atheistic society — and they succeeded. However, in that period of Soviet Communism the natural law was not obliterated. Current-day gender ideology was unimaginable.

As was "same-sex marriage"...

During Communist times in Russia it would have been absurd to promote the homosexual agenda. In the Soviet Union, if you committed homosexual acts you were punished.

---

4 Mgsr. Henri Delassus, *La Conjuration Antichrétienne* (Lille: Sociéte Saint Augustin, 1910), 1:146.

5 Lenin was a Freemason of the 31st degree ("Grand Inspecteur Inquisiteur Commandeur") and a member of the lodge "Art et Travail" in Switzerland and France. See Oleg Platonov, *Russia's Crown of Thorns: The Secret History of Freemasonry* (Moscow, 2000), part II, p. 417.

Your Excellency, for over two centuries the Church has condemned Free-
masonry, beginning with Clement XII (1738), through Leo XIII's many
interventions in the late nineteenth century, up to the Congregation for
the Doctrine of the Faith (1983). Even in our own time, Pope Francis has
spoken about the Church's work against Freemasonry a number of times
(e.g., Address to Young People in Turin, 21 June 2015). Could you say a few
words about what the popes have written against this secret society?

From the very beginning of the official appearance of Freemasonry
in 1717, the Church condemned it as a dangerous and anti-Christian
sect. In his Apostolic Constitution *In Eminenti*, Pope Clement XII
gave the following striking characterization of Freemasonry: "Men of
any religion or sect, satisfied with the appearance of natural probity, are
joined together, according to their laws and the statutes laid down for
them, by a strict and unbreakable bond which obliges them, both by an
oath upon the Holy Bible and by a host of grievous punishments, to an
inviolable silence about all that they do in secret together.... If they
were not doing evil, they would not have so great a hatred of the light."

The next memorable condemnation of Freemasonry was made in 1751
by Pope Benedict XIV with the Apostolic Constitution *Providas Roma-*
norum, in which the pope enumerates several reasons for the irrecon-
cilability between the Catholic faith and Freemasonry. For instance:
Masonic religious indifferentism and doctrinal relativism; the occultism
of its rites; the refusal of the validity of the natural moral law; and the
support of immorality.

In 1766, Pope Clement XIII, in his Encyclical *Christianae Reipubli-*
cae Salus, indicated the four basic errors of Freemasonry: Materialism,
Naturalism, Deism, and Atheism — the last of which is deceitfully veiled
by their code word "Grand Architect of the Universe." The notion of a
naturalistic universal religion was already established in the first "Constitutions" of Freemasonry, published in London in 1723.

Pope Pius VIII, in his Encyclical *Traditi Humilitati Nostrae*, published in 1829, gave one of the most succinct and accurate definitions of
the ideology and work of Freemasonry, stating, "Their law is untruth,
their god is the devil, and their cult is turpitude."

The most comprehensive and thorough treatment of Freemasonry
may be found in the Encyclical *Humanum Genus* of Pope Leo XIII,
published in 1884. There, Leo XIII approved the pronouncements of
all his predecessors regarding Freemasonry and gave his own analysis of

the secret society. The last theologically and canonically most relevant pronouncement of the Church on the nature of Freemasonry is the *Declaration on Masonic Associations* issued by the Congregation for the Doctrine of the Faith on November 26, 1983. The crucial statement of the Declaration says: "The Church's negative judgment in regard to Masonic associations remains unchanged since their principles have always been considered irreconcilable with the doctrine of the Church and therefore membership in them remains forbidden. The faithful who enroll in Masonic associations are in a state of grave sin and may not receive Holy Communion."

For centuries, then, the Church has been opposed to Freemasonry, although this opposition has been forgotten by many. But this raises a more fundamental question: what is the essence of Freemasonry?

The nature of the Masonic religion consists in perversion, in the reversal of the order given by God. In transgressing the laws of God, the High Freemasons see the true progress of humanity, the spiritual construction of the temple of humanity. Divine revelation is replaced by Masonic secrecy and man ultimately makes himself god. Historians have recognized Freemasonry as the germ of political totalitarianism.[6] Already the well-known Freemason and philosopher Jean-Jacques Rousseau said, "The life of man is not only a gift of nature, but a conditional gift of the State."[7]

The candidate of the 33rd degree of the "The Ancient and Accepted Scottish Rite" of Freemasonry, for instance, will receive this instruction: "Neither the law, nor property, nor religion may govern man; and since they destroy man by depriving him of his most precious rights, the law, property, and religion are murderers to whom we have sworn to take the most terrible revenge; they are enemies against whom we swore an inexorable war at any cost. Of these three disreputable enemies, religion must be the constant object of our deadly attacks. If we have destroyed religion, we will have the law and property at our disposal, and we can regenerate society by building Masonic religion, law, and property."[8]

---

6 See A. Cobban, *Historia de las Civilizaciones*, quoted in A. Bárcena, *Iglesia y Masonería* (Madrid: Ediciones San Román, 2016), 71.

7 *The Social Contract*, II, 5.

8 M. Tirado y Rojas, *La Masonería en España. Ensayo Histórico* (Madrid: Imprenta de Enrique Maroto y Hermano, 1892), 1:170.

One can recognize that Freemasonry is the Anti-Church in the following astonishingly frank witness of Giuliano Di Bernardo, Grand Master of the Masonic Lodge *Gran Loggia Regolare d'Italia*, which he gave during his television appearance on April 11, 2001, on the Italian TV Channel, Rai 2. He said: "You become a Mason through an initiation. Initiation is a constitutive act that gives man a dimension he did not have before. An analogy we find in baptism. You are not born a Christian, you become a Christian through baptism. And so, you become a Mason with the initiation. This means that you remain a Mason for life. Even if one then rejects Freemasonry, he remains a Mason. Even if you are asleep, even if you become an enemy of Freemasonry, you are always a Mason because you have received initiation, and initiation is a sacred act."

We also have to bear in mind the following shocking words, written by the excommunicated Catholic priest Antonio Fogazzaro, a leading Italian Modernist, in a book published in 1905: "We want to organize our whole action purposefully. A Catholic Freemasonry? Yes, a Freemasonry of the catacombs. [...] One must work towards reforming Roman Catholicism in a progressive, theosophical sense through a pope who is convinced by these ideas."[9]

To put this into the perspective of salvation history, when Jesus Christ came into the world and the Apostles preached the Gospel, the world was governed by an evil, pagan society, and so it is again today. After some seventeen hundred years, Christian society in Europe, which began with Constantine, has collapsed. We are again in a neo-pagan society, but to some extent it is worse because the Gnostic and Satanic invention of gender ideology is now destroying the human being in his or her natural sexual reality and destroying the family as well.

In his intervention at the Synod on the Family in October 2015, Cardinal Robert Sarah called gender ideology and ISIS "two apocalyptic beasts."

It is apocalyptic, and we have to struggle against it. But as Christians we cannot be fearful.

Your Excellency, do you believe that Western civilization is collapsing?

Yes, of course. The civilization built by Christianity has already collapsed. One needs, though, to qualify what is meant by "Western

---

9 See *Il Santo* (Milan: Baldini e Castoldi, 1905), 44 and 22.

civilization." The Freemasons also use this term, saying: "*We* are Western civilization. We brought light to Europe." Hence, they called the eighteenth century — the century in which Freemasonry officially began — the century of "the Enlightenment." To the contrary, it was a time of obscuration, of increasing darkness, because the so-called "Enlightenment" was an attempt to think and to live without the light of supernatural faith.

Would you say this is reflected in the European Union, which as a political body refuses to acknowledge the Christian roots of Europe? In 2007, which marked the fiftieth anniversary of the founding of the EU, Pope Benedict XVI told European bishops that Europe was committing a form of "apostasy from itself" by abandoning its Christian identity.

Exactly. When the European Union speaks about "European values," they are speaking about Masonic moral and political principles. These new "European values" are anthropocentric and against the revelation of God, and therefore they are ultimately against man. They will not produce an authentic civilization. There is no civilization when you separate yourself from God, from the revelation of God, and from the natural law, which is the signature of God.

People sometimes wonder why it is so important to place God at the center of society. Why is it that when we divorce ourselves from God or the natural law, civilization itself collapses?

"Civilization" comes from the Latin, *civis*, citizen — it means citizens creating a *civitas*, a city. In a city, there has to be order, law, beauty, hierarchy. Without these, there is no city — only anarchy and chaos. When you eliminate the laws of God, either in the natural law, which is written by God, or in the supernatural law, in the divine revelation of Holy Scripture, you begin to dismantle this beautiful city, and then chaos ensues in the private and public sphere.

This brings us to another principle of the Freemasons, which is the principle of chaos. They say, "We must create chaos in society occasionally and then, from chaos, we will create our order." Significantly, one of the ideological and strategic mottos of Freemasonry is: "*ordo ab chao.*"

Civilization is only possible according to the law of God, either natural or supernatural. This implies that God is the ultimate lawgiver, not man. Prior to divine revelation in Christ, there were civilizations that to some extent followed the will of God according to natural law. For example, the

Confucian system in China and Korea upheld a very high standard for a beautiful civilization in the moral sense, as for example in the principle of living together in mutual respect and harmony. It was based on the natural law, and so, on God the Creator — not merely on man alone.

We have to return to an esteem and observance of the natural law and from there build a civilization as a first step. European society is no longer a civilization. It has no civilization, because they have divorced themselves from natural law and from divine revelation. The current European so-called civilization represents ugliness, chaos, and cruelty. We cannot call this a civilization. How can you speak of civilization when you are perpetrating a mass genocide of innocent people in the wombs of their mothers, which is extremely cruel and whose extent has never existed in all of human history — killing innocent people, your own babies on a mass scale? For me, the existence of abortion in society is already an indication that there is no real civilization. There is technology, but there is no civilization. True civilization is destroyed through the promotion of immorality, through the destruction of the family. This is because a family is a little city, and when you destroy the miniature, you destroy the real city, and then the entire civilization.

Like destroying cells in the body.

Exactly. We have to restore the family — which is, according to natural law, a husband and wife and their children. As Christian European civilization collapses, it is being replaced with cold technology. Pure technology is spiritually cold and therefore people are not happy, they are empty, they are continuously seeking pleasures to escape the inner void. To avoid the ugliness, the insanity, people are running after new pleasures, new technologies, and they become in their souls cold, egoistic, and cruel.

We must restore civilization by restoring the natural law and the natural family. Then we need to restore Christ the King to society. This would be the most beautiful civilization, where Christ is reigning as King of the society, even in the parliaments and the schools. Europe had a beautiful civilization in the Christian Middle Ages, until the Protestant revolution began to destroy its unity.

Would you say more about this period of history?

To start with, Constantine opened the doors for Christ in human society. It was really a very meritorious act from this emperor; therefore, the Orthodox Church considers him a saint and gave him the title "Equal to the Apostles," along with his mother St. Helena. However, the Catholic Church does not consider him a saint because he led a life that was not exemplary, with murders, adulteries, and so on. He received baptism only on his deathbed and from an Arian heretic bishop.

Nevertheless, we have to acknowledge his merits: he opened the doors to Christ in human society. He opened the door, and Christ slowly and gradually came to reign in society. As a consequence, a true civilization grew organically as a garden grows. This civilization reached the peak of its beauty in the Middle Ages: from the fourth century to the peak in the thirteenth or fourteenth century — almost a thousand years. In those times, Christ truly reigned in the whole of public and social life. Therefore, it was an authentic civilization.

But it was far from ideal...

Even then, there were many sins in society. This was inevitable because the consequences of original sin and personal sin were at work. We must distinguish the bad example of some Christian emperors, popes, and bishops from the objective salutary influence of Christ's teaching in the laws and public customs of European society. Public life and laws in themselves reflected the wisdom and the beauty of God's Revelation. It was, for example, Constantine who first abolished the branding of slaves on their foreheads like cattle, because, he said, this is against the dignity of man who was created, according to the Bible, in the image and likeness of God. Constantine also decreed that Sundays had to be a day of rest in honor of the Resurrection of Jesus Christ, the Savior of mankind. Later, the gladiator fights were forbidden, and so on — step by step. Society became more humane, because it became more Christian, obeying Christ's divine teachings even on the public and objective level.

The reign of Christ in society must be established through legislation along with other endeavors. Yet today it is commonly thought that we must separate church and state, and that religion has no place in politics.

This idea is an illusion, because when religion has no place in politics, then politics has no measure and no orientation. Then politics and the State become a kind of god. It will then go astray from the wisdom and the law of God. Therefore, when one says religion has no place in politics, it is the same as saying God has nothing to do with the public life of men — and then we have an atheistic society, with atheistic and hence anti-human policies. Human society as such is also created by God, and it was conceived and created for Christ (cf. Col 1:16–17). All things are created for Christ, even politics and human society. Of course, politics has its own competency, and the Church should not interfere with those who are responsible for ordering temporal affairs. The Church has the spiritual competency. God unites in Christ the temporal and the spiritual, the eternal, the supernatural. But both have to worship Christ and obey Him: the rulers of human society and the shepherds of the Church.

Would you say more about the proper role of the Church in the temporal sphere?

Temporal affairs are not the real and primary competency of the Church. She does not have the authority to govern the strictly temporal affairs of human society. God did not give the Church this competency and this mission. Christ said to the Apostles, "Go and preach the Gospel and teach the people to observe all that I have commanded you" (cf. Mt 28:20).

The relationship between the Church and political and human society is analogous to the relationship between the soul and the body. The Church represents the eternal and supernatural, thus she represents the soul. This truth, however, does not contradict the fact that the lay faithful should have their proper role in ordering temporal affairs. The social and political authorities and institutions represent the temporal and natural, hence the body. However, you cannot separate the soul from the body; you would then have a corpse. Therefore, a human political society will not have true progress and prosperity if it bans the influence and reign of Christ over it. This is our situation. Without Christ the King, human society in time becomes morally and spiritually a corpse, because of the absence of its soul.

The Church is superior because she is the soul. But the body has its own laws and the soul has to respect the laws of the body. The body has its laws: for example, the body needs a certain number of hours of sleep. What happens if the soul says: "I want to pray all night"? Were the soul to interfere and forbid the body the sleep it needs, chaos would ensue, because in time we would be unable to think and work and then we would become sick. According to this analogy, the Church has to respect the purely temporal, technical competencies of the State.

However, we also have to restore all things in Christ: "*instaurare omnia in Christo*," as St. Paul says (cf. Eph 1:10). There is no other way. With humanism in the Renaissance, man started to make himself the measure of all things. And then came the revolution of Luther, and the Freemasonic Revolution in 1789 (the so-called "French Revolution"). Now we are faced with the consequences: human society, especially in Europe, has in the end thrown off Christ. We therefore have to begin to restore at least the natural law and then start restoring once again the reign of Christ. His salutary divine teachings have to reign not only in individual souls, but also in schools, universities, and parliaments.

We have an arduous road ahead. What is the concrete path to bring Christ back to Western society?

Although the majority of our politicians are no longer Christians, and it will take time to re-enthrone Christ as King of society, the Church has to set the goal clearly once again — as Pope Pius XI in his 1925 encyclical *Quas Primas* so beautifully expressed it. We have to create Catholic, Christian families and they have to penetrate slowly once again into political, social, and cultural life. We have to rebuild our Christian culture, for there is no longer an authentic culture in Europe. We live now in Europe in a culture of ugliness. We have to create beautiful Christian theater, film, painting, music, and so on. But Christian art like this is a fruit of faith, so we have to start with the Catholic faith in its integrity. Without this, we will not succeed in building a new civilization. It will take some generations and perhaps centuries. But it is worthwhile.

One sees glimmers of this rebuilding in the homeschooling movement wherever it is allowed to flourish. There is a quiet garden growing in the United States, for instance, and in other parts of the world. It is more difficult here in Europe in countries like Germany, where homeschooling is against the law.

This is a dictatorship. Under Communism in the Soviet Union, education in the family was also forbidden, as it was under the Nazi regime. The prohibition against homeschooling is a dictatorial law.

We have this challenge and duty to restore civilization and the reign of Christ in our families, in our societies. In the end, God has not only the Church in His hands, but also world history. He permits much evil that good may shine more brightly. So, it will always be a battle, a fight — we have to keep this in mind. Then God will achieve the ultimate goal of creation in the new city, the New Jerusalem, which will be the everlasting civilization. We have to inaugurate it already here on earth. This is our Christian mission.

5

Islam and the
Dechristianization of Europe

Your Excellency, as a Catholic bishop living in a predominately Muslim country, how concerned are you about the influx of Muslims into Europe and its Islamization, particularly in light of your comments about secularism?

For several years now in Europe, we have been witnessing a massive influx and presence of Islam and its effect in supplanting, and in some cases overtly opposing, what remains of Christian European culture. This phenomenon began some decades ago — perhaps fifty years ago — in numbers not as large as we see today, but the presence of Muslims in Europe had begun then. This may have been the result of workers coming to work mostly in France, Germany, and Great Britain. But since the recent war in Syria, the influx of Muslims into Europe has been, at least in part, organized by those who plan to Islamize Europe. And to Islamize Europe means practically to destroy Christianity in that region, to de-Christianize Europe.

The plans of many global world powers are clear: to de-Christianize Europe. This has always been a stated aim of Freemasonry. We had the most striking example of it in the French Revolution. The Freemasons during the Jacobin dictatorship, which was called the "Reign of Terror," even changed the names of the days and months to wipe away every trace of Christian tradition. They didn't succeed, however, and Europe experienced a restoration. Efforts to further de-Christianize Europe by other means, however, continued: through anti-Christian legislation that destroys morality and the family. That is how you can destroy Christianity on a large scale. And this is what powerful influences in European governments have done in slow motion since the time of the French Revolution up to our day.

The Communist Revolution was a very apt instrument in the hands of powerful forces seeking to de-Christianize the world. The Communist revolution, with its global reach, was thus an efficacious opportunity for Freemasonry to further de-Christianize all of humanity and to build up a new temple to their god — that is, the divinization and adoration of man, which leads in the end to the adoration of Satan.

Nevertheless, Communism collapsed...

We do not know all the exact reasons for this collapse, but I will not rule out the possibility of strategic influence from world powers.

But Pope John Paul II, President Ronald Reagan in the United States, and Margaret Thatcher in Great Britain were working together to bring about the fall of Communism.

Certainly, this is a legitimate perspective, but this does not explain to me the entire and remarkable collapse. Of course, in every great moment of history, God has His influence also. Thus, to believe that, through the prayers to Our Lady of Fatima and the efforts of Pope John Paul II, the Eastern Bloc was weakened is laudable. But one cannot conclusively rule out that additional geopolitical factors were complicit with the Eastern Bloc collapse.

Are you suggesting that some world powers knew that Communism would fall and had a plan in place?

One cannot rule out the possibility that there was also a plan to carry out the last phase of Communism: that is, to use the collapse of the classical, directly atheistic system of the Soviet Union, as it had evolved up to that point, to plant the seeds of the final, most virulent phase of Marxism — which is now prevailing in Europe.

Woven into the fabric and vision of the European Union, as we know it today, is the social and political machinery that can be deployed as a means to realize this final phase or period of Marxism. The penultimate phase is gender ideology and the complete destruction of the family at its root. The final phase will be the adoration of Satan, of the idol, and the total and explicit prohibition of adoration of Christ. I am not a prophet, but one can discern the method, means, and levers to achieve the final phase. Regrettably, there are already signs of this in mainstream American and European society, which gives us a concrete basis to think in such terms.

Satanism, the occult, and a morbid fascination with death are increasingly more prevalent in Western societies today. Gender ideology allows you to control people at a very profound level, whereas under Communism — if you retained the faith — even though you had no religious freedom, you still had the faith and were interiorly free. Today they are wounding and perverting people — even children — at such a profound level that it becomes very easy to manipulate the masses.

Faith presupposes nature, so if you distort and destroy nature, faith has no foundation on which to build — *gratia supponit naturam* — and this is the strategy of the enemy. This is not, however, sufficient for those with diabolical global plans. Anti-Christian forces inexorably seek concrete tools to destroy Europe, and Islamization can be viewed as a useful tool in their grand designs. They know that powerful forces in Islam already seek to expand and by design marginalize Christianity to the periphery. Only then will Islam gain ever more political power. The Muslims in Europe are fast becoming greater in terms of numbers. Were they to gain political power and establish Sharia law, all other religions would be discriminated against. This can be observed already in Europe and has been the basis for the spread of militant Islam.

This Islamic "opportunity" — as volatile and self-destructive as it might be — is not lost on Freemasonry. And one can see the cunning deployment of Masonic efforts under the pretext of mercy and compassion, to emotionalize issues and implore us to accept refugees because Christ was a refugee, and on the grounds that the Church was always merciful to foreigners. This is propaganda to displace Christian Europe. So, we are in a full process and this will increase still more. I live in an Islamic country where Islam has no political power, thanks be to God. The members of our government in Kazakhstan are mostly ethnic Muslims, but many of them do not practice Islam. However, the Muslims have the support of the government in an indirect way, for instance when governmental authorities help them to build mosques or to appoint imams. A secular government has to control these Islamic tendencies, since Islam essentially tends to become a political system according to Sharia law, which by its express terms is intolerant towards all non-Islamic peoples, who are treated like second-class citizens.

Do you think Islam is a religion of peace or that ISIS is the true face of Islam?

Violence against so-called "nonbelievers" is openly justified in the Koran, but it seems to me that ISIS is not the true form of Islam. It is a political abuse of Islam. However, ISIS is seen by some who hold political power as an instrument to be exploited in order to further an anti-Christian agenda.

Not long after the election of US President Donald Trump, the United States military swiftly moved in to defeat ISIS and take away their land holdings.

Yes, thanks be to God, the new President and cabinet of the United States do not support ISIS. But if we think back, where did ISIS get their weapons, heavy artillery, and advanced technology? These are obvious and troubling questions to consider.

I say this only within the context of the Islamization of Europe, which we must look at from various perspectives. I believe history will ultimately reveal the truth of the matter, but the hard saying of French writer Honoré de Balzac comes to mind in such matters: "There are two kinds of history: official history, lying history, that which they teach in colleges, history '*ad usum delphini*'; and secret history, in which are the true causes of events, shameful history."[1] Recall that I am a survivor of the most evil, systemic, geopolitical movement in history — Communism — where the official "truth" was routinely a lie.

I don't wish to enter more deeply into this political issue but will only add that we must distinguish between Muslim people and Islam. In my country, Muslim people are not violent but want to live peacefully and let others believe as they want. I have Muslim friends, but they say, "We are Muslims because our parents and grandparents were Muslims, and we believe in God" — whether they say "Allah" or simply "God." Though they may know an expression here and there, they don't know the Koran. In my opinion, the majority of the Muslim people are simple and peaceful and do not know the Koran or the Sharia well, and they live a religion of natural belief in one God as Creator and Judge. This is natural and is inscribed in the soul of every human being. But when some of them start to deepen their knowledge of the Koran and Sharia law, they start to become radicalized and inclined to violent irrationality. Christianity depends upon both faith and reason, as the two wings of a bird, as John Paul II beautifully explained in his encyclical *Fides et Ratio*. In Islam, supernatural faith is absent, and the aspect of reason regarding religious matters even on a natural level is deficient.

---

1   Honoré de Balzac, *La Comédie humaine*, "Scenes from Parisian Life" (New York, 1899), 364.

And, according to Islam, God's will is arbitrary.

Yes. You cannot say this is faith! Islam in itself is not faith.

Why is it not faith?

It is not faith because the only faith is given in Christianity. Faith by definition is the theological virtue by which man, with the gift of divine grace, believes in God and believes all that He has said and revealed, and all that Holy Church proposes for our belief (see *Catechism of the Catholic Church*, 1814). Faith involves an intellectual act, by the grace of God, of accepting the supernatural world, which is divinely revealed through Jesus Christ, the Incarnate God, though it was prepared for in the Old Testament. There is only one revelation: the Old Testament and the New Testament constitute one indivisible unity, with its fulfillment in Christ.

Faith is applicable only to belief in the Holy Trinity—Father, Son, and Holy Spirit. Only when a person accepts this can you say that he has faith. When someone does not believe in the Holy Trinity, he has no faith but simply natural religion. By natural religion, one can reach the knowledge of one God, who is Creator and Judge.

Many people are wrong in considering the natural knowledge of God as sufficient for salvation. There are several cases—on the internet and set forth in books—of the conversion of Muslim people to Christianity, who were then persecuted by their own families and not only persecuted but killed by their own fathers, their own mothers. This is a pure demonstration of blind fanaticism, where the aspect of reason is absent or strongly deficient.

Do you think Pope Benedict's Regensburg Address confirms your thoughts on Islam?

We saw the reactions after the Regensburg Address. The reaction demonstrated that this is true.

In your opinion, what was the most important thing Pope Benedict XVI said in his Regensburg Address?

He said that in the absence of reason, people come to believe that God's will is blind and arbitrary. This is then reflected in our lives—we are blind and go only by our arbitrary will. Islam always has to be politically controlled. When it is politically not controlled, it becomes innately violent and systemically oppressive of all who are not Muslims through the implementation of Sharia law.

In Kazakhstan, Islam is controlled by the government. The government of Kazakhstan promotes a climate of mutual tolerance among religions and promotes the ideal of harmony in society and inter-ethnic and interreligious peace. This policy is implemented in part through frequent congresses and symposia and talks and round-tables on several levels. I think this is very important. It could be good for American and European countries to look at the system of Kazakhstan, of social harmony, and to promote this, especially in these times in which there is so much conflict.

Pope Francis has devoted several paragraphs of the 2013 apostolic exhortation Evangelii Gaudium *to the Church's stance on Islam. I'd like to ask your thoughts on several key passages. Here is the first: "Our relationship with the followers of Islam has taken on great importance, since they are now significantly present in many traditionally Christian countries, where they can freely worship and become fully a part of society. We must never forget that they 'profess to hold the faith of Abraham, and together with us they adore the one, merciful God, who will judge humanity on the last day' (Second Vatican Ecumenical Council, Dogmatic Constitution on the Church,* Lumen Gentium, *n. 16)" (EG, n. 252).*

To state, as the Council did in *Lumen Gentium* n. 16, that Muslims adore together with us the one God ("*nobiscum Deum adorant*"), is theologically a highly ambiguous affirmation. That we Catholics adore with the Muslims the one God is not true. We don't adore with them. In the act of adoration, we always adore the Holy Trinity, we don't simply adore "the one God" but the Holy Trinity consciously — Father, Son, and Holy Ghost. Islam rejects the Holy Trinity. When the Muslims adore, they do not adore on the supernatural level of faith.

So even our act of adoration is radically different.

It is essentially different. Precisely because we turn to God and adore Him as children constituted in the ineffable dignity of divine filial adoption, and we do this with supernatural faith. However, the Muslims do not have supernatural faith. I repeat: they have a natural knowledge of God. The Koran is not the revelation of God, but a kind of anti-revelation of God, because the Koran expressly denies the divine revelation of the Incarnation, of the eternal divinity of the Son of God, of the redemptive sacrifice of Christ on the Cross, and therefore denies the truth of God, the Holy Trinity. This ambiguous affirmation of the Second Vatican Council must be corrected. This affirmation is not infallible and was not meant by the Council to be such.

In some way, we can accept the affirmation of *Lumen Gentium*, but then we must give a long explanation. Of course, when a person sincerely adores God the Creator — as I assume the majority of simple Muslim people do — they adore God with a natural act of worship, based on the natural knowledge of God, the Creator. Every non-Christian, every non-baptized person, including a Muslim, can adore God on the level of the natural knowledge of the existence of God. They adore in a natural act of adoration the same God, whom we adore in a supernatural act and with supernatural faith in the Holy Trinity. But these are two essentially different acts of adoration: the one is an act of natural knowledge and the other is an act of supernatural faith.

The acts of adoration, and the acts of knowing on which they are based, are substantially different, though the object is the same in that it is the same God. The affirmation of the Second Vatican Council should have been written more precisely, in order to avoid misunderstandings. Perhaps it could be formulated in this way: "Muslims adore God in an act of natural worship, and thus in a substantially different way than we Catholics do, since we adore God with supernatural faith." If the phrase had been formulated in this or some similar way, it would have avoided wrong applications in interreligious dialogue and wrong teachings in so many theological faculties and priestly seminaries in our days.

Returning to the passage in question: the subjective act of adoration of the Muslims is also different because their understanding of God is different from ours. We should bear in mind the fact that Muslims, accepting propositions asserted of God that are not of divine origin, are in danger of offering a false worship to God even on the natural level. Those who follow Islam see God as distant, devoid of a personal interrelationship, and this is a very wrongheaded idea of God. A considerable portion of Muslims has a distorted and false image of God as One who is unable to communicate personally with us, and whom we cannot truly and personally love as our Father and as our Redeemer.

Is it correct to say that Muslims worship the same God as the Jews?

As I said: from the point of view of simply natural religion, a lot of simple Muslims have natural knowledge of the existence of God and adore Him in an act of natural religion. The Jews, on the contrary, received the supernatural revelation of God. This revelation given to the Jews in the Old Testament was given only in view of God's Incarnation in Christ, and not for its own sake. The Holy Ghost says through the Apostle Paul in Holy Scripture: "Christ is the end of the law" (Rom 10:4), and "The former commandment is set aside because of its weakness and uselessness" (Heb 7:18). So, the Jews today adore God with us because of divine revelation in the Old Testament. However, the Jews of our day who reject Christ, and hence the everlasting covenant of God, adore Him in an unfaithful manner, a manner which does not please God, since they reject the true meaning of His covenant with them, which consists in the new and everlasting covenant in Jesus Christ. Since the first centuries, therefore, from the time of the Fathers and Doctors of the Church onward, the Church in her prayers called the Jews "unfaithful."[2] This expression reflected the fact that they rejected faith in the Incarnation of God and in the redemptive work of Jesus Christ. Before Christ, all the just of the Old Testament adored God in a faithful manner, because they implicitly accepted the new and everlasting covenant in Jesus Christ. But, insofar as Jews are followers of the Pharisees and of the Talmudic rabbis who rejected Christ, they now adore God in a defective and unfaithful manner.

Let's look at the next passage from Evangelii Gaudium. *It reads: "The sacred writings of Islam have retained some Christian teachings; Jesus and Mary receive profound veneration and it is admirable to see how Muslims both young and old, men and women, make time for daily prayer and faithfully take part in religious services. Many of them also have a deep conviction that their life, in its entirety, is from God and for God. They also acknowledge the need to respond to God with an ethical commitment and with mercy towards those most in need" (n. 252).*

And Pope Francis says, just after what you have quoted, that we can "benefit from their treasures." True enough: we can learn from all people, even from pagans, because when something is good in itself, it

---

2 The ancient Roman liturgy for Good Friday included the following invitation to prayer: "Oremus et pro perfidis Judæis" (let us pray for the unfaithful or unbelieving Jews). The Church used this prayer from about the time of the third century until 1959.

is acceptable to all. For example, the pope mentions that they have the deep conviction that their entire life is from God and for God. We have the same conviction. They show fidelity to their prayers during the day. When a false religion is faithful in prayer, all the more do we need to be faithful in prayer. This could be acceptable. But the fidelity to prayer of the Muslims must not to be attributed to Islam as such, but to the fact that being faithful to prayer or being faithful to a duty is in itself a good, which as such does not depend on a false religion.

We must also consider the fact that the Muslim conception of Jesus is a rejection of the Christian idea: for the Koran states that God cannot have a Son, and so they reject the Incarnation even if they accept the Virgin Birth. Therefore, it is inaccurate to equate their veneration of Jesus with our adoration of Him as God Incarnate and the Redeemer of mankind; and their veneration of Mary is not the same as our veneration of her as the Mother of God and the Mediatrix of all graces. Hence, we cannot learn from them how to relate properly to Jesus or Mary. In addition, their understanding that life is "for" God is not the same as ours, for Jesus taught that God is our Father, that we live for Him, in order to increase our love for Him and be happy with Him forever, whereas their conception of living for God is as a slave lives to serve a powerful Master. Finally, the Muslim conception of mercy is different from the Christian conception of mercy, for we are merciful as God the Father was merciful to us, sending His Son to die for us when we were still His enemies, which the Muslims deny.

In the next paragraph of Evangelii Gaudium, *Pope Francis continues: "In order to sustain dialogue with Islam, suitable training is essential for all involved, not only so that they can be solidly and joyfully grounded in their own identity, but so that they can also acknowledge the values of others, appreciate the concerns underlying their demands and shed light on shared beliefs. We Christians should embrace with affection and respect Muslim immigrants to our countries in the same way that we hope and ask to be received and respected in countries of Islamic tradition. I ask and I humbly entreat those countries to grant Christians freedom to worship and to practice their faith, in light of the freedom which followers of Islam enjoy in Western countries!" (EG n. 253).*

The pope says that we have to accept with affection and embrace Muslim immigrants to our countries in the same way as we would hope to be accepted in their countries. To me, this is *theoretically* acceptable. In the current historical situation, however, it is naïve to accept this, because of what is going on right before our eyes through these so-called immigrants. In fact, the immigrants are mostly used as instruments of a politically orchestrated process for the Islamization of Europe. We cannot be so naïve. If Muslims become more "solidly grounded in their own identity" on a political level, they will become more intolerant towards non-Muslims. According to Surah 9:29, Muslims are to "fight those who do not believe in Allah or in the Last Day and who do not consider unlawful what Allah and His Messenger have made unlawful and who do not adopt the religion of truth from those who were given the Scripture — [fight] until they give the tribute [*jizyah*] willingly while they are humbled."

We must always keep in mind that Islam and the Catholic faith are not on the same level. For a believing Catholic, Islam is not the true religion; the Catholic faith is the only true religion. We cannot put them on the same level. And therefore, when there is a Catholic society, these governments have to arrange that Muslim immigrants and refugees in real need should be accepted first by Islamic countries. It would be more natural and harmonious even for Muslims to be integrated into Islamic countries. When we bring them here, there will be clashes of culture, and Islam will spread, which will make future generations Islamic in time. We cannot accept this outcome if we want to preserve what little remains of European culture.

The clash of cultures makes for chaos.

Exactly. That is why it is not prudent to accept Muslim immigrants on a large scale as Europe now does. In this sense, the Holy See and the pope could perhaps help find Islamic countries who would be able to receive immigrants — and there are such countries — or at least European countries could give aid to help those countries who take in Islamic migrants. But a condition for giving aid must be that the Islamic countries grant the same freedom of worship to Christians that we now concede to Muslims in Western countries. It is a very commonsense requirement.

The same passage in Evangelii Gaudium *continues: "Faced with disconcerting episodes of violent fundamentalism, our respect for true followers of Islam should lead us to avoid hateful generalizations, for authentic*

Islam and the proper reading of the Koran are opposed to every form of violence" (n. 253).

With all respect due to him, I do not agree with the pope when he says that a proper reading of the Koran is opposed to every form of violence. First, this is not true simply based on a plain reading of the Koran. The later Surahs of the Koran are very violent toward non-Muslims and call for the occupation of non-Muslim countries by violence. This is well understood by Muslims to be the legitimate method to read the Koran. Further, Muslims agree that the later (more violent) Surahs have more authority. Usually Muslims understand the Koran literally as they have no spiritual or allegorical exegesis. The Muslims have no authority to settle disputes with universal authority; they have no magisterium. Maybe some exceptional persons, some good Islamic scholars will do this, but they do not represent Islam as such. They have no ultimate authority. There is no central authority in Islam to decide doctrinal questions for all Muslims.

Your Excellency, how do you think the Church can best respond to the Islamization of Europe?

I will tell you a story. Once a Kazakh student of English saw me close to the church in Kazakhstan, as I am always wearing the cassock. He recognized me as a Catholic priest and he wanted to speak with me. We spoke for almost an hour. He was very intelligent and was seeking God. He said to me that he grew up in a practicing and strict Muslim family, but he started to seek God because as a Muslim he was yearning, longing for God as Love. And God as Love is rejected in the Islamic religion.

To be loved eternally: this is a desire that is prompted by God's grace. This young man came oftentimes to our church and, after sitting in the back of the empty church, he would come out and say that he always felt a deep peace, which he had never before experienced in a mosque. He was seeking God and already reading the Gospel, even though his mother prohibited him. But he was reading the Bible on the internet in English. And so, he said to me: "I oftentimes look at television and internet out of Europe." He was informing himself because he was seeking God. And he said, "The form of Christianity that I see in Europe does not attract me because they have no zeal, no convictions. Islam attracts young people because of the decisiveness, the commitment, its uncompromising nature. This attracts young people. This form of Christianity which I see in Europe does not attract me."

What a testimonial from a non-Christian! He couldn't take this soft Christianity seriously.

I heard a saying which has often been repeated in recent years, "We have not to fear a strong Islam in Europe but a weak Christianity." This is our problem. As this young Kazakh man observed, our answer to Islam must be to increase our convictions in the Catholic faith, to nurture a virtuous and chaste life, faith in the uniqueness of Christ, in the reality that there is no other way to salvation outside the Church, and that all who are not Christians and who are Islamic have to know Christ and, by God's grace, freely accept Him. It is our duty to tell them this with love, not with violence; with love, but with conviction. We have to be deeply convinced Christians. We have to foster and nourish in ourselves the spirit of martyrdom, and develop the beauty of a chaste and virtuous life. One of the best and most efficacious means of radiating the Catholic faith and of evangelizing is given when our young people, our families, our priests radiate the integrity of the moral life.

This is what will attract Muslims: our conviction, our uncompromising faith, and the purity of the moral life in our families, and among young people and priests. The unique historical contribution of the Second Vatican Council consists in this: the universal call to holiness, a call we have to take very seriously. To admit and to implicitly promote divorce in the Church — as many pastoral guidelines for *Amoris Laetitia* already do — is contrary to the call to holiness. To commit acts of adultery in a second union is not holiness. To present oneself for Holy Communion without a serious intention to avoid such sins in the future is not holiness. There are no circumstances that can justify even one act of adultery or even one sexual act outside of a valid marriage. This is always contrary to God and offends God. The wrong and ambiguous application of *Amoris Laetitia* is not a call to holiness! To the contrary — the call to holiness is a long path, a difficult way that requires sacrifice and patience. Yet it is the only way that leads to happiness.

You are saying that the Church's message has to be challenging.

We have to say this to everyone, including to people who are divorced and living in a second union: "We will accompany you with loving understanding, but we will say that your unchaste acts offend God, my dear. But we will help you, with patience, so that you will no longer offend God." And we will teach and talk to young people, to help them to live in purity before marriage. And we will tell priests to live a pure life in celibacy, to avoid pornography and so on, and to live a life of prayer, of basic asceticism, of zeal for the salvation for souls.

With the pope and bishops as zealous proclaimers of the uniqueness of salvation in Christ, we have to start a new missionary zeal *ad gentes* to non-Christians with love and conviction. We have to propose Christ and the Catholic faith to them. This is by no means "proselytism." The witness of our Christian life, the beauty of our Christian life and our liturgy, will surely attract Muslims. St. Paul tells the Corinthians that if an unbeliever or unlearned person comes to them and sees that they are truly worshipping God, he will "fall down on his face, he will adore God, affirming that God is truly among you" (cf. 1 Cor 14:24–25). When we restore beauty, truly reverent and venerable and sublime liturgies, Christocentric beauty and sacredness, this will strongly attract others, especially the Muslims. Their souls are penetrated by the natural sense of reverence, sometimes even more deeply than some Christians. This is our path. Overcoming the crisis of the Church will also have the missionary effect of attracting non-Catholics and non-Christians to the Church.

6

Religious Indifferentism

Your Excellency, I'd like to discuss the Church's relationship with non-Christian religions and the problem of religious indifferentism, i.e., the opinion that differences of religious belief are essentially unimportant. In our discussion of Islam, you suggested it might be good for American and European countries to look at the system in Kazakhstan for social harmony. Do you find this type of interreligious dialogue effective?

It is effective in our country, yes. We do not discuss religious topics but the necessity of living peacefully and respectfully together in society and maintaining harmony in social life and not abusing religion as a pretext for introducing physical violence into common life. Religious tolerance was always part of Catholic doctrine, even before the Council. But Catholics cannot be in favor of other religions propagating their errors, because all religions that are not Catholic are erroneous, and God does not approve them, and so they are contrary to the will of God. They contain within themselves spiritual poison. It is clear that we cannot let spiritual poison spread through society.

Therefore, Catholics must tolerate other religions but not promote them. This is an essential difference. For sixteen hundred years, ever since the Church gained its freedom under Constantine, the Magisterium has taught uninterruptedly that it was not permitted for religious errors to be spread freely in society, because people are vulnerable to being contaminated. Civil authorities therefore had the duty of preventing the spread of such spiritual maladies, and the Church gave instructions to the government, because civil authority has no competence in questions of religious truth.

Can you explain the difference, in this context, between toleration and approval?

Catholics must tolerate even erroneous religions in view of the common good. A Catholic state grants to other religions tolerance so that they can exist, so that they can have their own churches or prayer houses and schools. However, an official Catholic society and Catholic state cannot give to false religions the same rights that are due to the true Catholic religion. Otherwise the false religions would spread among the Catholic population and lead young and weak persons into a false religion.

Many people say that this view is outmoded, untenable, after Vatican II.

Before the Second Vatican Council, the Church had always taught the tolerance of other religions to some degree. However, with the Council's Declaration on Religious Freedom *Dignitatis Humanae*, there was in my opinion a drastic change regarding the previous and universal Magisterium of the Church, which had always said that error does not have the same right as truth to be propagated. Error has no rights by nature, just as we have no right by nature to sin. God has not given man liberty in order to carry out a moral evil (sin) or an intellectual evil (error).

The more we live in accord with God's will, with the truth, the freer we are — and the more our freedom grows. *Dignitatis Humanae* made a change that is difficult to reconcile with the perennial Magisterium of the Church. One might easily deduce from this document that truth and error have the same rights by nature, by contending that the choice of error, the choice of a false religion, is a natural right of the human person. There are some people who say, "My conscience dictates that I have to create a Satanic church to worship Satan. This is permitted by the freedom of my conscience and the freedom of religion."

Where would you locate the problem with the document? What is the "change"?

The text of *Dignitatis Humanae* says that the freedom to choose one's religion is a right which is founded in the very nature of the human person (n. 2: "*in ipsa eius natura fundatur*"), with just limitations when there is a danger to public order in society. However, man does not have the right by nature to commit a sin or to embrace error. There is no natural right to offend and to outrage God, since a religion of idolatry and any false religion is an outrage committed against God. We can tolerate sin and error, but they do not have a natural right; this would be a perversion of God's created order, since God created all human beings for the unique end of knowing and worshiping explicitly God the Most Holy Trinity. Creation, and natural right, are ordered to divine revelation. Therefore, there cannot be even a natural right to worship merely a "Supreme Being," as stated in *Dignitatis Humanae*, n. 4. In divine revelation, God positively commanded every human being to worship only the true God; namely, God the Father, Son, and Holy Spirit. Furthermore, the concept of "Supreme Being" is in itself unclear and is understood by non-Christian religions, even by Muslims, in diverging ways, and oftentimes in a disfigured manner. Besides, the original text in *Dignitatis Humanae* n. 4 does not say *"ens supremum"* (Supreme Being), but instead *"numen supremum,"* which usually means "supreme divinity." Other official translations of this expression are more accurate, e.g., "la divinité suprême" (French), "suprema divinità" (Italian), "la Divinidad" (Spanish). These expressions are highly ambiguous, because in idolatrous religions there is also a "supreme divinity" amidst a pantheon of so-called "divinities."

It is surely against revealed truth to say that God positively wills the worship merely of a "Supreme Being," and that the human person should have a natural right to it (*"in ipsa eius natura fundatur"*). The only right given by God to the human person consists in knowing and worshipping the one true God, the Most Holy Trinity.

Was there a legitimate concern on the part of those who drafted Dignitatis Humanae *that prompted their formulations?*

The question of religious freedom has been changed by the concrete historical situation. We now live in a completely secularized and non-Christian society, with de facto atheistic governments in Europe. We are in a new situation, comparable to that of Christians living under pagan, Roman society. We are now entering a kind of new persecution.

But we cannot change the principles. One principle is that only the truth has rights; another is that every human society, and even governments, ought to recognize Christ and worship Him. These truths are unchangeable; they are revealed truths, as Pius XI states in *Quas Primas*. The state, of course, should not interfere in Church affairs. However, as representatives of the people, they must publicly worship Christ, the true God, and practice the true religion, which is only the Catholic religion. This is the constant Catholic truth, which no ecclesiastical authority can change into its contrary. The concrete, practical application of this truth in a changed historical situation is another question.

What do you mean?

The social historical situation has changed in the sense that we have to ask the government, just as under Roman persecution: "please give us freedom to worship God." In this sense, we cannot say to the atheistic government that we alone have the true religion — because they are atheistic and would laugh this off, rejecting such an argument. We can only use an argument from the point of view of civil law: "Grant us religious liberty!" So, as citizens of an atheistic or of a non-Christian government, all persons, independent of their religions, have a right to worship according to their convictions, having the same civil rights regarding religion.

But these governments could say that Christianity is actually harmful to the common good and needs to be suppressed, in order to build the society and world they envision.

They can say this, and they might do this. The pagan Romans did so, for they considered Christianity to be a spiritual disease and a threat to the common good. During that time, even the Christian name was considered a crime.

A traditional interpretation of the Second Vatican Council's document on religious freedom could say that we Catholics can claim our religious liberty on the basis of being citizens — as citizens, we have the same rights as those of other religions. However, I hope that in the future the affirmation of the Council document about a natural right to choose a false religion will be changed, because the claim that "religious freedom is a natural right" is, in its present formulation, theologically incorrect and misleading. The Council says that the right to religious freedom, which ultimately also includes the choice of a false religion (which is, however, expressly prohibited by God), has its foundation "in the very nature" of the human person (*Dignitatis Humanae*, n. 2). Unfortunately, this statement relativizes the correct affirmation in the same document that says that man has the "moral obligation to seek the truth" (ibid.). Only the choice of the true religion, that is, the Catholic religion, is a natural right positively willed by God. God is the Creator of natural rights, hence He cannot positively will the diversity of religions or the worship of merely a "Supreme Being."

I have a natural right to do good and to know the truth, and the truth is the Catholic religion. I have a right to the true religion. Not every religion can be the object of this right by nature. We have no right by nature to adore idols. Some religions also venerate a "Supreme Being," and since they have no divine revelation, even their concept of the "Supreme Being" can be wrong and idolatrous and hence offensive to God. Idolaters can only have a civil right as citizens. So, as citizens — whether Catholic or Muslim and so on — we have the same right to life, to a just salary, and such things. Juridical matters have to be the same in the sense that these religious communities are simply civil associations, and civil associations have the same rights. We already live in a new pagan society, but we cannot change the constant traditional theological principles.

I want to press you on the line of argumentation you are using, because it sounds like you are saying, "The constant teaching of the Church is x, but given the particular, concrete historical changes, for practical reasons we need to alter our approach and the way we apply this doctrine." This sounds like the argument that was used in the debate about Amoris Laetitia: *"We keep the doctrine, but for pastoral reasons as historical circumstances change, we may need to adapt it."*

I have also considered this objection. In the case of admitting to Holy Communion those who are divorced and living in a second union in a marital manner (*more uxorio*), they are in the same situation as were all Catholics who lived before them. We have always had divorced people and there is substantially no new situation. We cannot say, for example, that we are now in a special situation in society, and that we can now allow people who are living in an adulterous union to receive Holy Communion in some cases. The commandment not to commit adultery belongs to the so-called negative precepts of the commandments of God, i.e., thou shall *not* lie, steal, commit adultery, and so on. These commandments are indispensable always. No authority in the Church, not even the pope, has the power to dispense even in exceptional cases from these divine commandments.

The case of religious liberty is a different question, for it is not a matter of denying a principle that the Church has always taught. Rather, in this case, it is simply impossible practically with an atheistic society or government to claim that they must give the Catholic Church privileges above those of other religions and that they limit other religions' spreading of their errors. This is not an exception to a principle, but the case in which the principle cannot be applied through no fault of our own.

Immediately after Evangelii Gaudium*'s treatment of Islam, which we have discussed, there follows a passage about non-Christian religions more generally. I wonder what your thoughts are on the text which follows: "Non-Christians, by God's gracious initiative, when they are faithful to their own consciences, can live 'justified by the grace of God' (International Theological Commission,* Christianity and the World Religions *[1996], 72), and thus be 'associated to the paschal mystery of Jesus Christ' (ibid.). But due to the sacramental dimension of sanctifying grace, God's working in them tends to produce signs and rites, sacred expressions which in turn bring others to a communitarian experience of journeying towards God (cf. ibid., 81–87). While these lack the meaning and efficacy of the sacraments instituted by Christ, they can be channels which the Holy Spirit raises up in order to liberate non-Christians from atheistic immanentism or from purely individual religious experiences. The same Spirit everywhere brings forth various forms of practical wisdom which help people to bear suffering and to live in greater peace and harmony. As Christians, we can also benefit from these treasures built up over many centuries, which can help us better to live our own beliefs" (n. 254).*

The formulation that "non-Christians, by God's gracious initiative, when they are faithful to their own consciences can be 'justified by the grace of God' and thus can be 'associated to the paschal mystery of Jesus Christ'" can lead to a relativizing of the unique and obligatory character of the concrete way to salvation which is the Church, the Mystical Body of Christ, and therefore the way of salvation that God gave us.

Can Catholics legitimately speak of a "sacramental dimension of sanctifying grace" in non-Christian religions?

It is false to say that God works with His sanctifying grace in non-Christians through a "sacramental dimension." When God works in non-Christians, He does so by other means which only He knows and which we do not know. "Signs and rites" as sacred expressions pleasing to God are found only in the new and everlasting covenant in the Church, which God Himself established. Outside the Church there are no salvific and religious rites pleasing to God. The first Commandment, that man should not worship other gods, i.e., should not use "signs and rites, sacred expressions" relating to other gods, is forever valid.

The pope speaks about "signs and rites, sacred expressions" in non-Christian religions. However, they are objectively false signs of false religions. The very existence of such religions is contrary to the will of God. With such expressions as the one quoted, other religions are ultimately placed on the same plane as the Church. It is an error to say: "The Church is one path with its own signs and rites and non-Christian religions are another path, which also have their own signs and rites that can communicate an experience of journeying towards God." This would mean that God positively wills the diversity of religions. This is very relativistic and confusing. We cannot accept this. The Apostles and the entire Church tradition never taught this. It leads to relativism regarding the uniqueness and visibility of the way of salvation found in Christ and His Church. Even in the case of the "unknown god" of the Athenians that St. Paul recognized as the Holy Trinity, he did not encourage the continuance of this altar; he called them to conversion and belief in Christ (Acts 17:22–33).

I thought "the gods of the nations are demons," as the Vulgate has it (Psalm 95:5)?

The altar of the "unknown god" was an example of natural religion; it was not a fallen angel, but God Himself. The rest of the gods are demons, and their rites are false worship. The Holy Spirit speaks through the Apostle St. Paul: "What pagans sacrifice they offer to demons and not to God" (1 Cor 10:20). In the Book of Revelation, the Holy Spirit reprehends some of the members of the church of Pergamum because "they eat food sacrificed to idols" (Rev 2:14). The Holy Spirit also reprehends the bishop of the church of Thyatira, because he allowed a teaching according to which it was lawful to "eat food sacrificed to idols" (Rev 2:20). In some way, the bishop of Thyatira had taught that diversity of religions is legitimate and willed by God. In those times, sacrifices of food to pagan divinities and its consumption represented objectively "signs and rites, sacred expressions" of a non-Christian religion. Our Lord Jesus Christ and His holy Apostles would abhor the affirmation that God's work tended in the pagan religion of their time "to produce signs and rites, sacred expressions, which bring others to a communitarian experience of journeying towards God," as Pope Francis affirms in the aforementioned passage.

It is true, isn't it, that non-Christians, "when they are faithful to their own consciences, can be justified by the grace of God"?

Indeed, someone who is following his conscience in invincible ignorance can be saved through the Blood of Christ, in ways which only God knows. Pope Pius IX left us a clear teaching on this theme: "There are those who are struggling with invincible ignorance about our most holy religion. Sincerely observing the natural law and its precepts inscribed by God on all hearts and ready to obey God, they live honest lives and are able to attain eternal life by the efficacious virtue of divine light and grace, since God who clearly beholds, searches, and knows the minds, souls, thoughts, and habits of all men, because of His great goodness and mercy, will by no means suffer anyone to be punished with eternal torment who has not the guilt of deliberate sin" (Encyclical *Quanto Conficiamur Moerore*: DS 2866). The affirmation, however, which claims that through the "signs and rites, sacred expressions" and "communitarian experiences" of non-Christian religion men journey towards God, is theologically wrong and contradicts the clear words of Holy Scripture, the words of the Apostles, and the constant teaching of the Church for two millennia.

Non-Christians do not "journey towards God" with their "rites" and "communitarian experiences." On the contrary: through objectively erroneous religious signs, they move away from God. The Apostles always preached this to pagan societies and to other religions. The Church has always taught this, for two thousand years.

We then read in the passage you cited: "While these lack the meaning and efficacy of the sacraments instituted by Christ, they can be channels of the Holy Spirit to bring non-Christians from atheistic immanentism. . . ." Such an affirmation is a break with the constant teaching of the Church and the Apostles themselves. These "rites" cannot be "channels for the Holy Spirit" because they are intrinsically against the will of God. All non-Catholic religions and their religious signs are *per se* contrary to the will of God. Therefore, they cannot as such be channels of the Holy Spirit. There is no diversity of religion or diversity of non-Christian religious rites that is positively willed by God.

But what about man's inclination by nature, as intended by his Creator, to offer worship to God insofar as he understands Him? Isn't this something good and positive, willed by God?

Here we are speaking not of natural religion but of other and hence of false religions. The natural act of worshiping God is an individual act of the conscience and not part of a concrete religious system. The natural knowledge of God is usually individual: in your soul, you know there is a God, independent of whatever religion you belong to. It could be that some of the individual members of other religions — for instance, simple Muslims worshiping in the mosque — in their souls are worshiping the one true God according to their own natural knowledge. In this external ritual, he may be offering true worship to God, however not *because of* the ritual, but because he is knowing and reverencing God in his soul according to his reason. These rituals might remind him that he must pray to God, but he prays to God in this moment according to his natural knowledge, in his own heart.

This could also occur, for instance, with an innocent pagan person who wants to worship the one God, whom he knows by his reason, but he participates in the rites and signs of his pagan religion (e.g., sacrifice of animals). That innocent pagan person can in his soul worship the true God, not in virtue of the pagan rites, but in virtue of his reason and pure intention. However, non-Christian rites as such — e.g., the sacrifice of animals among pagans, or the worship ritual in mosques — are not pleasing to God. Since this way is not what God asks for, these rituals cannot be in themselves channels of the Holy Spirit. This is irreconcilable with the teaching of the Gospel and the constant teaching of the Church.

To play "devil's advocate," might it not be better for some to follow an organized false religion, if this would "liberate non-Christians from atheistic immanentism or from purely individual religious experiences"?

This expression is also incorrect. It is wrong to make a person a member of an idolatrous religion in order that he will be no longer be an atheist. Why is this wrong? It is wrong because that person would then worship God in a false manner and thereby offend God with idolatry.

God has His ways to attract an atheist. Every human person possesses reason, and God has written His natural law on man's heart. A false religion can distort even the natural law in the hearts of people. It is better that such a person have an individual religious experience according to natural law, which God inscribed in his conscience and soul, than that he practice an idolatrous religion or participates in rites that are objectively displeasing to God. We are not authorized to do something objectively displeasing to God in order to achieve an allegedly good aim.

Of course, God can use situations which are objectively contrary to His will to touch souls with His grace, and to lead them out of these situations so that they may achieve truth and virtue. God will not abandon souls who sincerely seek the truth in false religions. However, God does this by ways which He alone knows. These statements of Pope Francis in *Evangelii Gaudium* foster relativism and trivialize the uniqueness of the Way to salvation: *the* Way, which is Christ and His Church, the Catholic Church, outside of which there are no ways, no religions, no religious rites, and no religious signs which are pleasing to God. Any religious rites and signs outside of the Catholic Church which *are* pleasing to God can only be the rites and signs of non-Catholic Christians, since insofar as they are true, they belong to the Catholic Church. Indeed, according to St. Augustine, non-Catholic Christians, upon leaving the Church, have made their own property out of what they have stolen from the Church (see *Sermo* 97, 2).

The natural act of adoration and of knowledge of God, which He inscribed in the human heart, also pleases God, since He created the natural light of reason. But, according to the express will of God, this is not sufficient for salvation. There can be no natural right to worship God with rites and signs of natural worship alone. God calls every human person to go beyond natural adoration and natural knowledge of Him and to accept explicitly with supernatural faith His revelation and His Son Jesus Christ as the only Savior of mankind.

People like to bring up St. Justin Martyr's teaching on "seeds of the Word," as if to say: God's truth may be found everywhere, not exclusively in the Christian religion.

But note what St. Justin actually said: "In order that we may follow those things which please God, choosing them by means of the rational faculties He has Himself endowed us with, God both persuades us and leads us to the true faith" (*1 Apol.*, 10). From the beginning, the Church has always distinguished between the truths that people can reach by natural reason, as for example many sane elements that non-Christian philosophers demonstrate, and the pagan religions as such. St. Justin taught this with his doctrine of the "seeds of the Word" (*"logoi spermatikoi"*) present in non-Christian thinkers, when he said: "Whatever things were rightly said among all men are the property of us Christians" (*2 Apol.*, 13). For this very reason, St. Justin considered the rites and signs of pagan religions not only senseless but even insulting to God. He thought they were mostly invented by demons in order to enslave humanity (cf. *1 Apol.*, 14). For St. Justin, Christianity is the "only sure and valuable philosophy" (*Dial.*, 8).

On February 4, 2019, Pope Francis signed the "Document on Human Frater-nity for World Peace and Living Together," with Ahmad el-Tayeb, Grand Imam of Egypt's al-Azhar Mosque, during an interreligious meeting in Abu Dhabi. The joint statement incited controversy for affirming what many took as a quintessential expression of religious indifferentism. It reads: "The plu-ralism and the diversity of religions, color, sex, race and language are willed by God in His wisdom, through which He created human beings." During an inflight press conference on his return from the United Arab Emirates, Pope Francis told journalists that "the document did not go one millimeter beyond the Second Vatican Council." What do you make of this claim?

The root of the current religious indifferentism, or the theory of the alleged divinely-willed character of other religions, is to be found in some ambiguous phrases of the documents of the Second Vatican Council — especially in its Declaration on the Church's Relation to Non-Christian Religions, *Nostra Aetate*. Describing Buddhism, for exam-ple, the Council states uncritically that "it teaches a way by which men, in a devout and confident spirit, may be able either to acquire the state of perfect liberation, or to attain, by their own efforts or through higher help, supreme illumination" (n. 2). Pope Benedict XVI himself pointed out the weakness of this conciliar document, saying: "It speaks of religion solely in a positive way, and it disregards the sick and distorted forms of religion."[1] Also ambiguous is the already-mentioned statement from *Lumen Gentium* n. 16, which says that we Catholics and the Muslims together adore the one God ("*nobiscum Deum adorant*").

The other root, which we also mentioned, is to be found in the affirmation of *Dignitatis Humanae* that the choice even of a false reli-gion — including the worship of the "supreme divinity" (*Dignitatis Humanae*, n. 4) — is a natural right of the human person ("*in ipsa eius natura*": *Dignitatis Humanae*, n. 2). However, the natural right of the free will of the human person consists only in the choice of what is morally and intellectual good, i.e., the choice of virtue and of the one true religion, not just of the "supreme divinity." The abuse itself of free will, however, in choosing evil (sin) and error (false religion), is never positively willed by God. Hence the choice of a sin or of an error, such as a false religion, can never be the expression of a natural right ("*in ipsa eius*

---

1 Reflections of His Holiness Benedict XVI, published for the first time on the occasion of the 50th anniversary of the opening of the Second Vatican Council, *L'Osservatore Romano*, October 11, 2012.

natura"). Otherwise one has to say that committing adultery, homosexual acts, murder, lying, idolatry, blasphemy would be a natural right of the human person. There is no natural right to insult and blaspheme Jesus Christ, as is done, for example, in certain "sign and rites" of non-Christian and even Monotheist religions. One has to recall in this context the words of Pope Pius VI who in 1794 condemned the ambiguous language of the so-called Synod of Pistoia, stating that ambiguous language "can never be tolerated in a synod of which the principal glory consists above all in teaching the truth with clarity and excluding all danger of error" (Bull *Auctorem Fidei*).

The interreligious meetings held in Assisi by Pope John Paul II greatly contributed to a further growth and spread of religious indifferentism and of the view, even within the Church, that all religions are ultimately equal. These interreligious meetings in Assisi attained their logical consequences in the interreligious document of Abu Dhabi, dated February 4, 2019 and signed by Pope Francis, which says that "the pluralism and the diversity of religions, color, sex, race and language are willed by God in His wisdom."

In the preparatory documents for the upcoming synod of bishops on the Amazonian region (being held at the Vatican October 6–27, 2019), great emphasis has been placed on listening to the "voice" of the indigenous peoples. Some would say they are moved by the Holy Spirit simply by their social life. It has also been suggested that their very cultures are "epiphanic" and ought to evangelize Catholics. From your experience of several years of pastoral work in Brazil, and from the perspective of the Catholic faith, do you see danger in such statements?

We have to bear in mind the fact that pagan religions as such, and cultures founded on idolatry, cannot be a seed or a fruit of divine revelation, since idolatry, animism, and witchcraft, which are prevalent in Amazonian indigenous cultures, are spiritual deceptions that preclude the evangelization and eternal salvation of their adherents. It was Our Lord who coined the term "evangelization" (see Mt 11:5; Mk 16:15; Lk 4:18) and gave it a precise meaning: the mandate to spread His divine revelation to the people of all cultures and religions (see Mk 13:10; Mt 28:19). This is the mandate of the Church of all time and cannot be changed. Cultures and religions which did not receive the divine revelation and mandate of Christ are not able to "evangelize" the Church.

It is of course true that the common, sound human values and behavior of any culture can teach us Catholics as well. I remember a moving experience from my pastoral experience in Brazil. Once, a pious, indigenous Catholic woman came to me, crying, and told me about her sufferings. She told me that her tribe had the custom of greeting a distinguished guest with hands that had been washed. She always practiced this whenever she greeted such a guest in her home. Some years after the Second Vatican Council, her parish priest, who was a European missionary, made an announcement, saying that from the next Sunday forward, "you must all receive Communion in the hand, because this is the will of the Church." This pious indigenous woman was very shocked, since she could not imagine — based on the experience of her culture — that a person would greet Our Lord during Holy Communion with unwashed hands. So, she went to the parish priest and explained her concern, saying, "Reverend Father, I am unable to receive Our Lord in my hands, because this contradicts the cultural practice of my tribe." To which the parish priest responded, "You should know that Our Lord never gave Holy Communion on the tongue." The indigenous woman answered, "Reverend Father, where is this written?" He replied, "You don't know Holy Scripture! At the Last Supper, Our Lord gave Holy Communion in the hands of the Apostles." The good woman said, "Reverend Father, but I do not belong to the number of the Apostles." He answered her, "I will not accept your reasoning, based on your tribal custom. I will give Holy Communion to you only in the hand."

This European priest, who in other cases advocated the necessity of accepting elements of the spiritualities of the pagan cultures of Amazonian peoples, rejected in a despotic manner — as a true new Pharisee and Pelagian — such a sign of an authentically inculturated faith. I hope the upcoming Synod will be able to listen to those elements of the cultures of the Amazonian people that bolster the truth of the Catholic faith, the true supernatural spirit, and the deep reverence in the liturgy that has been practiced in the Church by people of all cultures.

How can the Church best respond to growing religious indifferentism?

We have to call all non-Christians to the one true path to God, which is the Catholic Church. The Apostles and the entire Church taught this for two thousand years. The Church could not err for two thousand years.

Something that should prompt us to reflection in the Church today is the real danger of religious indifferentism and dogmatic relativism, which are being promoted through a false ecumenism and ambiguous interreligious statements. In reading various books, the following two statements have especially remained in my memory.

In 1862, Éliphas Lévi—born Alphonse Louis Constant, an apostate Catholic deacon, who later became a Freemason and an occultist—put down in writing a dream he had: "A day will come when the pope, inspired by the Holy Spirit, will declare that all the excommunications are lifted, and all the anathemas are retracted, when all Christians will be united within the Church, when the Jews and Muslims will be blessed and called back to her. While keeping the unity and inviolability of her dogmas, she will permit all sects to approach her by degrees and will embrace all mankind in the communion of her love and her prayers. Then Protestants will no longer exist. Against what will they be able to protest? The Sovereign Pontiff will then be truly king of the religious world, and he will do whatever he wishes with all the nations of the earth. It is necessary to spread this spirit of universal charity."[2] In another place Lévi wrote: "When will the crown be returned to the Pope? When he will be reconciled with progress. The cross is cut to the game of their knives. The martyrs will worship the world. By whom will come the end of our miseries? By a great pope assisted by a great king, to bring together progress and faith."[3]

Lévi's dream reminds me of a highly thought-provoking affirmation in the apocalyptic novel *Juana Tabor 666*, written in 1942 by Gustavo Adolfo Martínez Zuviría (alias Hugo Wast), an Argentinian novelist and devout Catholic. One of the main protagonists in the novel, Fray Simon, a religious priest from Buenos Aires, was striving with all his might to become pope. To achieve his goal, he even accepted the help of Juana Tabor, the most powerful woman of the anti-Christian world alliance. Standing in his monastic cell in Buenos Aires, Fray Simon pronounced this soliloquy: "I bear within myself all the energies of a new belief. My mission is to bring religions up to date in the fields of dogma, politics, and society. I feel myself a priest unto the marrow of my bones, but I

---

2 *Cours de philosophie occulte d'Eliphas Levi*, 21 January 1862. The text was published in the review *Initiation et Science* 58 (July–September 1963).

3 *Philosophie occulte. Première série. Fables et symboles avec leur explication* (Paris, 1862), 471–72.

have received from the Lord a divine secret: the Church of today is only the seed of the Church of the future, one that will have three circles: in the first will belong Catholics and Protestants; in the second, Jews and Muslims; in the third, idolaters, pagans, and even atheists. I myself will begin, in myself, the perfect kingdom of God ... I am the first son of a new covenant."

Earlier you mentioned the Assisi meetings. Do you see them as somehow bringing to life the visions of Éliphas Lévi and Hugo Wast?

Since the Council, one of the greatest dangers inside the Church has arisen out of interreligious dialogue. The way such dialogue was conducted, especially in the Assisi meetings of John Paul II and Benedict XVI — seen in their results — were expressions of a relativizing of the uniqueness of Christ and His Church for the eternal salvation of souls. It is a relativizing of the biblical truth that Christ is the unique Savior and that all who are not Christians have to accept Christ as their God and Savior and adore Him in order to be saved. It is a relativizing of the obligation and indispensable mission of the Church to proclaim this truth clearly to all non-Christians. In this way, clerics in the Church in our days are committing, in my opinion, a great sin of omission in neglecting to proclaim Christ to all non-Christians, as the Apostles did. Interreligious meetings like those held in Assisi convey to the entire world the message that the Catholic religion stands on the same level with other religions, as a member of a kind of "Parliament of the World's Religions." In 1893, in Chicago, for the first time in Christian history, an interreligious meeting of leaders of the world's religions was held; it was called the "Parliament of the World's Religions." At the conclusion of the meeting, Pope Leo XIII disapproved of the participation of Catholics in such meetings and forbade future activities of a similar nature.

St. Paul in the Areopagus in Athens spoke about Christ to the pagans. He spoke about repentance and the Resurrection of Christ. And what was the reaction? They laughed at him, they mocked him, while others said to him: "about this we will hear you on another occasion" (Acts 17:32). This is the reaction of the world. But Paul continued, as did all of the Apostles, to preach Christ to unbelievers. With the same zeal, we too have to preach Christ to other religions, with love, of course — without pressure. This is not proselytism. When I preach with respect and love that Christ is the only Savior and that He is the only way to eternal salvation according to the will of God, I am not engaging in proselytism. We have to proclaim this truth to all non-Christians: first to the Jews, then to the Muslims, the Buddhists, to everyone.

Interreligious dialogue, in the way it has been conducted since the Second Vatican Council, creates the impression that we are all travelling on parallel tracks to the same God and will all reach the same end, and that we don't have to be bothered if there are still people of other religions who do not know or do not accept Christ. We have only to be nice and tolerant with one another, promoting goals such as "Human Fraternity for World Peace and Living Together." However, such a reductive attitude is a betrayal of the Gospel. We have to change the method of interreligious dialogue. If the Apostles used this method, they would not have converted so many people to Christ. They would not have died as martyrs but in their beds.

How would you change the way the Church conducts interreligious dialogue?

First, I would not use the expression "interreligious dialogue." This expression is confusing. It has a relativizing impression and effect. The Church's official public relations and meetings with non-Christian religions should be carried out under the aspect of culture, as Cardinal Joseph Ratzinger once suggested. We have to be aware that several non-Christian religions adore idols and engage in a cult of worship which offends God. Indeed, all non-Christian religions are engaging in wrong worship, a worship which displeases God, with the exception of those individuals who worship God by virtue of their natural reason and not by virtue of their false religion. We spoke of this earlier. Nevertheless, it is not the will of God that they adore Him only by reason. It is the will of God that they should adore Him as the Triune God, as the Holy Trinity by supernatural faith in His revelation.

Only those who are baptized have faith in the Holy Trinity.

Or those who desire and seek baptism.

So, first, we have to clear up the issue of so-called interreligious dialogue and ignite a new missionary zeal to preach Christ to the Jews, to the Muslims, to the Buddhists, to the Hindus, to all who do not yet know Him. And second, when we enter into a serious dialogue with non-Christians, it should be well prepared. We should not simply meet, issuing a joint statement and giving the impression that we are relativizing the uniqueness of Christ and His Church. We should say: let us meet in order to present to one other, with respect and love, the truth of what each one believes; let us speak about the common values of morality and culture in order to build up public life that is truly worthy of human dignity.

This would be productive.

I would be in favor of meetings with representatives of other religions to discuss common issues of human life, the natural law, and living together in harmony on the civil level. We do this in Kazakhstan. Recently, for example, our government organized a round table discussion on the immorality of corruption in public life and invited representatives of all the various religions. I took part in that meeting. We spoke together about the immorality of corruption, and on this issue, we agreed one hundred percent. To my amazement, the Muslim government officials who were presiding at the meeting quoted the Bible and even the New Testament in their interventions. We can certainly have interreligious meetings on such themes, for instance.

Issues such as family, abortion . . .

Exactly, and there we could do a great deal of work — not engaging in interreligious dialogue which relativizes Christ; this is confusing. It would be better to hold study meetings. We could also invite a non-Christian to study Catholic theology at a Catholic university, so that he may become more familiar and understand more deeply the Catholic religion. However, one would have to choose carefully a Catholic university that still maintains the integrity of Catholic doctrine and liturgy. We could say, "Please, our Muslim or Buddhist or Hindu friends, come, and we can help you to know what the Catholic religion is." In some cases, we could even offer a scholarship for a non-Christian person who is sincerely seeking the truth.

We have to use every possible means to proclaim Christ. It was always so in the Catholic Church since the time of the Apostles and the great missionary saints over the past two thousand years. We should develop a sincere human friendship with non-Christian citizens in our respective nations. Of course, we have to avoid even the slightest appearance of syncretism or relativization. Thus, we would not engage with them in things like common prayers. This is contrary to our faith, because they do not pray to the Holy Trinity and we on the contrary always pray to the Holy Trinity.

What about common prayer with the Jews?

The practicing Jews, who are the spiritual descendants of the Pharisees and the Talmud rabbis, rejected Jesus as the Messiah and still reject Him, and they expressly reject the Holy Trinity. As Christians, we always pray to the Holy Trinity. You cannot say: "Today I will pray only to the One God of the Old Testament or to the Creator." It would be an apostasy. The central mystery of our faith says that the Three Divine Persons are ineffably and mutually united. Each Person is present and living in the other. Catholic theology calls this truth the "*circumincessio*" of the Three Divine Persons. Every prayer you make begins with the sign of the Cross and the invocation of the Holy Trinity. Therefore, we cannot pray with the Jews, who reject the Holy Trinity and the Cross. We could maybe exceptionally recite with them the psalms, which are common to us, on a special occasion, for example when there is a disaster or natural catastrophe. We could join and pray to God with a specific psalm invoking the mercy and help of God.

On the basis of His covenant with them, God called the Jews to accept Christ, His divine Son. God continues to be faithful to His covenant with the Jews, calling them still to accept the fulfillment of this covenant in the new and everlasting covenant of His Son. Divine revelation declares through the mouth of the Apostle St. Paul that the first covenant was only temporary and served as a "schoolmaster" (cf. Gal 3:23–25), and that "by works of the law, of the Old Testament, no human being will be justified, since the justification of God comes through faith in Jesus Christ for all who believe, for there is no distinction" (cf. Rom 3:20–21). The entire Old Testament, the first covenant, was the *typus futuri*, the type and prefiguration of the future new and everlasting covenant, according to an expression of St. Ambrose. St. Leo the Great transmitted the same teaching of the Apostles, declaring that with the death of Our Lord Jesus Christ there occurred a transfer from the Law to the Gospel, from the Synagogue to the Church, from many sacrifices to one Victim (cf. *Serm.* 68, 3).

St. Thomas Aquinas formulated the same truth succinctly, when he said: "Just as it would be a mortal sin now for anyone, in making a profession of faith, to say that Christ is yet to be born, which the fathers of old said devoutly and truthfully; so too it would be a mortal sin now to observe those ceremonies which the fathers of old fulfilled with devotion and fidelity" (*Summa theologiae* I-II, q. 103, a. 4). The Council of

Florence presents the unchanging and constant teaching of the Gospel, stating that after the Passion of Christ nobody can place his hope in the legal prescriptions of the Old Testament and submit himself to them as necessary for salvation. If someone after the promulgation of the Gospel does not believe in Christ and instead observes the legal prescriptions of the Old Testament, he will lose eternal salvation (cf. Eugene IV, Bull *Cantate Domino*).[4] Pius XII transmitted the same constant doctrine, teaching: "The New Testament took the place of the Old Law which had been abolished" (Encyclical *Mystici Corporis*, 29).

The present-day Jews are not faithful to God's covenant when they continue to reject its aim and end, which consists in the covenant of His Son Jesus Christ. The words of St. Stephen, the Protomartyr, addressed to the Jews of his time who refused to believe in Jesus Christ, remain valid and refer to the Jews today: "You stiff-necked people, uncircumcised in heart and ears, you always resist the Holy Spirit. As your fathers did, so do you. Which of the prophets did your fathers not persecute? And they killed those who announced beforehand the coming of the Righteous One" (Acts 7:51–52).

Let me press you on the question of whether Catholics should pray with Jews. Could you envision a prayer meeting with Jews where there were psalms and readings from the Old Testament, as well as readings from the New Testament?

It would be confusing and relativizing, because we would be saying that there are parallel ways to salvation. There are not parallel ways. The whole meaning of the Old Testament consisted in its fulfillment in Christ, in the New Testament. It was the will of God that that entire People of God pass to His new and everlasting covenant. This is the covenant of God which is still valid; God calls all Jews to accept the new covenant. The Old Testament is still valid as the revelation of God, which has been fulfilled in the New Testament. Therefore, it isn't the case that the Jews who reject Christ are still living the covenant of God. No, they have rejected the divine fulfillment of God's covenant, they have disobeyed the will and call of God, becoming unfaithful to His covenant, since the old and the new covenant are inseparable and form ultimately only

---

4 Indeed, this document says, "whether or not they place their hope in it [circumcision], it cannot be observed at all [i.e., done as a religious observance] without loss of eternal salvation."

one covenant according to divine revelation. We have to state this with
all clarity and love. Therefore, Catholics should not pray with the Jews
in the way you describe.

I had an experience of prayer during an event with the Jewish community in Kazakhstan. On the anniversary of the Holocaust, the Israeli
embassy in Astana organized a memorial event at the theatre. During the
event historical slides on the Holocaust were shown and several speeches
were delivered. Then there was a prayer for the deceased victims of the
Holocaust. The embassy asked me to lead the prayer for the victims. I
agreed and chose Psalm 129, the *De Profundis*, which is a specific prayer
for the departed souls, and also Psalm 42, *Iudica me Deus*. It was a secular
event but also had a religious moment. There was no common prayer.
I alone recited the psalms and said a prayer for the eternal peace of the
departed souls.

*In this situation it was clear that you were not confusing Jewish and Chris-
tian worship. Everyone knew who you were, and you thoughtfully chose
words that implied nothing incompatible with Catholicism.*

That is right.

The confusion spread by incorrect interreligious events and discussions is one of the deepest crises in the Church today. In some ways, it is
a betrayal of Christ. Practically, and hopefully not intentionally, Christ
is put on the same level with other religions. This implies a loss of the
real missionary zeal which inspired the Apostles, the Church Fathers,
and the great missionary saints. We have an urgent need to return to this
missionary zeal. The lack of zeal is a deep wound in the Church. This
is the question of all times: either Christ or nothing. The uniqueness
of Christ and of His Church is the core of the entire Gospel. Truly, we
must return to the Catholic missionary zeal of all times.

III

The Moon Shall Not Give Her Light

7

Loss of the Supernatural

It seems that so many of the problems in the Church and society today come down to the loss not only of a sense of nature, as we spoke about earlier, but also of grace — of the supernatural — and even the distinction between nature and grace.

I think that the deepest root of the problems and the crisis in the Church is the weakening of the supernatural, and in some cases a loss of it. One can say that the deepest consequence of Original Sin, of the first sin of man — of Adam and Eve — expresses itself as a flight from God. They fled. When you flee from God's presence, you abandon the supernatural — the essence of God is supernatural. God is supernatural. The basic distinction between God and creation, or creatures, is supernatural and natural.

The most dangerous deceit and the most basic lie which the devil, the father of lies, sowed in the minds of Adam and Eve was to tell them: "You will be like God." Where is the deceit? To be like God as the devil tempted them is to seek to be like God *without God*. That is the deceit and the danger.

In one of the audio sermons he has left us, Archbishop Fulton Sheen described the deceit and danger into which humanity slowly sank beginning with the Renaissance, and then openly with the radical secularism of the French Revolution. "From now on men will divide themselves into two religions, understood again as surrender to an absolute. The conflict of the future is between an absolute who is the God-Man and an absolute which is the man-god; between the God who became Man and the man who makes himself god; between brothers in Christ and comrades in the anti-Christ."[1]

Christ brought us the only way to be like God, that is, *with God*, according to the way of God and *only* according to the way of God — this

---

1   Audio sermon "Signs of Our Times" on Anti-Christ, in the radio program "Light Your Lamps," broadcast on January 26, 1947.

is the invitation to salvation, to grace, to the supernatural. We can become like God, not *as* God but by being "divinized," as the Fathers of the Church, such as St. Athanasius, stressed. The devil, Satan, deceived our first parents into imagining that they could be like God *without God*.

The loss of the supernatural consists in trying to abolish a distinction that cannot be abolished between God and creatures. All attempts to minimize this distinction or to obfuscate it lead to a loss of the supernatural. To declare that nature and temporal realities are God is paganism and pantheism. This means that there is no supernatural. The creature, nature, and the earth are then declared to be supernatural, which is a lie and contrary to reality. This temptation has always been with man throughout history. All attempts at paganism and idolatry involve an identification of the supernatural with the natural — either by abolishing the supernatural or declaring nature to be divine. Naturalism unduly elevates the creature, or man, to be God, to be the Lord, in place of the only One who is God and Lord. As we already said, secularism is an attempt to sever the connection between human life and the supernatural order, and to reject any submission to the supernatural. Independence, autonomy, false autonomy: this started with humanism in the Renaissance and continued with Martin Luther, in so far as Luther made natural and temporal realities unduly independent from the life of grace — for example, in calling marriage "a worldly thing" ("*ein weltlich Ding*").

Luther also regarded human nature as fundamentally corrupt...

He despised nature. And so, in despising nature with his doctrine of *sola gratia*, he destroyed the foundation of grace. Grace has its foundation in nature. Grace beautifies nature, transforms it from within, elevates it and brings it to perfection. Here we can see a basic error in Luther's thought: by despising nature, he ultimately despised the reality of the Incarnation and the objective power of the sacraments.

The movement of descending, entering, transforming, and elevating is precisely the movement of Christ's redemptive Incarnation.

Yes, that is true. A form of Protestantism which despises nature ultimately despises the Incarnation, under the pretext of stressing only the supernatural with the axioms *sola fide* and *sola gratia*. It ends not in the supernatural, but in a distorted supernatural. The distortion of the supernatural manifests itself in the subjective theories which Luther and the other Protestant communities developed regarding the religious world.

The way of Protestantism does not observe the whole of divine revelation and the official Magisterium of the Church, the "incarnational" way, which means that the signs of the supernatural are present in nature, just as Jesus Christ Himself, in His sacred humanity and in the sacraments and in all the details of the liturgy, uses natural realities as instruments or vehicles of grace. Protestantism thus becomes a kind of *gnosis*, meaning that you build up your own mental world of religious ideas that is not supernatural in the true sense. I am not saying that a normal Protestant believer is a Gnostic. What I mean to say is that Protestantism always carries subjectivism inside of itself, and with subjectivism comes the tendency to the phenomenon of *gnosis*.

Granting one should not confuse nature and grace, is there not a tension between them?

In Catholicism, we have of course St. Augustine, the Doctor of Grace, who greatly stressed the existence of the supernatural and grace, against the heresy of Pelagius. Pelagianism abolished the distinction between grace and nature, exalting nature to such an extent that it declared nature itself to be grace-giving. This is a heresy and the Church condemned it. St. Augustine fought against this and stressed the supernatural so much that in some places in the polemic he had the tendency to stress grace to the detriment of nature; it is a slight tendency. St. Augustine's detractors saw him as destroying nature to save grace or the supernatural, but we have to look at the entirety of St. Augustine's writings.

The Catholic and divine path is *et . . . et*, "both . . . and." The union: nature and grace, natural and supernatural, the creature and God. Of course, on this path the primacy belongs to God, who is supernatural, who is the fountain of grace. Through grace we have a participation in His divine life, which He infuses into our souls, in order to elevate us to His supernatural world. Grace is His divine supernatural help, which constantly supports us. We cannot reach our heavenly homeland without this support. We are too weak, and we always need the support of grace, of this divine help for our soul and our mind, so that our mind might be purified and elevated, that our will and affections might be strengthened and conformed to the good, and that our love might increase.

How do we receive grace?

The primary means of obtaining grace is prayer, since we are not marionettes, we are not puppets. God, in a very mysterious and elevated manner, respects our freedom and dignity as free persons. Therefore, He does not impose His grace, His divine help, upon us. He waits for us to ask. In the first moment, when we ask Him for grace, God has already mysteriously moved our will to ask for grace. God pours His grace into our soul according to our capacity and according to our prayers, without violating our freedom. Therefore, we have to pray. This is our basic and first duty — not the prayer of petition only, to ask for graces, but the prayer of adoration. The first task of all creation is to adore God, to acknowledge His divinity, His majesty, His greatness. Man has to recognize this and to submit himself to God. Adoration is always — according to the Christian understanding — our respectful submission in awe, as creatures, and the recognition of the immense majesty of God, but in a loving and filial manner. Because of this characteristic love and filial relationship to God, Christian adoration differs substantially from the adoration, for example, of Muslims or pagans.

We have already touched on Islam, but in this context can you say more about what distinguishes the Christian understanding of adoration from the Islamic?

Islam is submission with servile fear, but we Christians surrender with filial fear and love. We continue to be creatures and servants of God — even though we have the dignity of adopted sons of God through baptism. We must recognize nature, which we cannot abolish, and which tells us that we are His creatures, that we are servants, that we are nothing, as well as faith, which tells us that by baptism we are beloved children of God in Christ.

In the spiritual classic, The Dialogue, *God the Father says to St. Catherine of Siena, "Do you know daughter, who you are and who I am? If you know these two things, the devil will not harm you and you will have beatitude in your grasp: 'You are she who is not, and I Am He Who Is.'"*

Exactly. Creation is *ex nihilo* and we are *pulvis* — dust and ashes — and this is our reality. We have to recognize this, while we have hope and love in the faith that we are children of God. Even though we are nothing — we are servants — by our nature, we are elevated to be the children of God, to love God, and to adore Him with reverence and with filial devotion.

This adoration does not destroy our nature, and it should not be offered in a servile manner, but with respect, love, and devotion, recognizing that "I am not God." I am a child of God, but still a creature and I will remain a creature forever. We have a moving example of this in the Book of Revelation: the elect, the saints, the twenty-four elders who take off their crowns and cast them on the earth, prostrating themselves in the presence of the Lamb. The Lamb is Christ, and the Lamb signifies also the mystery of the Eucharist. This is already the attitude of adoration in the Heavenly Jerusalem, which will remain for all eternity: total surrender, devotion, respect, love, and adoration.

And this is what we enter into during the Holy Mass, even though we don't see it with our eyes.

Exactly. Returning to our theme of the supernatural, St. Augustine and the Church condemned Pelagianism, which is a kind of naturalism. Since the time of the Apostles, the Church has always stressed the primacy of grace, of the supernatural. It must be stated: God is more important, and eternity is more important, than the creature and temporal realities, just as the soul is in itself more important than the body, for the soul is immortal. And prayer is more important than activity. Our Lord Jesus Christ taught this truth when He said to the active Martha that her contemplative sister Mary "has chosen the better part, which shall not be taken away from her" (Lk 10:42).

Secularism implies a denial of the supernatural — a denial of the possibility that God, who is supernatural, can intervene in this world and in souls through the efficacious power of the sacraments. Secularism, the philosophy of naturalism, and the entire Masonic movement's influence on the Church has expressed itself inside the Catholic Church in the Modernist movement. Since the Second Vatican Council, the Church in her life has yielded in large measure to the influence of secularism and naturalism.

Modernism is ultimately a denial or weakening of the supernatural, as it declares that pure reason and pure history are the ultimate criteria of truth. This is essentially Hegelianism. It was Kant who, through the primacy of pure reason and the impossibility of having access to what is metaphysical and supernatural, prepared the way for the Hegelian movement. This all entered the Catholic world and rebranded itself in religious language as Modernism.

The Modernist movement, which has been present in the Church since the nineteenth century, used the Second Vatican Council as a catalyst for expansion. Thus, after the Council, the Church became immersed in a deep crisis marked by naturalism. It seems that, to a certain degree, there has been a victory of the natural over the supernatural in so many aspects of the life of the Church. However, it is only an apparent victory, since the Church cannot be overcome by the powers of Hell. But temporarily, we are witnessing an eclipse, an obfuscation of the supernatural, of the primacy of God, of eternity, of the primacy of grace, of prayer, of sacredness, and of adoration. All these signs of the supernatural have been extremely diminished in the pastoral life and liturgy of the Church in our days. On a global scale, the deepest crisis in the Church is the weakening of the supernatural. This is manifested in an inversion of order, so that nature, temporal affairs, and man gain supremacy over Christ, over the supernatural, over prayer, over grace, and so on. This is our problem. As Jesus Christ said, "Without Me, you can do nothing" (Jn 15:5). The whole crisis in the Church, as seen after the Council, was manifest in an incredible inflation of frenetic human activity to fill the void or the vacuum of prayer and adoration, to fill the void created through the abandonment of the supernatural.

Which is a void that can never be filled . . .

Exactly. Nonetheless, efforts to fill this void have been tried, for example, in continual Church meetings and gatherings at different levels and in different forms — continuous synods. This is oftentimes busy work with a very pious mask. It is a waste of money; it is a waste of time that could be used for prayer and for direct evangelization. The phenomenon of permanent meetings, assemblies and synods on various levels is a kind of parliamentarization of Church life and is therefore worldly, although masked with the impressive word "synodality." There are episcopal meetings on the continental, regional, and national level, on the subnational level, on the diocesan level, and so on. We are suffocated with continuous meetings and every meeting has to produce papers. So, we are really submerged by the weight of papers and papers and papers. This is pure, frenetic Pelagianism. Not only is this taking money and time away from evangelization and prayer; it is also an extremely cunning method of Satan to take away the successors of the Apostles and priests from prayer and evangelization — under the pretext of a so-called "synodality."

There is only one parallel in the history of the Church to such excessive episcopal meetings, and that is the fourth century, precisely when the Arian heresy was dominant and reigning. They would gather together and hold meetings, and in those times St. Gregory of Nazianzus said: "I am resolved to avoid every meeting of bishops, for I have never seen any synod end well, nor assuage rather than aggravate disorders" (*Ep. 130 ad Procopium*).

Nowadays St. Gregory would be called a pessimist and would probably be disciplined for his uncooperative spirit.

To be honest, I am bored with episcopal meetings and synods. As much as I love my brother bishops and love to meet them, this method of continual synods and assemblies, which are often dominated by frenetic activity, are influenced by the spirit of Pelagianism and Modernism. They are often sterile and give the impression of an enormous show of clerical vanity.

What would you do instead?

It would be far more beneficial — personally, psychologically, pastorally, and ecclesiastically — to meet with the simple Catholic faithful. We bishops would do better to meet young people and young families with children who are thirsting for the beauty of God, the beauty of Catholic truth and life, and for the beauty of Catholic liturgy. To meet them and to pray with them and to instruct them and also to learn from them as a bishop. I also learn from them as a bishop, from their example, when I observe the faith of these beautiful Catholic young families, of exemplary Catholic youth. I have also often been edified by Catholic children. For me personally such meetings with the little ones in the Church are incomparably more fruitful and spiritually more enriching than participating in synods or in official meetings of bishops in the form in which they are held in our time.

Sometimes it seems to me that such meetings are a gathering, more or less, of bureaucrats. I will not say that every bishop in those meetings acts or thinks like a bureaucrat. However, one gets the impression that they are bureaucratic events, which do not bring a true clarification in doctrine or an improvement of Church discipline, i.e., a true progress of holiness in the life of the Church.

I am not against synods or other episcopal assemblies as such, provided they happen infrequently, are of short duration, have minimal bureaucracy and transparent and fair rules of procedure, and above all, guarantee and safeguard the integrity of doctrine and discipline in the discussion papers and in the final document. Every member of a synod or of another important episcopal assembly should be required to pronounce each time a clearly articulated oath of fidelity to the immutable doctrines of faith and morals, and to those norms of canon law and the discipline of the sacraments that originate in apostolic tradition and are thus perennially valid.

Could you say more about your meetings with the Catholic faithful? What do you find?

Indeed, I have had so many beautiful meetings with the simple ones in the Church. I call them "the little ones," which does not always correspond to the physical age written in their passport. The "little ones" in the Church are those of all ages who have the pure, profound Catholic faith, who have no administrative power in the Church. These, for me, are the little ones. They can be children, young people, families, also elderly people; age is not important, but rather the spiritual characteristics.

Once I had an unforgettable experience. I was in the United States in a parish celebrating a beautiful Pontifical Mass in the traditional form. There were a lot of altar boys of all ages and after the Mass I was in my choir dress, and a little altar boy wanted to be photographed with me on his own. So the entire parish was in the hall looking at us — I in my choir dress and this little boy at my side. It was a nice picture. I think this was a holy child because he radiated so much innocence. He was, I suppose, nine years old, more or less. Everyone took photos. Then from the crowd several parishioners shouted to the boy, "You will become a bishop!" And he was so serious and said, "I want to become a saint!" This is for me a much deeper experience, with this little child, than to participate in a synod of bishops for two or three weeks, which will probably not have much of a concrete impact on the sanctification and evangelization of people and the glorification of God.

I was reflecting upon the words of the little altar boy. One could have the impression that he contrasted being a saint with being a bishop! I don't think he really meant that, but it was funny for me, it sounded like: "I will not become a bishop, but a saint." As if to say that becoming a bishop endangers becoming a saint or contradicts it. Sometimes, it does appear this way, especially in our days.

Isn't it ironic that one of the Second Vatican Council's messages was the universal call to holiness — the call to every member of the Church to live out fully his baptismal vocation — and then, precisely at that time, we have experienced a profound and widespread loss of the sense of the supernatural?

This is precisely the essence of Modernism, which gained considerable strength during the Council. After the Council, people with the spirit of Modernism increasingly occupied the administrative structures of the Church. Modernism is a form of naturalism, which often carries with it the elimination of the supernatural.

I gave the example of these continuous meetings. I will tell you a story. Once I participated in a meeting for the Asian bishops in Manila. They prepared a very long document, and so I said, "We have to shorten this document by half and, even then, no one will read it." And the bishops were laughing. In my private conversations with several bishops, they acknowledged honestly that up to now they actually did not read the documents produced at these meetings, even though they received them.

I participated in several other meetings with my brother bishops and I asked several of them, once the documents were approved, "Have you read the final document?" And some of them answered me, "Sincerely, no." One of these meetings lasted one week and produced a document, which, at least in our region, no one has read. Later we got the financial report for this meeting. The meeting cost $250,000 from church funds. Imagine! Basically, it was $250,000 thrown to the wind. Really, to the wind. We had minimal time for prayer. Is this the "Church of the poor," which was so stressed during the Second Vatican Council and afterwards? The continuous meetings and assemblies of bishops: they are spending so much money, it's incredible. If we would reduce drastically the frequency of these meetings, we could give millions of dollars every year to the poor around the world. To me, this is a sin that churchmen are committing today. Even setting to the side for a moment the problems with these excessive meetings, which are ultimately a manifestation of Pelagianism and undermine the supernatural — to say nothing of the problem of the almost continuous stream of doctrinally ambiguous documents they produce — I believe it is sinful to spend so much money, which we could give to the poor in our world. We have to stop this. But it seems that the frequency of synods and meetings is only going to increase under the pretext of a so-called "synodality."

Under the current pontificate, Vatican synods are now being held annually.

Yes, the number of meetings is increasing. For me it is a sign: when there is a lack of faith and desire for the supernatural, a lack of love for prayer, for works of penance and direct evangelization, then the bishops and those who govern in the Holy See cast themselves into frenetic activities: synods, documents, continuous events.

Didn't this happen in religious life after the Council? Congregations that had an active apostolate but whose life was still primarily contemplative, though not cloistered, took on activism.

This phenomenon has invaded and infected the entire life of the Church. I compare it to the situation you have with a bicycle when the chain falls off and you just spin in place and don't move from the starting line. Just spinning in place, an exterior activism with a spiritual lethargy and passivity.

One of the means for coming out of this crisis, and which will heal the crisis, is to rediscover the supernatural and to give primacy to the supernatural in the life of the Church. This means giving time to prayer and Eucharistic adoration, making time for the beauty of Holy Mass and the liturgy, for the practice of corporeal penance, for the proclamation of the supernatural truth of the Last Things and the truth of the Gospel. We have to put Christ and His supernatural revelation back at the center, because this alone can heal all mankind.

8

Vatican II

The Second Vatican Council had an incalculable effect on the Church and the world, perhaps most significantly in the prayer of Catholics. As is well known, a committee under Paul VI made radical changes to the liturgy after the Council. Critics say the Council and its aftermath led to an undermining of doctrine and morals. How did you experience the "fruits of the Council"?

After two years at boarding school, I returned to my parents' home and attended the German gymnasium. I never received Holy Communion standing and in the hand. It was impossible for me. I was oftentimes the only one in the Church who knelt, since my interior conviction did not permit me to receive the Lord standing. I cannot explain this. This conviction was so deep in my soul. In those years, it was in the 1970s, even though the priests were very liberal, they did not refuse me Communion when I knelt, since they knew that I had come from the underground Church, from the persecuted Church. This was in some way my protection. They did not dare humiliate me publicly by telling me to "stand up." And so, it was a kind of protection for me and for my family also.

When I was fifteen or sixteen years old, I started to read more about the current situation in the life of the Church. I started to think about the crisis in the Church when I first heard about Archbishop Lefebvre. It was in 1976. I was 15 years old. That was the year that Archbishop Lefebvre was publicly suspended by Paul VI.

At the time, Archbishop Lefebvre celebrated several Masses with huge crowds, and in 1976 one was close to our home, close to the Bodensee, on Lake Constance. The bishops of all the surrounding dioceses, there were five bishops, issued a common pastoral letter advising and warning people not to go to the Mass of Archbishop Lefebvre. The letter was read while I was at Mass in my home parish. In that letter, the bishops said that Archbishop Lefebvre was disobedient, that he was a rebel and was against the

Council and the pope. I started to become interested in this issue. I then began receiving circular letters from the Society of St. Pius X. A neighbor sent them to our home. I always read them. In my soul I experienced a dilemma. On the one hand, I noticed that there was much truth in the letters, especially when I read about the Holy Mass and saw the liturgical celebrations portrayed in beautiful photographs. My intuition as a 16-year-old youth told me that what Archbishop Lefebvre said was substantially right. But I was in a quandary because I had a deep veneration for the pope. From one side, I saw the truth and the beauty of the Catholic faith and specifically of the Holy Mass presented by Archbishop Lefebvre, and from the other side, he was condemned by the pope. I was profoundly devoted to the pope, and so I could not understand this. It was very difficult for me. I started then to read more intensely about Vatican II.

Did you read the documents of Vatican II as a young man?

I did not read them in full. There were good conservative people who, using the documents of the Council, published very good texts to defend the tradition against the radical liberals in the Church. There was a book, a kind of "catechism of the Council," with quotations from it, which was very clear and defended the tradition of the faith. The author was a priest, Dr. Ingo Dollinger.[1] In the 1970s, he published several books to defend Church teaching against the liberal moral theologians, using the documents of the Second Vatican Council. I read these, and so I had no concern or suspicion that there might be problems with the texts of the Council.

At the same time, I was reading the texts of Archbishop Lefebvre, in which he argued that there *were* problems in the texts of the Council, especially concerning religious liberty. This was his main doctrinal concern, as was the theme of collegiality. Nevertheless, I continued to believe that there was no substantial problem with the Council texts. On one side, I observed the Council texts being abused by the liberals, and on the other side, it seemed to me, in those years, that the criticisms of Archbishop Lefebvre were exaggerated. It was for me impossible to think that a Council or a pope could make any mistake. Implicitly I considered every word of the Council and the pope as infallible, or at least without error.

---

1   He died in 2017. He lived in Wigratzbad and was my professor of Moral Theology in Brazil. He was a priest of the diocese of Augsburg. —*AS*

Any kind of error?

It was for me a kind of unconscious and total "infallibilization" of the Council—unconsciously, not on the theoretical level—and of all pronouncements of the popes. I was uncomfortable when there were critics, and I did not like to follow or study the critics because I was afraid of going in a direction that would be unfaithful to the Church and to my devotion to the pope. Instinctively, I repressed every reasonable argument which could, even in the slightest, be a critique of the Council texts. Nowadays, I realize that I "turned off" my reason. However, such an attitude is not healthy and contradicts the tradition of the Church, as we observe in the Fathers, the Doctors, and the great theologians of the Church over the course of two thousand years.

How were your views affected when you entered the seminary?

I entered the Congregation of the Holy Cross, the Canons Regular, who were—and still are—very faithful to the doctrine of the Church, with a very reverent manner of celebrating the liturgy, even the new Mass, but *ad orientem*, with Communion kneeling and on the tongue. I remember experiencing a kind of blind defense of everything that was said by the Council, which seemed sometimes to require mental acrobatics and a "squaring of the circle." Even now, the general mentality of good and faithful Catholics corresponds, in my opinion, with a de facto total infallibilization of everything the Second Vatican Council said, or that the current Pontiff says and does. This kind of extreme ultramontanism, an unhealthy papal-centrism, had already been present for several generations in Catholics. I was also educated in this mentality. But criticism has always been present and allowed within Church tradition, since it is the truth and faithfulness to divine revelation and tradition that we should seek, which in itself implies the use of reason and rationality and avoiding erroneous acrobatics. Some explanations of certain obviously ambiguous and erroneous expressions contained in the Council's texts now seem to me to be artificial and unconvincing, especially when I reflect upon them in a more balanced and intellectually honest manner.

What was the first time you came to think there might be prudential or theological errors in the merely ordinary teaching of either the popes or of Vatican II?

I think it was when I became a bishop thirteen years ago, because the task of a bishop is to be a teacher. The study of the Church Fathers also helped me very much. I have been teaching Patrology since 1993. Almost every year, I have given lectures in Patrology, either in Brazil or, since 1999, in Kazakhstan. So, I had to continue to read the texts of the Church Fathers. For some time, I had noticed that some expressions of the Council could not so easily be reconciled with the constant doctrinal tradition of the Church. I noticed that some teachings — let us say, on the topics of religious freedom, collegiality, the attitude towards non-Christian religions, and the attitude towards the world — were not in an organic continuum with previous tradition.

The crisis in the Church, as you know, has grown in recent years, especially with the pontificate of Pope Francis. This has obliged me to reflect more deeply. When I was charged by the Holy See with visiting the Society of St. Pius X almost four years ago, I had to prepare and study the issues more deeply and examine the arguments. I started to notice that we need to take the objections offered by Archbishop Lefebvre more seriously. I saw that the Holy See dismissed all of these objections and presented their way of interpretation through the method called "hermeneutic of continuity." Unfortunately, the Holy See did not take Archbishop Lefebvre's arguments seriously. The representatives of the Holy See simply said to the SSPX: "You are wrong, our position is the only correct one and it represents the continuity with the previous tradition of the Church." A kind of argument from authority, but not rooted in deeper theological reasoning, and without going to the substance of the arguments. This was my perception.

With the growing crisis in the Church, and especially the situation created after the two Synods on the Family, the publication of *Amoris Laetitia,* Pope Francis's approval of the pastoral guidelines of the bishops of the Buenos Aires region (which foresee, among other things, the admittance to Holy Communion of unrepentant adulterers), and the declaration on diversity of religions he signed in Abu Dhabi, I realized that we need to take the arguments of the SSPX more seriously.

Do you see the same pattern today of a top-down approach, without consulting or considering opposing views?

Yes. They often dictate by administrative power. There is no argument. The argument is power.

Force of will?

Yes, it seems to be a force of will, under the motto "we have the authority and therefore we are always right." I noticed that, from the side of the Holy See, there is no will to delve deeply into the essence of the questions presented by Archbishop Lefebvre. Maybe there is an unconscious fear that if one were to accept that some of the non-definitive teachings of the Council are ruptures with the constant previous tradition of the Church, then the era of a blind ultramontanism-as-a-substitute-for-orthodoxy will collapse. An honest examination shows that in some expressions of the Council texts there is a rupture with the previous constant tradition of the Magisterium. We have to always bear in mind the fact that the chief end of the Council was pastoral in character, and that the Council did not intend to propose its own definitive teachings.

What were the main arguments against Archbishop Lefebvre and critics of Vatican II?

It was said: "Your position is taken only from a few popes, from Gregory XVI, Pius IX, Pius X, Pius XI, Pius XII, while our position is the position of 2,000 years. You are fixated on a very brief span of nineteenth-century thinking." This was substantially the argument of the Holy See against Archbishop Lefebvre and against those who raised several legitimate questions about dubious points in the Council texts.

However, this is not correct. The pronouncements of the popes before the Council, even those in the nineteenth and twentieth centuries, faithfully reflect their predecessors and the constant tradition of the Church in an unbroken manner. One could not claim any rupture in the teachings of those popes (Gregory XVI, etc.) regarding the previous Magisterium. For example, concerning the theme of the social kingship of Christ and of the objective falsehood of non-Christian religions, one cannot find a perceivable rupture between the teaching of Popes Gregory XVI to Pius XII on the one side, and the teaching of Pope Gregory the Great (sixth century) and his predecessors and successors on the other. One can really see a continuous line without any rupture from the time of the Church Fathers to Pius XII, especially on such topics as the social kingship of Christ, religious liberty, and ecumenism.

Some keen proponents of Vatican II say the Council is a means for the Church to go back to the roots, to the pre-Constantinian model.

It is precisely in this argument that they reveal or "out" themselves, and thanks be to God that they say this. I will return to your argument, but I just wanted to add that usually the arguments from the Holy See against Archbishop Lefebvre were that the disputed points of the Council were in complete continuity with the Church's earlier teaching. In this way, men working for the Holy See have implicitly accused Gregory XVI, Pius IX and all the popes until Pius XII of being in some way an exotic phenomenon in the two-thousand-year history of the Church, a rupture with the time before them.

A 150-year rupture, a parenthesis in Church history...

They have not said this explicitly, but de facto it is so. And what they say now, as you mentioned, is that the parenthesis encloses not only 150 years, but the period from the fourth century (with Constantine) to Vatican II — a 1700-year parenthesis! However, such thinking is clearly not Catholic. This is, in substance, the theological position of Martin Luther. His main argument was that with Constantine the Church strayed from the path of the true doctrine of the Gospel, a parenthesis which lasted until his own emergence in the sixteenth century. This argument is the position of liberals today, and especially also of the Neocatechumenal Way. Such a theological position is ultimately Protestant, and heretical, because the Catholic faith implies an uninterrupted tradition, an uninterrupted continuity without any perceivable doctrinal and liturgical rupture.

Perhaps today's crisis with *Amoris Laetitia* and the Abu Dhabi document forces us to deepen this consideration. In the *Summa Theologiae*, St. Thomas Aquinas always presented objections ("*videtur quod*") and counterarguments ("*sed contra*"). St. Thomas was intellectually very honest; you have to allow for objections. We should use his method on some of the controversial points of the Council texts that have been under discussion for almost sixty years. Of course, the majority of the texts of the Second Vatican Council present no rupture and are clearly in continuity with the constant tradition of the Church. There are a few expressions we are all aware of, however, and we need to clarify them.

To this end, I think that the Society of St. Pius X can be of help and make a constructive contribution. Maybe in some positions they are too one-sided; they also have to acknowledge that the majority of the Council texts are in organic continuity with the previous Magisterium. However, ultimately, the papal magisterium has to clarify in a convincing manner the controversial points of some of the expressions in the Council texts. Were it necessary, a pope or a future ecumenical Council would have to add explanations (a kind of "*notae explicativae posteriores*") or even amendments and corrections of those controversial expressions, since they were not presented by the Council as a definitive teaching.

Do you think the Council was a mistake?

I think history will tell us this from a distance. We are only fifty years out from the Council. Maybe we will see this more clearly in another fifty years. However, from the point of view of the facts, of the evidence, from a global point of view, Vatican II did not bring real spiritual progress in the life of the Church. After the Council, a disaster occurred at almost every level of the Church's life. The plan and intentions of the Council were primarily pastoral, yet, despite its pastoral aim, there followed disastrous consequences that we still see today.

Of course, and I repeat, the Council had many beautiful and valuable texts. But the negative consequences and the abuses committed in the name of the Council were so strong that they overshadowed the positive elements which are there.

What are the positive elements you see in Vatican II?

If we look at the span of Church history, it was the first time an ecumenical Council made a solemn appeal to the laity to take seriously their baptismal vows to strive for holiness. The chapter in *Lumen Gentium* about the laity is beautiful and profound. The faithful are called to live out their baptism and confirmation as courageous witnesses of the faith in secular society. This appeal was prophetic.

Immediately after the Council, this appeal to the laity was abused by the progressivist establishment in the Church, and also by many functionaries and bureaucrats who worked in Church offices and chanceries. Oftentimes the new lay bureaucrats were not themselves witnesses but helped to destroy the faith in parish and diocesan councils and in other official committees. Unfortunately, these lay bureaucrats were oftentimes misled by the clergy, by the bishops and pastors.

It seems as if the Council called for holiness, and instead we got more employees on the payroll, more artificial "ministries," and more committees to tell Father what to do.

Never in history did the Church have so many administrative structures as after the Second Vatican Council. The Roman Curia, the diocesan chanceries, and the offices of religious orders were never so bureaucratized as in the postconciliar period, and this phenomenon has reached its peak in our days. The bureaucratization of the life of the Church brought in a strongly worldly spirit and suffocated true spiritual life, supernatural vision, and missionary zeal for the salvation of souls. The time after the Council left one with the impression that one of the main fruits of the Council was bureaucratization. While it is true that the Church, as any human society, needs rules and an order and a precisely formulated *Code of Canon Law*, nevertheless this worldly bureaucratization in the decades since the Council paralyzed spiritual and supernatural fervor to a considerable extent, and instead of the announced springtime, there came a time of widespread spiritual sterility, a spiritual winter. Well known and unforgettable remain the words with which Paul VI honestly diagnosed the Church's state of spiritual health: "We thought that after the Council there would come a day of sunshine for the history of the Church. Instead, there has come a day of clouds, of storms, of darkness" (Sermon on June 29, 1972).

Within this context, it was Archbishop Lefebvre in particular (though he was not the only one to do so) who began, with a frankness similar to that of some of the great Church Fathers, to protest the destruction of the Catholic faith and the Holy Mass that was occurring in the Church and being supported, or at least tolerated, even by high-ranking authorities in the Holy See. In a letter addressed to Pope John Paul II at the beginning his pontificate, Archbishop Lefebvre realistically and aptly described in a brief synopsis the true extent of the crisis of the Church. I am continually impressed by the clear-sightedness and prophetic character of the following affirmations: "The flood of novelties in the Church, accepted and encouraged by the Episcopate, a flood which ravages everything in its path — faith, morals, the Church's institutions — could not tolerate the presence of an obstacle, a resistance. We then had the choice of letting ourselves be carried away by the devastating current and of adding to the disaster, or of resisting wind and wave to safeguard our Catholic faith and the Catholic priesthood. We could not hesitate. The ruins of the Church are mounting: atheism, immorality, the abandonment of churches, the disappearance of religious and priestly vocations are such that the bishops are beginning to be roused."[2] We are now witnessing the climax of the spiritual disaster in the life of the Church to which Archbishop Lefebvre pointed so vigorously already forty years ago.

Obviously the Council remains controversial. How do we get past simplistic or one-sided views of it?

In approaching questions related to the Second Vatican Council and its documents, one has to avoid forced interpretations or the method of "squaring the circle," while of course keeping all due respect and the ecclesiastical sense (*sentire cum ecclesia*). The application of the principle of the "hermeneutic of continuity" cannot be used blindly in order to eliminate unquestioningly any evidently existing problems. Indeed, such an approach would transmit artificially and unconvincingly the message that every word of the Second Vatican Council is infallible and in perfect doctrinal continuity with the previous magisterium. Such a method would violate reason, evidence, and honesty, and would not do honor to the Church, for sooner or later (maybe after a hundred years) the truth will be stated as it really is. There are books with documented and reproducible sources, which provide historically more realistic and true insights into the facts and consequences with regard to the event of the Second Vatican Council itself, the editing of its documents, and the process of the interpretation and application of its reforms in the past five decades. I recommend, for instance, the following books which could be read with profit: Romano Amerio, *Iota Unum: A Study of Changes in the Catholic Church in the Twentieth Century* (1996); Roberto de Mattei, *The Second Vatican Council — An Unwritten Story* (2012); Alfonso Gálvez, *Ecclesiastical Winter* (2012).

You said you believe one of the bright lights of the Second Vatican Council was the way it stressed the universal call to holiness. What was happening among concerned laity at the time of the Council? And are we beginning to see its fruits?

At that time, there emerged a movement of laity who said: "We protest the dilution of the faith and the trivialization of the Holy Mass. What we observe is not the faith that was always and everywhere transmitted to our forefathers." This lay movement inside the Church was growing

2   Letter from December 24, 1978.

independently of Archbishop Lefebvre's work, and today it is continuing to grow in strength and numbers in response to the pontificate of Pope Francis. I think that with the tremendous and almost unprecedented interior crisis in the Church we are witnessing today, the hour of the laity has arrived. They also feel responsible for the conservation and defense of the faith. The true intention and teaching of the Second Vatican Council on the laity is being realized now in our days ever more clearly, in many meritorious and courageous lay initiatives for the defense of the Catholic faith. We have arrived at a grotesque situation, in which the sheep are beginning to unmask the infiltrating wolves in sheep's clothing, i.e., the unbelieving, apostate, and debauched cardinals, bishops, and priests.

Is the internet an important tool for the laity in defending the faith?

Yes, to be sure. I see the internet and social media as providential tools that give lay people who want to defend the faith a unique possibility to be united. This was not possible thirty years ago. I now see lay men and women who have the courage to say to their pastor, or bishop, or even to the Holy See: "Please, we are concerned about these facts. This does not correspond with the faith of our forefathers. We want to defend the faith of our Mother, the Church." However, the ecclesiastical liberal establishment — I call them the "ecclesiastical *nomenklatura*"[3] — is now accusing the lay people of interference, saying "this is not your task, shut up!"

It smells of clericalism, wouldn't you say?

Yes, such an attitude of these clergy towards faithful lay people is a demonstration of enormous clericalism. But the lay faithful have to respond to these arrogant clerics. That is what Vatican II taught about the duty of the laity to witness to and defend the faith. They can say to these clerics: "If you love Vatican II so much, you should let us critique you! Let us stand up and speak freely in the Church in defending the faith of our forefathers. We have the right to express our concerns even to the pope, because we are one family." In this new and courageous attitude of many lay people, I see a realization of the intention of the Second Vatican Council. God permitted the evils after the Council and uses them in order to draw a greater good from them.

---

3   The "nomenklatura" were Communist bureaucrats who held various key administrative positions and who ran all spheres of public life.

Do you think that, maybe looking back fifty years from now, the Council will be seen as a step toward getting rid of the Modernist heresy in the Church because unintentionally it exposed the infestation of this heresy and showed it for what it is?

Yes, I wanted to mention that as well. God always uses negative phenomena to produce an even greater good.

The current vigilant and committed participation of traditionally-minded lay people in the life of the Church expresses the true meaning of Vatican II regarding the laity. In the difficult times of persecution under Communism, it was the laity who primarily transmitted the pure Catholic faith. I received the faith in the clandestine Church from lay people, from my grandparents, from my mother and father and from other lay men and women. Our own time is the hour of Catholic families, large families. In fact, a very positive contribution of the Council was the beautiful doctrine of the family as a domestic church. We find this thought already in the Church Fathers, in St. Augustine for example, but it was renewed by the Council. I think the true fruit of the Council will be borne in the future, once the crisis is over, in renewed Catholic families, in domestic churches, and in the courageous witness to the faith by the laity.

I want to mention another positive contribution, the chapter about Our Lady in *Lumen Gentium*. It was the first time that an ecumenical Council spoke so extensively and deeply about the role of Our Lady in the Church and in the history of salvation. The title "Mother of the Church," *Mater Ecclesiae*, which Pope Paul VI gave to Our Lady during the Council, was based on the teaching in *Lumen Gentium*. Since the time of St. Irenaeus, Mary has been called "the new Eve." Pope Benedict XVI taught: "Mary is the Spiritual Mother of all humanity, because Jesus on the Cross shed his blood for all of us and from the Cross he entrusted us all to her maternal care" (*Homily*, January 1, 2007). Her role as spiritual Mother of humanity is manifested through these specific motherly functions, as she cooperates "in the work of the Savior in restoring supernatural life to souls" (*Lumen Gentium*, n. 61), as the Mediatrix of graces, dispensing Christ's graces, and as the Advocate with her interceding power.

These points — the universal call to holiness, the role of the laity in defending and witnessing to the faith, the family as the domestic church, and the teaching on Our Lady — are what I consider the truly positive and lasting contributions of the Second Vatican Council.

Didn't the Council begin on the liturgical feast (later suppressed) of the Divine Motherhood of Our Lady?

Yes, exactly. And the patron of the Council was St. Joseph. Even though it had disastrous consequences, we need to have respect for the event—it was an ecumenical Council.

The Church defined herself for the first time at Vatican II as the "servant of the Word."

But on the contrary, when one looks at photographs from that time, Vatican II as a phenomenon appeared as a huge show of clerical triumphalism. I am not comfortable with this. The motto "We are the Church" leaves one with the impression of great triumphalism. One observes here a lack of modesty. When I look at the historical pictures and reports from the Council, I have the impression that in some way the bishops put themselves at the center. However, we are only servants.

The Magisterium has been so overloaded in the last 150 years with an insane ultramontanism that there emerged an atmosphere of "ecclesiocentrism," which in turn is a hidden anthropocentrism, and this was not healthy. The Council, which was unfortunately a demonstration of a very rare "ecclesiocentrism" and "Magisteriocentrism"—this Council itself gave a beautiful description of what the Magisterium is, which had never before been given in the history of the Church. It is found in *Dei Verbum*, n. 10, where it is written: "The Magisterium is not above the Word of God, but serves it." That is beautiful. I have never read this before in a text of another Council.

Paul VI has been accused of abusing papal power in his implementation of Vatican II. Critics say that, acting of his own accord, he changed the liturgy in a way that had never occurred before. This seems to lend credence to what you said about a manifest triumphalism, with the bishops and the pope focusing too much on themselves. What opened the door to this exaggeration or hypertrophism of power? Was it a lack of centeredness on the Lord?

Exactly, this is what I mean by "ecclesiocentrism" and "Magisteriocentrism." By this, I mean that the human and administrative elements were put at the center of the life of the Church and above the constant tradition of the Church. The liturgical reform of Paul VI is a striking example. In some ways, Paul VI put himself above Tradition—not the dogmatic Tradition (*lex credendi*), but the great liturgical Tradition (*lex orandi*) which is inseparably linked to doctrine. Paul VI dared to begin a true revolution in the *lex orandi*. And to some extent, he acted contrary to the affirmation of the Second Vatican Council in *Dei Verbum,* n. 10, which states that the Magisterium is only the servant of Tradition. We have to put Christ at the center: the supernatural, the constancy of doctrine and of the liturgy, and all the truths of the Gospel which Christ taught us.

Through the Second Vatican Council, the Church began to present herself to the world, to flirt with the world, and to manifest an inferiority complex towards the world. Yet clerics, especially the bishops and the Holy See, are tasked with showing Christ to the world — not themselves. Vatican II gave the impression that the Catholic Church has started begging sympathy from the world. This continued in the postconciliar pontificates. The Church is begging for the sympathy and recognition of the world; this is unworthy of her and will not earn the respect of those who truly seek God. We have to beg sympathy from Christ, from God, and from heaven.

Some who criticize the Council say that, although there are good aspects to it, it's somewhat like a cake with a bit of poison in it, which needs to be thrown out.

I have heard this comparison from the Society of St. Pius X. We cannot accept it because the Second Vatican Council was an event of the entire Church. In such an important phenomenon, even though there were negative points, we have to maintain an attitude of respect. We have to evaluate and esteem all that is really and truly good in the Council texts, without irrationally and dishonestly closing the eyes of reason to what is objectively and evidently ambiguous and even erroneous in some of the texts. One has always to remember that the texts of the Second Vatican Council are not the inspired Word of God, nor are they definitive dogmatic judgments or infallible pronouncements of the Magisterium, because the Council itself did not have this intention.

We need to recall, for example, the fact that the Ecumenical Council of Florence in its decree for the Armenians, which was not meant to be a definitive dogmatic judgment, made an objective doctrinal error in saying that the matter of the sacrament of Order is the "handing over of the instruments." Whereas according to the longer and previous and unanimous tradition of the entire Church in the East and West, it was not the handing over of the instruments, but the imposition of the hands that was regarded as the decisive element (matter) of the diaconal, presbyteral, and episcopal ordinations. Even though it was not the mind of the Council of Florence to claim the necessity of the *traditio instrumentorum* for validity — as it was stated later by Pius XII — the Council incomprehensibly omitted to add any explanatory remark, so that its intention would be clear and would not lead to error and ambiguities. In such a grave matter as officially teaching about the essence of the sacraments, a Council is obliged to speak in a most unambiguous way. In fact, the Council spoke plainly, "The sixth is the sacrament of Orders. Its matter is the object by whose handing over the order is conferred. So the priesthood is bestowed by the handing over of a chalice with wine and a paten with bread; the diaconate by the giving of the book of the gospels." This affirmation taken alone, by itself, is erroneous, independently of the intention. It later caused some Catholic theologians to assert in their dogmatic manuals that the *traditio instrumentorum* is necessary for validity. Even the Holy See did this in some of the editions of the *Pontificale Romanum*, in which one can find it stated that, if the handing over of the instruments had been omitted, it had to be supplied for the sake of the validity of the ordination. In 1947, Pope Pius XII officially corrected the objective theological error of the Ecumenical Council of Florence, which was also the error of St. Thomas Aquinas, by stating that the imposition of the hands is the only valid matter for diaconal, presbyteral, and episcopal ordinations. After the magisterial intervention of Pius XII, the dogmatic manuals and the rubric in some of the editions of the *Pontificale Romanum* had definitively to be corrected.

To come back to the comparison — "it's somewhat like a cake with a bit of poison in it" — I would not apply this to the Second Vatican Council. For me, that betrays a lack of a supernatural perspective. Another example is *Amoris Laetitia*. There are certainly many points we need to criticize objectively and doctrinally. But there are some sections which are very helpful, really good for family life, e.g., about elderly people in the family: *in se* they are very good.

I will not reject the entire document but receive from it what is good. The same with the Council texts. St. Thomas Aquinas accepted many philosophical insights of Aristotle in spite of the fact that not all things in Aristotle are perfect. There are some things St. Thomas did not accept from Aristotle, but, nevertheless, he quotes him often. This principle applies even more to those ecclesiastical documents that may contain some imperfections.

You were saying earlier that the Second Vatican Council inaugurated an era of unprecedented "ecclesiocentrism." Do you see this phenomenon still at hand today?

Yes. This attitude manifests itself in organizing continuous clerical meetings, synods, and almost countless committees — a grand display of continuous clerical anthropocentrism. It is unhealthy, really.

When bishops meet, shouldn't prayer be the main priority?

Exactly. The bishops' first task is to pray. During the meetings there should be a really beautiful and worthy liturgy to glorify and adore God and a true and constructive fraternal sharing of experiences and suggestions for improving the faith and discipline in the Church and for promoting authentic spiritual life. The bishops' meetings and synods do not primarily have to produce documents and present themselves to the media. I am convinced that in the future, maybe in fifty years, after the crisis has passed, the Church will draw a lesson from this.

But now, I would like to come back to your earlier comment about exposing Modernism. The Council was a catalyst for bringing out all that was latent in the Church before it in the Modernist movement. Pope St. Pius X issued an encyclical and an oath against Modernism. But afterward, the Modernists who were hidden in their holes during his pontificate started slowly to come out by means of ecclesiastical personal politics. During the subsequent pontificates there was, in my opinion, sometimes a lack of care in the selection of candidates for the episcopacy and cardinalate.

Since the pontificate of Pius X?

It is no secret that his successor Benedict XV was not happy with the pontificate of Pius X. This is a historical fact. He was a pupil of the famous Cardinal Rampolla, who was a very mysterious personality and more inclined toward political liberalism and friendly with the radical anti-clerical and Masonic French Republic of those times. I don't know if Cardinal Rampolla was a Modernist or a Freemason; however, he was clearly inclined to political liberalism. This attitude of Rampolla and his ecclesiastical pupils, chief among them Monsignor Giacomo della Chiesa, who then became Benedict XV, manifested itself in a new policy towards the world. They were of the mind that the Church had to make political compromises with the world. Such an attitude, however, over time, led to a worldly mentality among high-ranking and influential clergy in the Church, especially in the Roman Curia. Benedict XV started to change the policy, not doctrinally but in practice, through some ecclesiastical appointments of men who were not zealous defenders of the faith. Even though they all had to take the Anti-Modernist Oath, some of them did it with mental reservations, as subsequent historical facts have proven.

With the pontificate of Benedict XV, there began a slow and careful infiltration of ecclesiastics with a worldly and somewhat Modernist spirit into high positions in the Church. This infiltration grew particularly among theologians, so that later Pope Pius XII had to intervene by condemning well-known theologians of the so-called "*nouvelle théologie*" (Chenu, Congar, De Lubac, etc.) and by publishing the encyclical *Humani Generis*. Nonetheless, from the pontificate of Benedict XV onwards, the Modernist movement was latent and continually growing. And so, on the eve of the Second Vatican Council, a considerable part of the episcopacy and professors in theological faculties and seminaries were imbued with a Modernist mentality, which is essentially doctrinal and moral relativism and worldliness, love for the world. On the eve of the Council, these cardinals, bishops, and theologians loved the "form" — the thought pattern — of the world (cf. Rom 12:2) and wanted to please the world (cf. Gal 1:10). They showed a clear inferiority complex towards the world.

Pope John XXIII also demonstrated a kind of inferiority complex towards the world. I don't believe he was a Modernist in his mind, but he did have a political way of looking at the world and strangely begged sympathy from the world. He surely had good intentions. He convoked the Council, which then opened a floodgate for the Modernist, Protestantizing and worldly-minded movement inside the Church. I am impressed by the following acute observation, made by Charles de Gaulle, President of France from 1959 to 1969, regarding Pope John XXIII and the process of reforms started with the Second Vatican Council: "John XXIII opened the floodgates and could not close them again. It was as if a dam collapsed. John XXIII was overcome by what he triggered."[4]

The talk of "opening the windows" before and during the Council was a misleading illusion and a cause of confusion. From these words, people got the impression that the spirit of an unbelieving and

---

4   See Alain Peyrefitte, *C'était de Gaulle* (Paris: Gallimard, 1997), 2:19.

materialistic world, which was plainly evident in those times, could transmit some positive values for the Christian life. Instead, the authorities of the Church in those times should have expressly declared the true meaning of the words "opening the windows," which consists in opening the life of the Church to the fresh air of the beauty of divine truth, to the treasures of ever-youthful holiness, to the supernatural lights of the Holy Spirit and the saints. Over time, during the postconciliar era, the partly opened floodgate gave way to a disastrous flood which caused enormous damage in doctrine, morals, and liturgy. Today, the flood waters that entered are reaching dangerous levels. We are now experiencing the peak of the flood disaster.

Surely, ever since Paul VI, ecclesiastics with a liberal Modernist spirit and with a worldly and careerist mentality began to dominate in the positions of power in the Church. Many of them were and still are united among themselves in true clerical old-boy networks.

Earlier we discussed Modernism and the way in which it sets aside intelligible truths in favor of a religious sentiment that can be expressed in different concepts from one age to the next. St. Pius X explains and condemns this heresy in the encyclical Pascendi Dominici Gregis. *Is this document still relevant today?*

Of course! *Pascendi* is very relevant. As Pope Pius X said in *Pascendi*, Modernism is the most dangerous phenomenon in the entire history of the Church. He said that Modernism is the collection basin, the "synthesis" of all heresies of all times, due to its relativism and lack of faith. Today we are experiencing the complete predominance of Modernism in the life of the Church, and in theological faculties. To some extent, Modernism has even penetrated documents of the Magisterium.

But God has permitted this. So, to your question, the face of Modernism has revealed itself from the time of the Council to our own day. We can now see it for what it is. Cardinal Christoph Schönborn, the archbishop of Vienna, has for example said that until Pope Francis the entire Church had taught only one side of moral theology, the objective side, and that Pope Francis brought to the Church the other side, the subjective and individual view of morality. For me this is a clear example of rupture, of Modernism and of relativism. To say that we now have a new category, i.e., the subjective, which determines truth, is wrong. This does not correspond to the truth that the Church has proclaimed for two thousand years. God gave objective norms to the individual, to the subject: "Thou shalt not kill. Thou shalt not lie." That is individual: "Thou shalt not!" And the Church has always preserved this individual aspect of moral truth. To present the category of the "subject" in order to abolish sin is a dishonest method. It comes close to the method of Gnosticism, of Martin Luther, and ultimately also of the Freemasonic ideology.

Other cardinals and bishops talk about a "paradigm shift." It is a very cunning expression to deny everlasting truth. It is insidious.

Now to your observation: today the veil has been lifted and Modernism has revealed almost all of its hideous face. Once the crisis in the Church is over, we will have the task of rejecting all of these phenomena which are present in the life of the Church. And the Church will do this, because she is divine. She cannot leave this undone. She will do it precisely and will correct all of the errors which have accumulated, beginning with several ambiguous expressions in the Council texts. She will then correct the errors that have spread and grown to our own day.

Modernism is like a hidden virus that has now manifested itself and is going to be expelled.

Yes, that's a good comparison. After the crisis, after the serious spiritual viral infection, the clarity and preciseness of doctrine will shine more brightly.

You initiated and were one of the main contributors in the editing process of the "Declaration of truths relating to some of the most common errors in the life of the Church of our time," which you signed together with two cardinals and two bishops on May 31, 2019.[5] Is this something you hope a future pope or Council will adopt, or something similar to it?

I not only hope that a future pope or Council will publish something similar; I am convinced that the Church will do this in an unambiguous manner, as she did in times of serious doctrinal and moral crises over the past two thousand years. To teach clearly the truths of the divine deposit of faith, to defend the faithful from the poison of error, and to lead them in a sure way to eternal life belongs to the very essence of the divinely appointed task of the pope and bishops. Therefore, I think it is not a matter of "should." In the future a pope *must* do this, because

5   The text is reproduced in the Appendix.

the Church is divine, and she has always condemned errors. Like a good physician, a future pope has to diagnose and provide medicine to cure the disease, otherwise he will not be a good physician.

Before Vatican II, that was always the reason for a Council to be called, wasn't it?

Yes, exactly. It was a spiritual medical procedure to protect souls from spiritual diseases. In this sense, I think that the Second Vatican Council has a positive meaning, insofar as the doctrine will be clarified and the positive points of the Council will shine forth — i.e., the call to holiness, the role of the laity in spreading and defending the faith, the family as the domestic church, and Our Lady, the Mother of the Church, and the spiritual Mother of all men.

In the meantime, while we are waiting, what happens to the souls who are lost because of all this confusion?

Yes, this is a very important question. I think that a great part of the faithful are misled by clergy in our days. In the Gospel, the Lord says that those who have received more have to give a stricter account. "That slave who knew what his master wanted, but did not prepare himself or do what was wanted, will receive a severe beating. But one who did not know and did what deserved a beating will receive a light beating. From everyone to whom much has been given, much will be required; and from one to whom much has been entrusted, even more will be demanded" (Lk 12:48). These lay people received less, because they received no formation and even a distorted formation by those who were supposed to form them well. And so, they have a lesser responsibility in my opinion. I believe they will be judged by Our Lord more leniently than the clergy. But the higher the clergy, the stronger and stricter will be the judgment, because they had the task of being vigilant and protecting the flock from disease and danger and did not, and they even collaborated in spreading disease and danger, and acted as wolves in sheep's clothing.

9

Papal Power

Your Excellency, the Catholic Church holds that Jesus gave special preroga-
tives to St. Peter, the first bishop of Rome, and that each successor of Peter
is the divinely-protected guardian of the faith, who has an unparalleled
role to play as the supreme visible head of the Church. However, does this
mean that the pope has unlimited power? Would you say that there are
limits to papal power?

This is a very good question. It is connected with the previous
theme we spoke about, on the Council and the Magisterium. Papal
authority is a subordinate magisterium. It is subordinate to the written
Word of God and to the transmitted Word of God in Sacred Tradition, and also to the constant teaching of all of the pope's predecessors according to the perennial sense of the entire Church (*perennis*
sensus ecclesiae). Papal authority therefore has an essentially vicarious
character. The pope is ultimately the person in the Church with the
least freedom, because his authority is very limited, since he is only
an administrator of something which does not belong to him, but
to Christ. The pope is the last person in the Church who could say,
"Now I will do what I want!"

Since the time of St. Gregory the Great, the popes have adopted
the title *servus servorum Dei. Servus* means, not minister, but servant
or slave. *Servus* is a very humble expression. A *servus* has to execute the
orders of his Lord. The pope is not the Lord, despite the expression
Sanctissimus Dominus. He continually has to be aware of being a *servus,*
a slave, a servant, like Our Lady at the moment of the Incarnation.
In her response to the Angel Gabriel, the Blessed Virgin Mary gave
to all mankind, especially to the clergy, the perfect example of being
a "servant" of the Lord: *Ecce ancilla Domini* ("I am the handmaid of
the Lord"). This attitude of Our Lady must first and foremost be the
attitude of the pope, of the bishops and the priests.

Another title of the pope is Vicarius Christi, *the "substitute" or "representative" of Christ.*

I once heard an amusing joke about the meaning of the Latin word *vicarius*. When you write "*vicarius*" vertically, you can get this decipherment: V (*vir*, man); I (*inutilis*, useless); C (*carens*, lacking); A (*auctoritate*, authority); R (*raro*, rare); I (*intelligens*, intelligence); U (*umbra*, shadow); S (*superioris*, of the superior). The most useful of the decipherments of this joke is the expression "*umbra superioris*" — to be the shadow of the superior. This should be the interior attitude of every priest and bishop and of the pope himself, since their superior is Jesus Christ. The pope has constantly to point to the Lord and decrease, like John the Baptist did. The pope should not obscure the Lord by his actions, he is to be the shadow of his Superior, the pope is to be *umbra superioris*, who is Christ.

This is the task of the Magisterium and the pope: to be faithful stewards. In the Gospel, Our Lord says: "Who is then the faithful and wise steward, whom his master has set over his household, to give them their food at the proper time" (Mt 24:45). The great clerical temptation is to consider oneself a Lord and to behave as such, and not as the steward. The higher the clerical rank, the more dangerous is this temptation. Therefore, it is especially the pope who must take the utmost care in every expression of the magisterium and also in his gestures and actions. The pope should weigh very carefully every word he speaks. I think that in the future there must be a pope who will explicitly and officially correct the unhealthy ultramontanism and papolatry which has infected the life of the Church in the last centuries, and which has reached its peak in our days.

It seems he would have to do so in both a doctrinal and a pastoral way.

Of course. I think that popes should speak rarely, in part because the inflation of the pope's words obscures de facto the magisterium of the bishops. By his continuous pronouncements, the pope has become the pivotal point for daily life in the Church. However, the bishops are the divinely-established pastors for their flock. In some way, they are quite paralyzed by an unhealthy papal-centrism. This is also contrary to the constant Tradition of the Church, as witnessed by the Fathers of the Church and especially by Pope St. Gregory the Great. The Fathers of the Church, almost all of whom were bishops, greatly stressed the importance of the episcopal ministry. Until the Second Vatican Council, the bishops took more seriously their magisterial function by means of pastoral letters, which were usually doctrinally very clear and pastorally useful.

Isn't that ironic? Nowadays we get the impression that the bishops are supposed to be more important and do more, but they seem rather passive and ineffective.

The Second Vatican Council strongly emphasized so-called episcopal collegiality. However, we can observe in recent decades that this teaching and its practical implementation contain some ambiguities and dangers. The danger is that collegial organisms, especially bishops' conferences, often obfuscate and limit the divinely established authority of individual diocesan bishops. Collegiality and so-called "synodality" are defective in their implementation if they harm the divinely established structure of the Church.

The extreme papal-centrism in the Church today has made it almost impossible for bishops publicly, fraternally and, of course, respectfully, to admonish the pope, if he manifestly deviates from the constant teaching of all his predecessors and from the unchanging sacramental practice of the Church. In admittedly very rare cases, when a pope by his non-definitive teachings or by his omissions is considerably damaging the clarity and integrity of the doctrine of faith and the discipline of the sacraments, the possibility exists for the bishops to express not only a private but also a public fraternal admonition towards the pope. If such an act of fraternal admonition were not considered scandalous, and if the bishops who expressed the admonition did not have to fear reprisals, and if their act would not be wrongly labeled "schismatic," then the true spirit of collegiality, which Vatican II theoretically intended, would be also practically realized — principally and only for the universal spiritual good of souls.

I think that a future pope has to issue a document on the papal ministry itself, correcting the errors of papolatry, but also stating that it is sometimes possible and necessary for bishops — of course with respect and prudence — to publicly admonish the pope, when he departs from the uninterrupted and constant Tradition of the Church, and that such an act should not be considered irreverent, disobedient, or schismatic. I am thinking, for instance, of the case when four cardinals published the *dubia* addressed to Pope Francis in 2016, an act which was none of those things.

Do you think the current crisis will induce a correction of papolatry?

Yes, I think that after this crisis the Church will correct the situation.

You asked about the role of the pope. In Kazakhstan, I quite frequently have contact with the Orthodox, who represent twenty-five percent of the population. I have contacts with some Orthodox bishops and priests. Recently, I met with an Orthodox priest. He is very kind to me and has invited me several times to dinner with his family. An Orthodox theologian was also at the dinner. This theologian said to me, "I believe in the dogma of the primacy of the pope." He went on, "But we Orthodox could never accept the papacy in the form in which it is now lived and practiced by Pope Francis. It is for us an incredible papal-centrism and papolatry." The Orthodox priest and the theologian said to me: "We could even accept Vatican I, the primacy and infallibility, but as it was practically lived out by Leo the Great and Gregory the Great, for instance."

It must be said that treating the pope like a rock star did not begin with Pope Francis.

As I mentioned before, this comes from a movement in the nineteenth century called "ultramontanism." In those times there was still no television or internet, or even radio. However, had these media existed in the nineteenth century, Pope Pius IX might have been a star — and even perhaps Pius X, I don't know. This extreme papal-centrism was done in good faith, because when the enemies of the Church, with the French Revolution, started to attack the rock of Peter, the faithful instinctively began to defend their common father. And the rock of Peter was truly a rock in those pontificates. Thus, I think it is a matter of historical context.

Pope John Paul II already said this in his encyclical *Ut Unum Sint*, on ecumenism: "I even ask my brethren to help me to exercise the Petrine ministry in a manner that would be more convenient for the unity of the Church" (n. 95). However, the correction of papolatry is something the pope himself has to do, first by his example, but also through a document. An example is not sufficient. One pope dies and then another one comes. But if a papal document on the Petrine ministry were written, also regarding these practical aspects, there would be a concrete reference for future cases of manifest and objective abuse of the Petrine ministry.

Do you see the current pontificate of Pope Francis as the fruit of Vatican II?

This pontificate is a logical consequence of the so-called "spirit of the Council" and of the ambiguous elements in some of the Council texts. In the past fifty years, many statements of the Council were interpreted and implemented in the wrong way, oftentimes against the authentic intentions of the Council Fathers. Today we have reached the peak of this development, especially in the field of moral doctrine on the issue of the divorced and civilly remarried, and in regard to the so-called "diversity of religions." A doctrinal, moral, and liturgical relativism is reigning in the life of the Church at almost every level. Not so long ago, the vice-president of the German Bishops' Conference, for example, publicly stated that the Church has to earnestly and seriously reflect on giving blessings to homosexual unions. A vice-president of a bishops' conference publicly stated this, and the Holy See does nothing! What is worse, in past years bishops have been raised to the cardinalate and priests to the episcopacy who were already known for active homosexuality in their private lives, and for publicly advocating the moral legitimacy of homosexual activity.

But what's the path out of this quagmire?

I think it is good that these clerics are now coming out from their holes and presenting their faces. Divine Providence has permitted this. I think that the next pope should be a pope who will be ready to die in defense of Christ, of the truth. The pope should ask a heretical bishop or cardinal publicly to retract his errors, and if such a bishop or cardinal would refuse to do so, he should be deposed. Were a pope to act in this manner, bishops and cardinals would not dare to say or teach doctrinal errors and heresies, thereby spiritually poisoning the faithful.

Do you know what a great number of bishops and cardinals, even the liberals, love most in their life?

What is that?

More than anything else in the world they love their chair, i.e., the career position they occupy. Yes, this is what they love more than their life. For the sake of this they will even offer the sacrifice of making a retraction from their heresies — to keep their position.

Do you see the Church being secularized, and would you say the current pope is promoting it?

Yes, we are witnessing this. Secularism is very strong, because Pope Francis is mostly addressing — and, in my opinion, in an exaggerated manner — issues which do not of themselves belong to the task of the Apostles, of the Successors of the Apostles, since he mainly promotes purely worldly realities.

Such as...

Such as climate change, the environment, the care of plastic waste disposal, immigration. These are not the proper competencies of the Church; they belong to the government. Oftentimes, before the Council, the liberals or the world would accuse the Church of interfering unduly in affairs that properly pertain to secular powers. Today this is really taking place through the pope's excessive concern for secular and temporal affairs. The pope is interfering and occupying himself with duties that belong to secular powers.

Looking at history, we had examples of popes who occupied themselves mainly with secular issues. I think of Pope Julius II, who spent a great deal of his time in warfare, leading on horseback and dressed as an army commander; or Leo X, who spent his time dealing mostly with arts and amusements, unconcerned about the dangerous increasing conflagration of the Lutheran heresy in the Holy Roman Empire, especially in Germany and in northern Europe.

It could also be that — in the case of climate change, for instance — secular powers are infiltrating and using the Church in order to gain moral authority and to promote their own agenda.

Exactly. When the bishops and the pope neglect supernatural realities and the primary care of souls, they sometimes turn to caring for the body. The Apostles refused to do this, as we read in the Acts of the Apostles, chapter six. St. Peter, the first pope, said it is not right for them to "serve tables," i.e., to focus on the bodily and temporal needs of people, while neglecting prayer and the ministry of the Word, and the proclamation of revealed truths. I would agree that in our days there is a very strong process of secularization underway in the life of the Church and in the policy of the Holy See.

Is the Church also being Protestantized?

The Protestants strictly separated the spiritual and secular domains. They said: "I am living my faith subjectively and what is happening outside is not my concern." Historically, most Protestants did not have a strong lay movement to present Christ in society, to defend Christ and the Gospel in public life. Now, thanks be to God, there are Protestant groups who publicly protest against abortion, homosexuality, etc.

A Protestantization is happening in the Church through Modernism, because Modernism is born from a Protestant spirit. Luther said, "I am now interpreting the entire tradition in a new way." The Catholic Modernists also say that they are interpreting tradition in a new way. The mindset of Modernism is ultimately Protestant. With the promotion of relativism and Modernism in the Church today, Protestantism and its subjectivist principles end up being promoted as well. We can observe this very clearly in the issues raised by the papal document *Amoris Laetitia*. Many pastoral guidelines for its implementation allow Communion to unrepentant adulterers on the basis of the subjective decision and discernment of the conscience. This is plainly a Protestant principle.

Moving to another topic related to papal power, how should we consider canonizations in relation to papal infallibility?

To illustrate these issues, I would first look to the historical example of the status of St. Philomena, the favorite saint of St. Jean Marie Vianney, who is one of the greatest saints. He performed miracles, and he attributed these miracles to St. Philomena; he even had several visions of this saint. The tomb of St. Philomena was discovered in the catacombs at the beginning of the nineteenth century and devotion to her spread very quickly. However, there are almost no historical documents about her life. Nonetheless, she was given a proper Mass and Office by Pope Pius IX in 1855, and devotion to her was showered with papal favors by Leo XIII and Pius X. Pope John XXIII later had her removed from any and every liturgical calendar whatsoever. With this act, veneration of a popular saint was suppressed. She was venerated as St. Philomena for almost two hundred years and then she disappeared in the wind. She was recognized as a saint with a public *cultus* and then she was gone. Whether we agree with the decisions or not, it was historical reasoning that put her into the liturgical calendar, and it was historical reasoning that took her out. The canonization therefore was not infallible, but contingent on historical information.

Canonizations happen in different ways: names are inscribed in the list of the saints either by a decree of the pope without a previous canonical process of canonization, or by a formal process of beatification and canonization. In the sixteenth century, some names of saints were simply inserted by Cardinal Caesar Baronius, the redactor of the *Roman Martyrology*. Thus, thanks to Cardinal Baronius, we have many saints in the *Martyrology* for whom the pope did not order a canonical process. The pope just accepted the names proposed by Cardinal Baronius and granted his pontifical approval.

As the history of the *Martyrology* demonstrates, when we look at two thousand years of history, beatifications and even canonizations have no definitive dogmatic value in the sense of infallible papal *ex cathedra* decisions, as defined by the First Vatican Council.

Turning from saints in heaven to the Church here on earth, what do you think is the proper role of papal jurisdiction in the Church, and what spiritual relationship should the pope have with the bishops and the faithful?

The pope is the Vicar of Christ and the Supreme Pastor in the Church. He has jurisdiction over the clergy and the faithful. But in the Gospel, when the disciples were discussing who was the first, Our Lord said: "whoever would be the first among you must be your slave" (Mt 20:27). That is the pope. He has to serve his brothers. Just before, Our Lord said to the Apostles, "You know that the rulers of the Gentiles lord it over them, and their great men exercise authority over them. It shall not be so among you" (Mt 20:25). He said this within the broader context of who would be the first among them, so this was an indication for the pope. I think the pope has to keep this in mind: "I shall not lord it over my brother bishops."

It is a regrettable fact that, with the increase of the political power of the Roman Pontiffs as temporal Sovereigns of the Papal States, they also adopted over time the attitude of a worldly monarch in their relationship even towards their brother bishops. Such a worldly political attitude sometimes had the characteristics of a papal absolutism, under the motto "The Church, that's me"—"*l'Église c'est moi*," similar to the political motto of King Louis XIV of France, "*l'État c'est moi*." In cases where popes were infected with the spirit of worldly absolutism, the relationship between the pope and the bishops oftentimes became a relationship between a boss and his employees. Such a relationship contradicts the words of Our Lord and the essence of the Petrine ministry.

Therefore, the intention of the Second Vatican Council to stress the divinely established office of bishops and episcopal collegiality was meaningful. However, the affirmation in *Lumen Gentium* n. 22 that there are two supreme permanent authorities for governing the whole Church — the pope on the one side, and the entire episcopal college with the pope on the other side — is doctrinally ambiguous and needs a further clarification.

The Orthodox churches fear papal absolutism that exists in a worldly manner. They fear that if they recognize the pastoral authority of the pope, he will dominate and lord it over them, as secular lords do. Of course, the pope has to exercise authority, for example, when bishops and priests spread heresies, sacramental abuses, and moral scandals. However, when a bishop with a personally high moral standard works with zeal for the integrity of doctrine and discipline in his diocese, the pope has to leave freedom to such bishops, since they are doing their work well. The pope should not hinder but must encourage such bishops. This is his task.

The pope's task regards the entire flock and all the faithful. He has to be a good shepherd who defends the flock from the wolves. The pope must be the first defender against the wolves. He has to be watchful and expel the wolves who have crept into the Church sometimes disguised as cardinals, bishops, and priests. The pope has to defend the Church from the wolves, even to the point of giving his life, as Jesus says: "The good shepherd lays down his life for the sheep" (Jn 10:11).

A pope can of course lay down his life as a sacrifice by persevering to the end and dying in his bed. But, I think here Our Lord meant that a shepherd must defend his flock even to the extent of being killed, if that is inevitable. The pope lays down his life for his flock also when he is morally attacked or when he is calumniated. His name "Petrus" says that he has to be a rock, to be firm. The pope has no authority to change doctrine, but only to hand on what he has received. That is the meaning of "confirming" the brothers in the faith and the truth, since that is the power he has, merely to "confirm"; he has no power to change or invent the truth. The true honor of a pope was articulated in what St. Paul said: "*Tradidi quod et accepi*," "For what I received from the Lord I also delivered to you." I very much like this quotation from St. Paul (cf. 1 Cor 11:23). This phrase is also written on the tomb of Archbishop Marcel Lefebvre.

10

The Society of St. Pius X

Our last conversation ended with a mention of Archbishop Marcel Lefebvre. Let's turn to the Society of St. Pius X directly. You were chosen in 2015 as one of the visitators to the SSPX. Why do you think you were chosen?

I don't know the reasons. The Pontifical Commission *Ecclesia Dei* asked me to visit several houses of the SSPX in order to lead theological discussions with a group of priests and with the Superior General Bishop Bernard Fellay.[1] Perhaps I was chosen because I publicly celebrate the traditional Mass. It would be better to send such a bishop to the SSPX than to send Cardinal Kasper or Cardinal Marx…

What were your impressions of the Society of St. Pius X once you made the visitation?

In general, I had a positive impression. I lived the entire schedule of the day with the seminarians and the priests. I participated in the prayers, in the meals in the refectory, in recreation. At their request, I also spoke with seminarians and priests individually, and of course I spoke at length with Bishop Fellay and other superiors of the SSPX. In this way, I had enough experience to make a reasonable evaluation of the situation of the SSPX.

Of course, there are negative points in every community, otherwise we would already be in heaven. However, in general I had a positive impression. Humanly speaking, I experienced a pleasant atmosphere. I met priests and seminarians who were balanced and normal. They received me as a bishop with respect. I even saw a photograph of Pope Francis on the walls. In the sacristy I saw nameplates with the name of Pope Francis and the local diocesan bishop — not, however, the name of Bishop Fellay. This is ecclesiologically correct. I believe most people

---

1   Since the time of this interview, Pope Francis suppressed the Pontifical Commission *Ecclesia Dei* and entrusted its competencies to a section within the Congregation for the Doctrine of the Faith.

would be shocked to hear that the SSPX has the picture of the current pope on the wall in their houses, and the nameplates of the current pope and the diocesan bishop in the sacristy.

When I commented on it to the SSPX priests, they said to me: "We didn't just put up the picture of Pope Francis before you came."

Did you see many photos of Archbishop Lefebvre or Bishop Fellay?

I never saw a picture of Bishop Fellay in the sacristies, but just the name and sometimes even the picture of the pope and of the local bishop. There were photos of Archbishop Lefebvre and St. Pius X, of course.

And what did you find from examining the Society? People say that it's very wealthy now, and that there may be some corruption. Did you see any of that?

The houses I visited had good religious observance and fidelity and zeal for prayer. I did not notice any luxury in the places I visited. I *have* seen wealth and luxury in some seminaries and episcopal chanceries in Germany and the United States. I did not see that in the houses of the SSPX. I visited the General House in Menzingen in Switzerland and it was beautiful and simple. Where I visited, I did not see wealth and luxury.

And what did you find in your theological discussions?

Regarding the theological discussions, I noticed an attitude of mistrust towards Rome, towards others who are not from the SSPX. However, such an attitude is psychologically understandable. For forty years the SSPX has had no formal canonical relationships with Rome and with local bishops. Such a situation contains a danger, and I told this to Bishop Fellay and the other priests. I said, "This is your danger, that in time you will develop a spirit of ecclesiastical self-reliance and a kind of ghetto mentality." I suggested that they request canonical recognition from the Holy See. I avoided saying "reconciliation," but instead I spoke of "recognition." I said, "You have a right to be recognized by the Church," because you are training seminarians, preaching, teaching the catechism and celebrating the sacraments as the Church has always done.

In the houses I visited — the General House in Menzingen (Switzerland), the seminaries in Flavigny (France), in Winona (USA), and in Zaitzkofen (Germany), I participated in the prayers during solemn Exposition of the Blessed Sacrament. I was moved when I heard the solemn prayer for the pope sung in Gregorian chant: *Oremus pro pontifice nostro Francisco*. In many seminaries and churches in the Catholic world, they don't sing the solemn prayer for the pope, but the Society of St. Pius X does. On one occasion I met a group of families affiliated with the SSPX apostolate and the parents told me that their children pray the Rosary for Pope Francis. How can one consider such attitudes and acts to be those of schismatics?

Do you think they will come back into full communion, whatever that means?

"Full communion" is not the correct expression in my view. They are already in communion with the Church, since they recognize the current pope, mention him in the Canon, pray for him publicly, and pray for the local diocesan bishop. The SSPX has received faculties for absolution from the pope, and the priests of the SSPX may now obtain faculties from the diocesan bishop or from the parish priest canonically to assist at marriages.

"Regularized"?

Regularized, that is better. Full recognition is better than the expression "full communion," because the members of the SSPX are not excommunicated. I encouraged them very much to ask the pope to give them canonical recognition.

We also discussed their assertion that the new Mass is "evil" or "bad." I told my interlocutors from the SSPX: "You should not speak in this manner." I told them that I am also not happy with the new Mass. I suggested that they use the expression "The new Mass has defects but is not an evil." I also said to them: "When you say that the new Mass is evil, you are accusing me of committing an evil, a sin, because I, too, celebrate the new Mass." I said to them: "You have to write down and present your criticisms, that is good, but do it with more careful language." The priests with whom I spoke demonstrated a good theological training. However, they also have to consider objectively what was good in the Council, and this does not mean that they must accept the entire Council. What is, *in se*, true and good — even in the new Mass — could be accepted.

In my opinion, the SSPX should be recognized and, if they were, it would be a true spiritual and pastoral help to the entire Church, to strengthen doctrine and tradition in the Church. The SSPX offers good priestly formation.

What is your view of the most recent attempt made at reconciliation?

There were very ambiguous signs coming from Rome in June 2017. Cardinal Müller presented them with a formula of agreement, which was not acceptable. During our visitation, the other bishops and I sought to present a more realistic and pastorally-minded formula. To my knowledge, the Pontifical Commission *Ecclesia Dei* promoted the proposal that I made. Unfortunately, the formula was changed, and I don't know what the current situation now is.

In November 2017, Archbishop Pozzo said that they have done everything they can, and the ball is now in the Society's court.

Yes, but the Holy See presented the last formula in 2017, and everyone knew that it would not be acceptable to the SSPX. Rome should have been more pastorally-minded and generous.

One of the requirements was that the pope should be given three names for the appointment of a bishop, and that he will choose one of those names. This prompts a concern that men will maneuverer to be favorable to Pope Francis's vision more than perhaps the Society's, so you'll get these men coming to the top and this will eventually weaken the Society.

It could be, but Pope Francis is not eternal. I told them, "You cannot pin your concrete situation to one pontificate and make it dependent on that. This is too human; you have to have a supernatural vision, that God is guiding His Church."

Were the SSPX recognized, and Rome afterwards obliged them to accept doctrinal and liturgical changes that would be contrary to their charism, the SSPX would have to reject such changes, even at the risk of again losing canonical status, as happened in 1975. In such a hypothetical case, the SSPX would only lose the canonical status and return to their former situation.

Traditionally, this is why religious Orders had a cardinal protector. He was to protect it from the world but also from the Holy See, from intervening in their life in a way that was inappropriate.

According to the proposed statutes of a Personal Prelature St. Pius X, the Prelate would be appointed by the pope from a list of three priests who are members of the SSPX and are proposed by the authorities of the SSPX.

Theoretically, the Roman Curia could try to interfere in the life of a future SSPX Prelature. We had the example of the Order of Malta, which was an extreme intervention into a sovereign state, and the pope ultimately removed the head of state — of course under the pretext that this head of state is also a religious with the vow of obedience. Theoretically, it could happen that after the erection of the Prelature, Rome could find a pretext to say: "We depose the Prelate and appoint an apostolic administrator and he will govern the Prelature with full authority in the name of the pope." However, these are human political possibilities and conjectures, and we have to overcome this attitude with a more supernatural trust in the providence of God and in His guidance of His Church.

I I

The Fourth Great Crisis

You have spoken in the past about the three great crises in the Church. How would you summarize them?

The first deep crisis in the history of the Church happened in the fourth century — the Arian crisis. It was a tremendous crisis that reached almost universal proportions, as the entire episcopacy collaborated with the heresy which denied the mystery of the Most Holy Trinity, by denying the true divinity of the Eternal Son of God and of the Holy Spirit. While nearly all the world's bishops, with different motivations and to varying extents, collaborated with this heresy — you could count the number of bishops who remained faithful on one hand — most of the laity remained faithful to the true faith in the Holy Trinity, the faith they received in baptism. This first crisis lasted approximately sixty years.

Then came the terrible crisis of the so-called "Dark Age" — the *saeculum obscurum* — in the tenth century, when the papacy was occupied by very wicked and immoral clans of Roman families. They put their corrupt sons on the papal throne.

The third crisis was the Avignon Exile, which led to the Great Western Schism. This crisis lasted some seventy years and greatly damaged the Church, for in some ways it prepared the way for the worldliness and publicly-known immorality of the Renaissance popes. The deep moral crisis of the Renaissance papacy was also one of the factors, surely not a decisive one but a factor nonetheless, that contributed to the Protestant revolution in the sixteenth century.

Are we now entering the fourth great crisis?

Yes — a tremendous state of confusion over doctrine, morals, and liturgy. The Church in our days is infected with the virus of an egoistic naturalism and an adaptation to the spirit of the unbelieving world. The clergy in positions of responsibility bend their knees to the world. The following observation, which St. Gregory Nazianzus made regarding the behavior of a great part of the bishops of his time, is definitely applicable to our situation as well: "We serve the times and demands of the masses. We leave our boat to the wind which happens to blow at the moment, and like chameleons, we know how to give our word many colors" (*De vita sua = Carmina* 2, I, II).

The current crisis is in my opinion the deepest and most danger-ous one because it expresses itself in a denial of the constant validity of *any* truth: dogmatic, moral, and liturgical. The religious relativism and indifferentism according to which God wills positively the diversity of religions ultimately entails the denial of the solemn and obligatory divine command of Christ to evangelize people of all nations and religions, without exception. This is at the very core of the current crisis in the Church. We have already been in this crisis for more than fifty years. Perhaps God will be merciful to us, and this crisis will slowly come to an end in ten, twenty, or thirty years. God knows, and He will intervene in due time, as He has already done so often in history.

John Henry Newman once wrote that, during the great Arian crisis in the fourth century, it was the faith of the laity rather than the faith of the bishops that saved the Church.

I would definitely apply Newman's words about the laity's contri-bution to preserving the integrity of the Faith to the current situation. I remember the following evocative words of St. Hilary of Poitiers — the Athanasius of the West — with which he underlined the fidelity of the lay faithful in light of the betrayal of the faith committed by the majority of the bishops during the Arian crisis: "The ears of the faithful people are holier than the lips of the bishops" (*Contra Arianos vel Auxentium*, 6). Along the same lines, I remember a very striking and apt observation of Archbishop Fulton J. Sheen: "Who is going to save our Church? Not our bishops, not our priests and religious. It is up to you, the people. You have the minds, the eyes, the ears to save the Church. Your mission is to see that your priests act like priests, your bishops, like bishops, and your religious act like religious."[1]

Today, too, the lay faithful — the "little ones" — by their simple and pure faith are carrying the Church on their shoulders. I often remember the following words of St. Ambrose which are contained in the Breviary,

---

1 Speaking to the Knights of Columbus, June 1972.

"*maior ambitioso eloquentiae mendacio simplex veritatis fides*," i.e., "the simple faith of truth is greater than the ambitious lie of eloquence" (*De Abraham*, 1, 2). When high-ranking clergy, through an ambitious and false eloquence, become careless in their zeal for Christ and His divine truth, the "little ones" step into the breach. What St. Bridget of Sweden once heard from the mouth of Christ is surely applicable to the liberal and worldly clergy of our days. He said to her: "They would rather speak a hundred words for the sake of the world than a single one in my honor. They would rather work a hundred times for the sake of their own profit and that of the world than once in my honor."[2]

Do you think the current crisis in the Church has to some extent been caused by the Holy See itself?

It is a fact that the Holy See has enacted a number of measures which considerably weakened the integrity of the rule of prayer (*lex orandi*), the rule of faith (the *lex credendi*), and the rule of life (*lex vivendi*). The drastic change of the millennia-old rite of Mass enacted by Pope Paul VI unquestionably weakened the essentially sacrificial, Christocentric, and latreutical character of the Mass, shifting it more towards the meaning of a fraternal banquet and a community-centered prayer meeting, which phenomenologically is more similar to Protestant prayer services.

How much is neglect of the first Commandment at the heart of the current crisis in the Church?

What you say is very apt. Our first duty is to adore God the Holy Trinity and the Incarnate and Eucharistic God in the sacrament of the Eucharist. To our situation I would apply the words of the prophet Jeremiah: "They have turned to me their back and not their face" (Jer 32:33). Indeed, many of the shepherds of the Church have turned their backs on their first duty: they have turned their backs on prayer and the proclamation of Christ. These words of the prophet are in some way a picture of the Church today and of the way the new Mass is usually celebrated: they have turned away from the Lord. The Apostles said, "We will devote ourselves to prayer and to the ministry of the word" (Acts 6:4). The Apostles said it was not good for them to deal with temporal affairs, to the detriment of their primary spiritual duties.

2 *Book of Revelations*, Book I, ch. 48.

Is there a particular image you would use to describe the state of the Church in the present crisis?

Cardiac asthenia — a sickly, weak heart. The Church is the Mystical Body of Christ and the Eucharist is the heart. The heart gives blood and energy to the body. We are more than fifty years out from the Council. Especially with the new form of the Mass, which by its undetermined structure opened the door to a variety of subjectivist celebrations, and particularly with the practice of Communion in the hand, we are suffering a kind of spiritual heart disease in the Church. When the heart is weak, there is a medical expression for it: heart failure, cardiac asthenia. The Church in our day is suffering from a strong Eucharistic "cardiopathology," and so the entire body is anemic and without energy.

Never in the bimillennial history of the Church were there perpetrated such horrible offenses against the Blessed Sacrament, so many trivializations of the Sacrifice of the Mass on the part of the clergy and on the part of the faithful, as in our time. The "reform" of the liturgy and its implementation had the effect of desacralizing and weakening faith in the Real Presence and in the sacrificial nature of the Mass. We see this above all in the practice of the reception of Holy Communion in the hand and standing, which reveals this deepest wound and disease in the life of the Church today.

At a conference in Paris several years ago, I noted five wounds in the liturgical life of the Church.[3] These five wounds are an expression of the Eucharistic heart disease of the Church. We have to begin again to renew the heart of the Church, which is the Eucharistic cult — that is, to take Our Eucharistic Lord seriously and to renew the manner of worship and celebration of the Holy Mass and how we treat the Eucharist, Our Lord Himself, especially in the sacred and intimate moment of Holy Communion.

The Church is alive but not fully living?

People who suffer from a weak heart will understand this. The Church in many of her members and especially in her hierarchy is weak, she has no energy, because her heart, the Eucharistic cult, is weak. Instead, she engages in frenetic external activities, as for instance synods, crisis and emergency meetings, addressing issues on climate change and migration, etc.

---

3   Talk "The Extraordinary Form and the New Evangelization" during the "Réunicatho" Conference in Paris, January 15, 2012. The text may be found at https://www.paixliturgique. org.uk/aff_lettre.asp?LET_N_ID=863.

More than a hundred years ago (1899), Pope Leo XIII — in a document addressed to the Catholic hierarchy in the United States — warned the Church of the danger of "activism." He was referring specifically to a phenomenon called "Americanism." After the Council, a spirit of activism took over religious congregations with an active apostolate in a particular way. To what extent does activism contribute to the current crisis in the Church and how far has it spread?

It is evident that since the Second Vatican Council the life of the Church has been dominated by a frenzied activism, which might aptly be called the "heresy of action."[4] As you mention, the "heresy of action" was already condemned by Pope Leo XIII in his Apostolic Letter *Testem Benevolentiae*. In this letter, Pope Leo XIII refuted the error of those clergy who, on the practical level, gave primacy to the active virtues and to temporal and natural realities to the detriment of supernatural realities, i.e., grace, prayer, and penance. Returning to our discussion about the loss of the supernatural, the "heresy of action" substitutes (practically speaking) the primacy of man and his actions for the primacy of God's action.

Where in the Church do you see a particularly dangerous manifestation of the "heresy of action"?

Today the "heresy of action" has reached its peak at almost every level of the Church's life. But it has been manifested in a most striking manner in the recent and incredible attack on the cloistered contemplative life of nuns. This attack came not from the enemies of the Church, but from the Holy See itself, through the Instruction *Cor Orans*, which obliges cloistered nuns to join existing federations or to create their own. You are right in saying that this heresy was adopted in many active religious congregations, particularly in the West, following the Council. But now the "heresy of action" is being imposed on the strictly cloistered contemplative religious life of nuns, the true gem of the Church, with its absolute primacy of prayer.

The instruction *Cor Orans* makes cloistered religious life more bureaucratic, since federation structures necessarily require administrative and financial work. It obliges nuns to leave the cloister periodically for federation assemblies and for compulsory formation meetings outside their convent. This all implies frequent travels, which bring with them always

---

4 Also referred to as the "heresy of activism."

a distraction and a loss of recollection and solitude, and considerable financial costs, which is against the spirit of poverty of cloistered nuns. The once strictly cloistered nuns will be transformed thereby into a kind of itinerant or travelling nuns with only the name "cloistered" or "contemplative." The uniformity foisted onto the cloistered life of nuns would be detrimental to the richness of true Catholic diversity and the different ways of living a zealous religious life. The tradition of the Church always respected the inspiration of God reflected in the rich diversity of religious ways of life. Man-made and insidiously imposed "uniformism" — as is the case with *Cor Orans* — is different from the necessary unity in faith.

It sounds like the nuns are being sent by the Holy See to "re-education camp"...

We have to keep in mind that the enemies of the Catholic Church have always hated a radical and exclusively cloistered contemplative religious life. First among them was Martin Luther, who made a propaganda journey among the cloistered convents in Germany, inviting the nuns to abandon the cloister. Then there was the naturalistically-minded Emperor Joseph II of Austria, at the end of the eighteenth century, who closed many cloistered convents. A kind of death blow to the cloistered religious life hit with the so-called "secularization" in 1803, which dissolved almost all cloistered abbeys and nunneries in the Holy Roman Empire (Germany). Prior to 1803, the French Revolution closed the cloistered female monasteries and tolerated at most the public charitable works of the Daughters of Charity of St. Vincent de Paul. A historical example of the blind hatred of the Masonic tyrannical Directory against enclosed female religious was the public macabre execution by guillotine in Paris, in 1794, of the Discalced Carmelite nuns of the Carmel of Compiègne.

In times of great crisis, the Church was spiritually sustained by the radical contemplative, cloistered, and eremitical religious life. During the time of the Arian crisis in the fourth century, there were the desert monks, and during Iconoclasm in the eighth century, the so-called "non-sleeping" (*akoimetai*) monks of the monastery of Studion in Constantinople, who by their prayer and penance helped to defeat the spiritual evil of this heresy. At the time of the pseudo-reform of Martin Luther and his Protestant followers, God gave to His Church the gift of a new radical cloistered life of prayer and penance with the reformed "discalced" Carmelite nuns through the work and mission of the great doctor of the Church, St. Teresa of Avila. She would never under any circumstances allow any weakening of the cloistered, recollected, solitary, prayerful, and penitential religious life of her nuns. Since then, the strictly cloistered life of nuns (Discalced Carmelites, Poor Clares, and other religious orders) has provided, and still provides, the secret spiritual power which sustains the active missionary and apostolic life of the other members of the Church, especially of the clergy.

But doesn't Cor Orans *say that such nuns have an irreplaceable role?*

In spite of its beautiful and partly sophistical rhetoric and its impressive theoretical assertions, in practice *Cor Orans* ultimately destroys the radicalness and exclusivity of the cloistered and contemplative life of nuns, destroying thereby the work of the great St. Teresa of Avila, since it transforms the cloistered life of nuns into the lukewarm and unrecollected state in which St. Teresa found it before her reform.

It has to be said that the strictly cloistered life, lived out of love for the Lord, represents and realizes in the Church the exclusively contemplative mission of Mary at the feet of the Lord (cf. Lk 10:39). The Lord forbade Martha from expecting or forcing her sister Mary to share in her own active life. Contrary to the clear words of the Lord in the Gospel, the instruction *Cor Orans* weakens the absolute primacy of a strict contemplative and cloistered life, taking away from cloistered nuns the "better part" (cf. Lk 10:42), i.e., their mission to be exclusively "Mary at the feet of the Lord," transforming them into a kind of "half-Mary" who is not always at the feet of the Lord. However, to be entirely "Mary" at the feet of the Lord is what choosing the "better part" means.

How has the "heresy of action" manifested itself in the hierarchy of the Church?

Many positions of responsibility in the Church today have de-emphasized the primary apostolic duty of worship, prayer, and the zealous proclamation of divine truth. The life of the Church on the official level (the Holy See and episcopates) has turned excessively to human activities through an enormous proliferation of ecclesiastical bureaucracy, an unprecedented quantity of structures, committees, episcopal assemblies, and federations on various levels, through continuous meetings and synods. In the last years, the activity of the Holy See and of many bishops' conferences has even turned predominantly to temporal affairs, which leads ultimately to naturalism, which is the essence of the "heresy of action." In recent times, some activities of the Holy See and of different bishops' conferences have given the impression that they are the daughter houses of the United Nations and are promoting its ideological agenda.

The "heresy of action" with its spirit of naturalism causes a void in the souls of ecclesiastics and especially of bishops. As we talked about before, these men attempt to fill this void with continuous meetings, assemblies, and synods on different hierarchical levels and geographical regions. All of these meetings produce a document, usually an excessively long document. It seems that there is a direct proportion between the spiritual void and the length of the documents produced. These lengthy documents contain much impressive rhetoric and beautiful theories, but little sound theology and practical usefulness.

How can the Church respond to the "heresy of action"?

The "heresy of action" is very strikingly expressed in the manner of celebrating the liturgy of the Mass: by turning towards one another in a closed circle. The Church must begin to turn to the Lord and celebrate not only interiorly but also exteriorly towards the Lord. At all levels of Church life, beginning with the bishops, in priestly formation, and in the life of the parishes, we must increase the life of prayer, of adoration, of petition to ask for grace, and a renewed missionary zeal for proclaiming the divine truth of Our Savior Jesus Christ for the sake of the eternal salvation of souls.

In terms of concrete means, besides the renewal of Eucharistic worship and of giving due honor to Our Eucharistic Lord, our priority in pastoral activity must be the formation and care of Catholic families and of a serious doctrinal, pastoral, ascetic, spiritual, and liturgical priestly formation. It is indispensable that these two axes — the formation of Catholic families and a true Catholic priestly formation — be promoted with the apostolic spirit of the constant tradition of the Church. We must really form new apostles, new missionaries, new saints in the priesthood. In the seminaries we have to renew the zeal and restore the purity of the priesthood. The Church urgently needs a new generation of chaste priests with an ardent zeal for the salvation of souls. This is for me one of the most important and concrete ways to reform the Church.

Will this come through the reform of the bishops and the Curia?

Of course, the entire body of the Church will ultimately be renewed only when the head is renewed. In the time before Luther and even during the Great Schism and the Avignon Exile, and then during the Protestant "Reformation," there was the continual clamor for a *"reformatio ecclesiae in capite et in membris,"* the reform of the Church in her head and in her members. In order to reform the Church, sanctity of life and apostolic purity must first be found in the head of the Church (the pope and the episcopacy) and then in its members. Therefore, it has to start with the authorities in the Roman Curia, with the College of Cardinals, and with the episcopacy. Concretely, however, we have to start with Catholic families and with a new, serious formation for the priesthood. It is indispensable to form new, zealous, apostolic, and holy men.

As a bishop, St. Athanasius was such a man. You received the name Athanasius at your profession. What meaning does it have for you now? Do you sense a call in this name?

As I mentioned before, as a young religious I could never have dreamed of this name. It was a complete surprise to me. But when I became a bishop, I started to understand this particular circumstance in my life. In my episcopal ministry, I was and still am forced to undertake the defense of the universal doctrine and liturgical tradition of the Church. I consider it a sin of omission to be silent in view of the evident and enormous crisis of doctrine, morality, and liturgy in the Church, in the current atmosphere of widespread spiritual confusion. Therefore, I cannot say, "It is none of my business. I have my duties in my diocese and so I shall say nothing." I would consider it a sin of omission before the judgment of God. If I recognize and can articulate the crisis which infects the entire body of the Church, I cannot say: "It is none of my business! In my little place, there are no considerable spiritual diseases."

It would be a kind of egoism for me as a bishop to be silent. A bishop is consecrated, as the Second Vatican Council said, as a member of the entire body of bishops, as a member of the college of bishops, and has to feel in his heart a care and preoccupation for the health of the entire body of the Church. The Council teaches that each of the bishops, "as a member of the episcopal college and legitimate successor of the Apostles, is obliged by Christ's institution and command to be solicitous for the whole Church, and this solicitude, though it is not exercised by an act of jurisdiction, contributes greatly to the advantage of the universal Church. For it is the duty of all bishops to promote and to safeguard the unity of faith and the discipline common to the whole Church" (*Lumen Gentium*, n. 23).

Of course, the task of being solicitous for the whole Church belongs first and foremost to the pope, but individual bishops have to help him fraternally in this regard. This is what St. Athanasius did, who not by his own choice was thrown into the turbulence of the global Arian crisis in the Church of his time. I too find myself in the midst of one the greatest crises in the history of the Church — a crisis which has reached proportions which I could never have imagined when I became a priest. I cannot stand by and stay silent. I try not to speak continuously — that is not my task — but when something is obviously damaging the entire Church, I have to raise my voice.

In this context, I recall the well-known saying of Julius Fučík, a Czech journalist who was murdered by the Nazis: "Fear not your enemies, at worst they may kill you. Fear not your friends, at worst they may only betray. Fear the indifferent, as all the most infamous crimes on earth are committed with their tacit consent."

How did St. Athanasius respond at the time of the Arian crisis?

More and more, I think of my patron. He raised his voice amid enormous spiritual confusion. St. Athanasius was part of a very small group of episcopal colleagues, as he was in his time often alone or at least numbered among very few in comparison with the entire college of bishops in the fourth century.

St. Gregory of Nazianzus painted the following realistic picture of the behavior of the bishops of his time. He wrote: "For in reality, as the Scripture says, 'The shepherds became brutish, and many shepherds destroyed My vineyard, and defiled my pleasant portion' (Jer 10:21)... For with very few exceptions — and these, either men who from their insignificance were disregarded, or from their virtue manfully resisted, being left unto Israel (Is 1:9), as was ordained, for a seed and root, to blossom and come to life again amid the streams of the Spirit — everyone yielded to the influences of the time, distinguished only by the fact that some did so earlier, some later, that some became the champions and leaders of impiety, while such others were assigned a lower rank, as had been shaken by fear, enslaved by need, fascinated by flattery, or beguiled in ignorance; the last being the least guilty, if indeed we can allow even this to be a valid excuse for men entrusted with the leadership of the people" (*Or.* 21:24).

I ask my patron St. Athanasius also to help me always to be faithful to Christ and to the unchanging Tradition of His holy Church. St. Athanasius had a very beautiful saying, which I love, and which helps us. He once wrote to a bishop, saying: "*non decet servire tempori, sed Domino,*" it is not fitting that we serve time, but that we serve the Lord (*Ep. ad Dracontium*). That is to say, we should not first and foremost serve those persons who now have temporal power in the world or in the Church, but we have to serve the Lord.

A Catholic bishop is first a servant of the Lord, as St. Paul often called himself in the opening words of his epistles, "*Paulus, servus Jesu Christi.*" St. Paul would never have written, "*Paulus, servus Simonis Petri.*" So, too, a Catholic bishop is first a servant of the Lord. A bishop is not a simple employee of the pope. We bishops have first to serve the Lord. This means that we have first to serve the Church of all times; in doing so, bishops also best serve the pope. When we serve Christ alone in truth, we help the pope and the papal ministry more than those who are silent or are adulating him. Adulating the pope is not worthy of a bishop, of a successor of the Apostles. Thought-provoking and memorable is the following observation of Melchior Cano, a faithful and erudite Dominican bishop from the time of the Council of Trent. He said: "Those who defend blindly and indiscriminately any judgment whatsoever of the Supreme Pontiff concerning every matter weaken the authority of the Apostolic See; they do not support it; they subvert it; they do not fortify it. Peter has no need of our lies; he has no need of our adulation."

I hope that the saint and great confessor, St. Athanasius, will help me to live out and exercise the episcopal ministry according to the example he left to the Church. Since I have been called to this episcopacy without my seeking or wishing it, I have to fulfill this ministry according to my conscience, as did so many holy bishops, especially my patron.

I 2

Doctrinal Confusion

Your Excellency, you said that the fourth great crisis is marked by doctrinal confusion. I'd like to look more deeply at that, beginning with a discussion of the new and increasing emphasis on "synodality" and the push towards what many see as the decentralization of doctrine. What do you think are the roots of this push, and what are your thoughts about it?

Doctrine is the truth and is the foundation for the entire life of the Church and Christians. Therefore, Our Lord Jesus Christ is called in the Gospel "Master," that is, "Teacher" (*magister*; *didaskalos*). Teacher means to give a teaching, a doctrine. Our Lord said: "My teaching is not mine, but his who sent Me" (Jn 7:16). And of the Holy Spirit He says: "He will teach you all things and bring to your remembrance all that I have said to you" (Jn 14:26). "He will not speak on his own authority" (Jn 16:13). The entire basis of our life is the truth, the *Logos*, the Word who became flesh. The Word (*Logos*) is the other name of the Second Person of the Holy Trinity. The Second Person of the Holy Trinity is called properly "Son," Son of the Father, the Son of the Living God. The Holy Scripture did not say, for instance, that the "act," the "action" became flesh, but that the "WORD" — the truth — became flesh. The famous German poet Goethe, who was a known Freemason, was not fond of the expression "In the beginning was the WORD" (Prologue of John's Gospel), but instead preferred to say, "In the beginning was the action."[1]

We might also ask: Why does Holy Scripture not say: "Love became flesh," but rather, "The Word became flesh"? Why does it not say, "Feeling or sentiment became flesh?" or "Mercy became flesh," but "The Word, the *Logos*, became flesh"? Indeed, the Truth became flesh. And

---

1   "It's written here: 'In the Beginning was the Word!' / Here I stick already! Who can help me? It's absurd, / Impossible, for me to rate the word so highly / I must try to say it differently / If I'm truly inspired by the Spirit. . . . It should say: 'In the beginning was the Power!' / Yet even while I write the words down, / I'm warned: I'm no closer with these I've found. / The Spirit helps me! I have it now, intact. / And firmly write: 'In the Beginning was the act!'" (*Faust*, I, 3).

so, the truth, and with it the faith, is the foundation, the rock of the whole edifice of Christian life. God based His work of saving mankind on truth. We must not separate truth from love. However, truth serves as the basis for love, like a rock, and protects love.

Love is the proper name of the Holy Spirit, the Third Person of the Holy Trinity, because He is the love proceeding from the Father and the Son (*amor procedens*), He is even the "subsisting love" (*amor subsistens*) as St. Thomas Aquinas says (see *In I Sent.*, d. 10, q. 1, a. 1, ad 1). In the visible divine missions, Love, the Holy Spirit, comes forth from Jesus. The Lord "breathed on them; and said to them: Receive the Holy Spirit" (Jn 20:22). The Holy Spirit, who is Love, is always the Spirit of truth, as Jesus said: "the Paraclete, whom I will send you from the Father, the Spirit of truth" (Jn 15:26). We see then that love comes from truth, since the Son and Word of God does not proceed from the Holy Spirit, but the contrary. The Holy Spirit, who is subsistent Love in the Holy Trinity, and at the same time the love of God which has been poured out in the hearts of the faithful (cf. Rom 5:5), continues the Magisterium of truth of the Incarnate Word (cf. Jn 14:26; 16:13).

The Apostles — and the constant Magisterium of the Church afterwards — considered the strength and clarity of truth as central and indispensable to the proclamation of the Gospel and the Christian life. St. Luke speaks in the prologue of his Gospel about the "the certainty of those things, wherein thou hast been instructed" (Lk 1:4); St. Paul admonishes the faithful to remain "steadfast in the faith" (Col 2:5) and St. Peter warns the faithful of the risk of losing their stability (*firmitatem*) "by being carried away with the error of lawless men (*iniquorum errore*)" (2 Pet 3:17). How relevant for our own times are the words which Pope Pius VI wrote some 250 years ago and which I recalled earlier: ambiguity "can never be tolerated in a synod, of which the principal glory consists above all in teaching the truth with clarity and excluding all danger of error" (Apostolic Constitution *Auctorem Fidei*).

The crisis in the Church today is due to a neglect of the truth and specifically a reversal of the order of truth and love. Today, a new principle of pastoral life is being propagated in the Church which says: love and mercy are the highest criteria and truth has to be subordinated to them. According to this new theory, if there is a conflict between love and truth, truth must be sacrificed. This is a reversal and a perversion in the literal sense of the word.

The right order of truth and love — as it is reflected in the life of the Holy Trinity, where Love proceeds from Truth — is the basic law of the Church and Christianity and all pastoral efforts.

The unchanging paradigm . . .

Exactly. This is the unchanging paradigm. Therefore, doctrine is like a rock on which the city of the Church is founded. The rock is Christ, the WORD, and Peter is the visible sign of this rock. Peter is the rock, but not by his own power. He is the rock *in* the true Rock of Christ.

"They drank from the supernatural rock which followed them, and the rock was Christ" (1 Cor 10:4).

Yes, and the truth of the Church is therefore based on Peter. His first task is to strengthen the brethren in faith, as Jesus said (cf. Lk 22:32). Of course, the task of the entire episcopal college and of every bishop is by divine right to be a *doctor fidei*, a teacher of the faith, a teacher of the truth, yet in union with the entire episcopal body and with Peter, i.e., with the Roman Pontiff. The pope himself cannot teach his own doctrine. He can only teach what the Church has always taught. In the same way, a synod or a bishops' conference can only teach what the Church has always taught.

So you are saying that doctrinal decentralization is contradictory to the nature of the Church?

There can be no decentralization in doctrinal matters; otherwise, the Catholic Church would be transformed into countless doctrinally different Christian denominations, as we can see occur daily in the Protestant world. There can be a decentralization in pastoral approaches, which of course always have to be in conformity with doctrine. To a certain extent, and within certain well-defined parameters, there could also be a certain decentralization in liturgical issues of minor importance. In some regions of southern Germany, Austria, and Eastern Europe, for example, on Good Friday and Holy Saturday, the Blessed Sacrament is solemnly exposed in the monstrance and covered with a white transparent veil for Eucharistic adoration. Some regions celebrate octaves or obligatory liturgical feasts which are not observed in the universal Church. Some nationally important and urgent issues which do not have a directly doctrinal character, and which do not touch on the common and constant universal discipline of the Church, can and would better be decided locally.

A healthy decentralization helps the pope not to be overloaded with non-essential issues. In this sense, I agree with some bishops who during the Second Vatican Council advocated a healthy decentralization regarding the Roman Curia. I would see it applied, however, to the administrative and pastoral spheres and never to doctrinal or major disciplinary issues.

A healthy decentralization would allow the pope to concentrate on the essence of his apostolic task, i.e., the defense and strengthening of doctrine and liturgy and the appointment of good bishops. These are the essential tasks the pope has to take very seriously, even to some extent scrupulously.

If doctrinal errors spread in the Church, if real abuses creep into particular churches, and if bishops commit grievous failures and omissions in their pastoral duties, the pope can and should intervene in virtue of his pastoral jurisdiction over the entire Church. Each pope should, therefore, always recall the principle formulated by Pope Celestine I in the age of the Church Fathers, and recalled by Pius VI in his Bull *Auctorem Fidei*, by which he condemned the so-called Synod of Pistoia: "It is almost just as much of a crime to close one's eyes in such cases, as it is to preach offenses against religion." The pope ought to have sufficient time to concentrate more on safeguarding the purity of doctrine, liturgy, and the discipline of the sacraments, and the appointment of good bishops.

If you were to reorganize the Roman Curia, would you keep the Congregation for the Doctrine of the Faith in place as is?

Yes, and strengthen it. The work of the Congregation for the Doctrine of the Faith is a help to protect the little ones in the Church from the wolves, who frequently today are bishops and priests, and who are promoting heretical or confusing ideas in the Church and are thereby giving scandal to the little ones. When in the Gospel Our Lord speaks about the little ones, He says regarding anyone who scandalizes them that "it would be better for him to have a great millstone fastened round his neck and to be drowned in the depth of the sea" (Mt 18:5). I remember that Cardinal Joseph Ratzinger once compared these little ones in the Gospel to the faithful. The faithful are the little ones, independent of their age. I also remember a conversation which I had with Cardinal Joachim Meisner, who was archbishop of Cologne (1989–2014) and one of the signatories of the *dubia*; he passed away in 2017. In the conversation he said that during one of his frequent visits to the Roman Curia under the pontificate of John Paul II, an influential cardinal of the Curia told him: "Here in the Roman Curia sometimes the faith wins, at other times diplomacy wins." When Cardinal Meisner asked him to be more concrete, he said: "When the CDF wins, faith wins; when the Secretariat of State wins, diplomacy wins."

We have seen a strong push for decentralization with the German bishops on the issue of intercommunion. The pope gave his tacit approval to a German Church handbook allowing Holy Communion for Protestant spouses in some cases. What are your thoughts on intercommunion?

The question of intercommunion touches on relations between Christians. This is again a question of truth. Non-Catholics are visibly not united with the Church, notwithstanding the fact that they were made, and many remain, members of the Mystical Body of Christ in virtue of their valid baptism. The dogma of faith says in the creed that there is only one baptism: *"confiteor unum baptisma."* The Catholic Church has always rejected the practice and theory of a re-baptism. Even St. Cyprian of Carthage in the third century was wrong on this point. The Church recognizes the baptism even of those who were baptized by schismatics and heretics, provided that the rite of baptism was correctly administered. A valid baptism impresses the indelible mark which testifies that this schismatic or heretic is the legitimate property of Christ and hence of His Church. To be a true Christian, a true Catholic, to live according to the will of God, you have to be visibly united with the Catholic Church, with the Apostolic See of Peter. The admittance of Protestant or Orthodox Christians to Holy Communion contradicts the nature of the sacrament of the Eucharist and the necessarily visible character of the Church. Unfortunately, the *Code of Canon Law* (canon 844) says that it is possible in "emergency cases."

Or on one's deathbed...

Yes, or in danger of death. However, we have to be truthful to the nature of the Church and the Eucharist. The reception of Holy Communion is the highest expression of the full and perfect union of the Church. By the Eucharist's very nature, Holy Communion produces the highest union with the visible Church of the one who communicates. The sacraments are by their very nature visible signs. In giving Holy Communion to non-Catholic Christians who have no intention of visibly joining the Catholic Church, we are perpetrating a contradiction, a lie, and hence performing a kind of pious show, even in so-called emergency cases. By receiving Holy Communion, a non-Catholic should demonstrate and proclaim that he is in perfect union with the Catholic Church, since the essential effect of Holy Communion is perfect union not only with Christ but also with the Church. Yet the visible sign a non-Catholic outwardly and publicly gives by receiving Holy Communion contradicts his interior conviction and intention of not accepting the integrity of all Catholic dogmas and canonical communion with the visible head of the Church, the pope. No honest person can deny that the reception of Holy Communion by non-Catholics represents *in se* — even in a case of emergency — a lie and a contradiction.

To receive Holy Communion properly, it is not sufficient to be free from mortal sin, i.e., to have the right disposition. It is also not sufficient to believe in the dogma of the Real Presence of Jesus Christ in the Eucharist, the sacrament of confession, and the ministerial priesthood. Certainly, these are all indispensable conditions. However, it is also necessary to believe in all of the dogmas of the Catholic faith. Since apostolic times, only those who accepted the doctrine of the faith in its entirety could receive Holy Communion. St. Justin bears witness to this apostolic rule in his *Apology*, writing that only those are admitted to Holy Communion who believe in all the truths in which the Church believes (cf. *1 Apol.* 65).

Cardinal Reinhard Marx, president of the German Bishops' Conference, made clear that their proposal did not require the Protestant spouse to convert to Catholicism before being admitted to Eucharistic Communion.

The *Code of Canon Law* states that they have to believe the Catholic truth about the Eucharist. I suppose there could be a Protestant who even believes in Transubstantiation and in the sacrificial character of the Mass. But that is not enough. He also has to believe in all the other dogmas of the Catholic faith, such as, for example, the Marian dogmas, the dogma concerning papal primacy — dogmas which a Protestant rejects, otherwise he would become officially Catholic. The same is true for the Orthodox. They may believe in all of the other Catholic dogmas, but they clearly reject the dogma of papal primacy and infallibility.

Even when a non-Catholic is dying, one has to ask him if he believes in the truths of the Catholic Church. If so, one can give him sacramental absolution and Holy Communion. We always have to remember that the reception of the Eucharist is not of absolute necessity for eternal salvation. Only the true faith and baptism are necessary for salvation (cf. Mk 16:16).

At that point, if a non-Catholic believes in all the truths of the Catholic Church, and submits himself to the Church's practices, at least interiorly he has converted to Catholicism...

But he also has to become a Catholic *visibly*, because the Church is essentially visible, and the sacrament of the Eucharist is visible as well. I would like to repeat once more that Holy Communion is not absolutely necessary for salvation. There is only one sacrament that is necessary for salvation, and that is baptism. We do not even give the sacrament of baptism to someone who is selecting truths à la carte. He has to believe in all the truths revealed by God and taught by His Church, and to submit himself to the Church's practices. When a Protestant, or an Orthodox Christian, desires to receive Holy Communion, he simultaneously has to have the desire to be Catholic.

Admitting a Protestant or Orthodox Christian to Holy Communion in the case of an alleged emergency or as an exception already expresses a relativizing of the dogma of the uniqueness of the Catholic Church, which we profess in the Creed: "*credo unam catholicam ecclesiam.*" It also expresses a relativizing of the necessity of belief in all Catholic dogmas precisely on account of their being revealed by God.

When a Protestant or an Orthodox Christian is in spiritual need or is dying, he can make a Spiritual Communion, if he truly longs to receive the Lord. He may receive in an invisible manner the consolations and effects of the Eucharist, yet in a manner which God alone knows, and which consequently corresponds to the truth of his objective state of visible separation from the Catholic Church.

You are implying that too much emphasis, or maybe the wrong kind of emphasis, is being put on sacramental communion.

How many Catholics died a holy death even without Holy Communion! In my experience, in the underground Church in the Soviet Union, many of my relatives, my grandfathers Sebastian and Bernhard, my grandmother Melania, some of my granduncles and grandaunts, died without receiving Holy Communion sacramentally, without viaticum. My parents told me that they still died a holy Christian death because of their custom of frequent Spiritual Communion. How many hermits in the desert lived for years and even died without Holy Communion, living in a state of continuous Spiritual Communion!

God will provide His graces to the soul of a sincere Protestant or Orthodox Christian who longs for Holy Communion. In giving them Holy Communion without asking them to become Catholics visibly, we are pressing the action of God's grace into our own categories, which are contrary to the rule that God set forth in the apostolic tradition and which has spanned two thousand years of the Church's history. The Church has no authority to change the substance of the sacraments and she also should not relativize the apostolic rule regarding the reception of the Eucharist, the rule which says that the Eucharistic can be received only by those faithful who visibly profess all the dogmas of the faith.

The issue of intercommunion came to the fore when Pope Francis visited a Lutheran Church in Rome with Cardinal Walter Kasper and was asked by a Lutheran woman married to a Roman Catholic what could be done so that they can receive Communion together—so that they could share everything in life—with no mention of conversion to the Catholic faith.

Such an argument is in itself wrong and insincere. Returning to what we discussed about truth being the foundation of love, unity does not come from ambiguity and lies. The Catholic spouse continues officially to profess his or her adherence to the dogmas of the Catholic Church, whereas the Protestant spouse professes officially the errors of his or her Protestant denomination. The common reception of the Eucharist, the sacrament of perfect and visible ecclesial union, constitutes in such cases an enormous lie.

If we analyze this honestly, logically and theologically, we discover the error present in the *Code of Canon Law* (can. 844) and in the Second Vatican Council's Decree on the Catholic Churches of the Eastern Rite, which prescribes that an Orthodox Christian may receive Holy Communion in a case of a spiritual need, a spiritual emergency, or in danger of death (see *Orientalium Ecclesiarum*, 27). The expressions "urgent spiritual need" and "spiritual emergency" are in themselves vague and subjectivist, since it is oftentimes impossible to establish and objectively verify an "urgent spiritual need" or a "spiritual emergency." However, the discipline of the sacraments demands by its visible and objective nature objectively verifiable conditions.

It seems like the error you are describing could have immense consequences if pressed to its limits.

In giving this permission, the Council and the *Code of Canon Law* laid the foundation for carrying out a theological contradiction and a visible ecclesiastical lie. The principle laid down in the aforementioned Council text, and in can. 844 of the *Code of Canon Law*, has its logical consequence in the recently introduced regional pastoral norms admitting unrepentant adulterers to Holy Communion in some cases, in an alleged "urgent spiritual need" or a "spiritual emergency." Some of these norms were even approved by Pope Francis on the basis of *Amoris Laetitia*. In fact, these unrepentant adulterers, who cohabitate *more uxorio* in a civil union with a person who is not their legitimate spouse, live in the visible and objective state of public sin.

However, one of the main arguments for admitting such persons to Holy Communion is very similar to the one (can. 844) for admitting to Holy Communion non-Catholic persons who visibly and objectively live in a state of schism and heresy. In both cases — that of public sinners who are living in an objectively adulterous union, and that of persons who are in objective schism and heresy — proponents cite the argument of an "urgent and deep spiritual need or emergency" which has to be evaluated individually on a case-by-case basis and with pastoral accompaniment and discernment.

The Church has always jealously guarded Holy Communion. In ancient times, certain categories of sinners were not even allowed to enter the main part of the church until their penance was fulfilled.

The ancient discipline of the Church, witnessed to by the Apostolic Fathers and all the great Fathers of Church, admitted dying persons to Holy Communion only when they repented and desired to be visibly reconciled with the Church. This discipline has been valid for two thousand years. There may have been a very few and temporally and locally limited exceptions in the cases of missionaries among an Orthodox population, in order to facilitate the process of becoming Catholics.

Even a member of the Catholic faithful, when there is no priest and he truly repents of his sins and desires to be absolved, is absolved by God by the force of his loving repentance and his desire to receive the sacrament, i.e., by force of the *votum sacramenti*. When someone dies desiring baptism, he is baptized by desire, by the *votum baptismi*. When a Catholic is dying and sincerely desires with a contrite heart sacramental absolution and there is no priest, he will be absolved by the force of his graced desire, analogous to baptism by desire. Let us also allow the Protestants to die in this way, desiring the forgiveness of sins, since God provides for their salvation by ways which He alone knows. If we grant sacramental absolution without them giving previous signs of a desire to be united with the Church, we are choosing a way for these souls which does not correspond to the objective sacramental way that God Himself established. We will, of course, provide the maximum spiritual help for such dying non-Catholic souls: remaining by their side, praying the Rosary for them, blessing them to protect them from the attacks of the devil, and so on. However, we cannot give dying non-Catholic persons the sacraments unless they manifest, at least implicitly, a sign that they wish to be united in truth with the Catholic Church.

How much do you think the current crisis is due to the weakening of the truth "extra ecclesiam nulla salus" (outside of the Church there is no salvation)? Ever since that doctrine has been weakened, some say, we have seen a decline of the Church, and a growing relativism.

This is somehow already present in the texts of the Second Vatican Council—in the declaration *Nostra Aetate* and also *Dignitatis Humanae* on religious freedom. Relativism is already implicitly there along with a false ecumenism, when, for example, the Second Vatican Council praises Hinduism as a religion, saying that "in Hinduism, men contemplate the divine mystery.... They seek freedom through a flight to God with love and trust" (n. 2). How can you praise a religion which mainly worships idols? The affirmation of *Dignitatis Humanae* n. 4, that every person has a natural right, a right from his nature, to choose his own religion according to his conscience, and to worship the *"numen supremum,"* i.e., "supreme divinity"—this affirmation is wrong. We do not have the natural right to commit sin and to commit error. All religions outside the Catholic faith represent as a whole a system of errors, and are thereby objectively offensive to God, the Supreme Truth. They contain some truth, of course, but this truth is due to the light of natural reason and not to the religion as such, which is against the will of God and constitutes thereby an offense to God. Subjectively we don't know about the eternal destiny of such persons, because only God knows their intentions and their heart. However, persons who adhere to false religions are in objective danger of not attaining eternal salvation. In such a decisive theological matter as the truth that God wills only the religion born of the faith in Jesus Christ, God and man, we must avoid any words of confusion and of a purely worldly wisdom. We have to avoid the "smoke of worldly wisdom" (*"fumus mundanae sapientiae"*), to use an expression of Pope St. Leo the Great.

Insofar as people are "good Hindus," as Hindus they are worshiping false gods.

Exactly, false gods. The policy of the Church after the Council with the ecumenical and interreligious dialogues contributed to doctrinal relativism regarding the unicity of salvation through Christ and His Church. However, as we mentioned, this wrong policy was already laid down in the principles contained in some passages in the Council texts.

Some would say that the discussion in Dominus Iesus *of the Church of Christ "subsisting in" the Catholic Church doesn't offer as clear a teaching as we had before the Council.*

Dominus Iesus in great part is very clear, and thanks be to God we have this document, especially regarding other religions. However, the affirmation that "the Church of Christ subsists in the Catholic Church," which comes originally from *Lumen Gentium*, is insufficient. It is not wrong, but it is insufficient. It would be clearer to state, for example: "The only Church of Christ *is* the Catholic Church, and only in her are realized and subsist in fullness all the truths and all the means of salvation of the Church of Christ." Even now, a lot of bishops say that you can continue to be Muslim or Lutheran. Such affirmations promote relativism, in the sense that every religion is relative, including the Catholic religion. We surely are weakening the doctrine on *extra ecclesiam nulla salus.*

We might also ask: "What does *extra ecclesiam nulla salus* mean?" It means, in fact, *"Extra Christum nulla salus,"* outside Christ there is no salvation. The Church is not the center; Christ is the center. According to the teaching of St. Paul, "the church submits to Christ" (Eph 5:24) and "He is the head of the body, the Church. He is the beginning, the firstborn from the dead, that in everything He might be preeminent" (Col 1:18). The Fathers of the Church underlined this truth by comparing the Church symbolically to the moon and Christ to the sun. St. Augustine says, "The moon is understood to be the Church, because she has no light of her own, but is lighted by the only-begotten Son of God" (*Enarr. in Ps.* 11, 3). The Church is the necessary instrument and means of salvation in the hands of Christ, who is the only way to eternal supernatural salvation.

Perhaps we may turn to another topic. In 2016, four eminent cardinals submitted several questions (dubia) to Pope Francis asking for clarity on certain points of the Post-Synodal Apostolic Exhortation Amoris Laetitia. *Their questions regarded the validity of the divine moral law and the indissolubility of marriage. Chapter 8 of this document appears to allow Holy Communion in certain cases to those living in adultery. Is this really what chapter 8 says?*

Surely, I agree with the four *dubia* cardinals: clarification is needed on *Amoris Laetitia*, especially chapter 8, which appears to allow Holy Communion in singular cases to those who live in civil or irregular unions as husband and wife (*more uxorio*) and who have not procured a canonical declaration of the invalidity of their prior marriage. Pope Francis approved the pastoral norms of some local churches which allow in singular and special circumstances the reception of Holy Communion in such cases. Even if these local norms do not represent a general norm for the entire Church, they nevertheless signify a denial in practice of the divine truth of the absolute indissolubility of a valid and consummated sacramental marriage. This issue is very serious and has to be addressed in all honesty and clarity. We can never consent and be silent in view of the fact that, in the Catholic Church in our days, divorce and in a certain sense also polygamy is being introduced through such norms — if not in theory, then certainly in practice.

On the fiftieth anniversary of Humanae Vitae *in 2018, efforts in the Church over the past half century to undermine this encyclical reached a crescendo when a relatively new member of the Pontifical Academy of Life, Italian moral theologian Father Maurizio Chiodi, argued on the basis of* Amoris Laetitia *chapter 8 that responsible parenthood can obligate a married couple to use artificial birth control. What would you like to say about* Humanae Vitae *to married couples and those preparing for marriage?*

The Encyclical *Humanae Vitae* concerns the divine law about the transmission of human life, which God gave to husband and wife. "Be fruitful and multiply," He told them. Each human life is precious and unique. Parents receive from God the unique privilege of being collaborators in giving new life. To give life is a prerogative exclusive to God, and God in His mercy and wisdom decided that human parents, husband and wife, should also participate in His divine power of giving life.

The act of transmitting human life is therefore not an issue exclusively between the two spouses, but refers always to God, the Creator of life. Hence, this act has to be accomplished as God intended it and created it. God in His eternal and infinite wisdom, and not man, established the structure and order of human sexuality. In virtue of the created order of human sexuality, the meaning of the sexual act is by its nature procreative, it is meant to give life. Therefore, it is not within the domain of a couple to decide to change the God-given meaning and structure of sexual union, which by its very nature is open to life. In this way, God wisely connected sexuality with giving life.

Giving life is something completely selfless, and this should always be the disposition of man and wife in the marital act—selflessness.

Because marital union is not turned in on the couple; the act of giving life goes out of itself . . .

Exactly. This is a very good observation. Openness to life protects the couple in their sexual union from selfishness. Selfishness is the deadly poison of love. Consequently, when a husband and wife exclude the giving of life in the sexual encounter, they ultimately do not perform an act of love in the way God intends it, but an act of mutual selfishness. And this deeply wounds their love, because every time they exclude new life in the sexual encounter, they become increasingly more selfish.

God wisely made the life-giving act of procreation inseparable from the marital act in order to protect conjugal love. Human nature is wounded because of original sin. The wound of original sin also touches the sexual encounter between husband and wife. They are not immaculate. They were not conceived immaculate. They have the consequences of original sin, which has left its imprint in the sexual encounter also. Indeed, openness to life protects spouses from the negative, selfish consequences of original sin. The words of Our Lord about the indissolubility of marriage, "What therefore God has joined together, let not man put asunder" (Mt 19:6), may also aptly be applied to the truth about the indissolubility of the two ends of the marital act. Let not man put asunder the procreative and unitive ends of the marital act of husband and wife.

By inscribing openness to life into the nature of the marital act, God declared that the first end of sexuality is to give life, and the Church has always taught this uninterruptedly for two thousand years. The first end of sexuality, and consequently of marriage, which is obviously inscribed into nature, is to give life and to propagate the human race. For Christian couples, to give life means to give life to possible new citizens of heaven. The natural end of giving life is elevated, and incomparably so: to give life to new citizens *of heaven*. In this we see once more the truth that *grace presupposes nature*, elevates and perfects it. How beautifully this truth is realized in the marital act of a Christian couple!

Therefore, couples should really trust in God and let Him decide to call into existence a new human person and a new possible citizen of heaven. Why limit the number of citizens of heaven? Why not have more citizens of heaven, who for all eternity will see God, love, adore, and glorify Him? How could parents by their own decision limit the number of children, preventing thereby the existence of a possible citizen of heaven, who for all eternity will know God and love Him and who will also for all eternity thank his parents that they gave him life?

Therefore, even the so-called natural methods...

Natural family planning...

I think that the expression "natural family planning" is not correct. This expression seems to be coined in response to the abortion-focused organization "Planned Parenthood." It sounds too technical and, in some way, bureaucratic. One makes an economic plan for grain production, or cultivating and raising chickens or cows, a kind of "plan for the breeding of chicken or cattle." This is planning. I applaud the couples who have heroically avoided contraception, and who have sacrificed in order to practice conjugal life according to the design and will of God. However, for me it is unworthy to apply the word "planning" to human persons and to new possible citizens of heaven, to the children of God. We need to avoid the expression "natural family planning."

Would you use the expression "responsible parenthood"?

I don't like it much, either. We must all be responsible, of course, but the phrase is quite often misused and can be very subjective, so that by your own criteria you decide what is responsible and what is not responsible. In some way, the expression "responsible parenthood" contains the danger of falling into a contraceptive mentality, even when you use natural methods, which God provided in the cycle of the woman's body. The observation of the natural cycle of a woman's fertility can be used with a contraceptive mentality, as a contraceptive method. Therefore, this expression is already in some way ambiguous, because there is at least an implicit lack of trust in God, in His providence, a lack of trust and confidence that it is ultimately He who determines the calling into existence of a new possible citizen of heaven. In using specific terminology — particularly in such a delicate matter as the transmission of human life — we have to think about the ultimate consequences.

If I may go back to something you said — namely, that the Church has always taught that the procreation of life is the first end of marriage. I think some people today would contest this, arguing that with the Second Vatican Council, the two ends of marriage — the unitive and the procreative — were put on the same level. From what you are saying, it seems that keeping procreation as the first end — in addition to being objectively true — also protects the second end, protects the unitive aspect of marriage. In the sexual encounter, if husband and wife are not open to life, can they truly be open to God? It would seem that if they are open to life, in encountering one another in selflessness and chastity, in a certain sense they encounter God because there are three who are present when a child is conceived. A husband and wife who impede the procreative aspect seem more like our first parents in the garden who have turned themselves away from God and shut Him out.

Exactly. The procreative aspect of the sexual encounter of husband and wife, with their unconditional openness to life, allows God to enter into this moment of their intimacy. However, when the spouses purposefully eliminate the procreative aspect, they are eliminating the presence of God in this moment, saying to God: "Please, leave! We want to be alone now, only us two and no one else." Such an attitude is very sad. It is the core of what we call "sin." When the first sin in human history was committed, Adam and Eve did exactly the same: they wanted to be alone without the presence of God, therefore they fled from the presence of God after committing sin.

Then it is impossible for their union to be unitive if it is not procreative. A husband and wife cannot truly become closer if they have closed themselves off to God, especially in a sacramental marriage, since He is the source of their love.

Yes. When the spouses separate the unitive and procreative aspects, only pleasure and feelings remain. As we can observe over the last fifty or sixty years with the widespread contraceptive mentality, this attitude has far-reaching consequences for sexual morality within society and within the Church.

Cardinal Gerhard Müller, the former prefect of the Congregation for the Doctrine of the Faith, has argued that anyone who believes that contraception is all right ultimately has no argument against homosexuality.

I agree with this statement. You cannot separate sexual pleasure from the possibility of bestowing life. When you do this, first by supporting contraceptives within marriage — as unfortunately has become widespread in the lives of Catholic couples in the Western world, with the indirect support of some bishops' conferences — then you are opening the door to legitimizing and justifying a simple sexual encounter for pleasure, either before marriage, in adultery, or even in same-sex relationships, and so on.

In this sense, the encyclical of Pope Paul VI was a very important, highly necessary, timely and prophetic encyclical to save the dignity of human sexuality and the dignity of spouses. It was a protecting dam against the flood of sexual immorality and disorder in human society in the twentieth century. It was a dam to hold back this flood. Unfortunately, some bishops drilled a hole in this dam by allowing couples to decide themselves, "according to their consciences," whether or not to use contraception, to decide on the basis of an "emergency case" or a "deep urgent spiritual necessity." We have already seen this argumentation used to admit unrepentant adulterers and formal schismatics and heretics to Holy Communion, "in special cases" and because of a "deep urgent spiritual necessity."

It was a very irresponsible attitude of some bishops and bishops' conferences to allow the use of contraceptives on the basis of a decision "in conscience" or in "urgent and special cases" and in a "discernment process," as they said. Now, fifty years later, the bishops of the Catholic Church and the pope must not only restate the immutable truth about the meaning, order, and nature of human sexuality, but also make reparation for the infidelity of certain bishops and bishops' conferences, especially of those famous 1968 statements which ultimately undermined the encyclical *Humanae Vitae* and the perennial teaching of the Church concerning contraception. Among the most well-known and disastrous statements about *Humanae Vitae* were the Winnipeg Statement (Canada), the *Königsteiner Erklärung* (Germany), and the *Maria Troster Erklärung* (Austria). I think those bishops and bishops' conferences whose predecessors issued these fatal statements fifty years ago have to make acts of reparation for this. I hope that it will be done.

I believe you once mentioned that when a couple meets the Lord for their particular judgment, He will show them the children they would have had, had they been more open to life. But the same could be said of the bishops. Perhaps He will show them how many children were not conceived and brought to heaven because they failed to teach young people and married couples the truth about human sexuality.

It is my personal opinion that when the spouses appear before the judgment of God, He will show them all the possible children to whom He wanted to give life, so that they might be future citizens of heaven, and whom the parents by their selfishness in their sexual encounter refused. Children whom God would have called into existence. Perhaps this child who was prevented by his parents from coming into existence, either through contraception or through natural means used with a contraceptive mentality, was to be a great saint for the kingdom of God. Or perhaps the couple prevented talented people or geniuses from coming into existence who would have contributed greatly to the good of human society. Therefore, God will show them all the children they purposely avoided having — either through artificial or natural methods.

It is a matter of trust in God. It is a matter of faith. In my opinion, it would usually be better for a husband and wife to say: "O Lord, we allow you to decide. You are wiser than we are." Therefore, I would not say that it is irresponsible to have many children. There are many cases in human history and Church history of very large families.

St. Catherine of Siena (1347–1380), one of the greatest saints and mystics of the Church, who was instrumental in restoring the papacy to Rome after the Avignon Exile, was among the youngest of twenty-five children. St. Pius X (1835–1914) was one of ten.

These couples did not use "natural family planning." They said: "May God decide." I am therefore very careful and wary of the expression "responsible parenthood," because I believe it opens itself to misunderstanding and to subjective criteria. Certainly, natural methods could be used in extremely difficult cases, such as illness, but these would need to be very grave situations.

We see that the issue of *Humanae Vitae* touches on the essence of family and marriage. We therefore have to restate that the first end of marriage and of the sexual encounter is the giving of new life.

What do you say to those who argue that the teaching on the two ends of marriage was changed at Vatican II—that they were put on the same level?

The Pastoral Constitution *Gaudium et Spes* did not change this directly, but avoided speaking of the distinction between the primary and secondary end. By avoiding these expressions, the Council left some ambiguity regarding the first end of marriage. This caused erroneous interpretations and applications. However, *Gaudium et Spes* also left us the following traditional teaching about the nature of matrimony: "By their very nature, the institution of matrimony itself and conjugal love are ordained for the procreation and education of children and find in them their ultimate crown" (n. 48). The Magisterium of the Church has constantly taught that the life-giving procreative end is objectively the first or primary end. Yet it is inseparably united with its second aim, the subjective unitive end.

Unfortunately, in the current *Code of Canon Law* (can. 1055), the secondary end of marriage is mentioned first and only then the primary one, thus opening a new questionable understanding and practice. When the subjective unitive end is the first aim, couples might argue that "this is the first aim of our marriage, so we can use contraception," because procreation was listed second after the unitive end. This attitude can be in the minds of the spouses, because procreation was mentioned by the Council and also by the *Code of Canon Law* in second place—not saying it is the secondary end but mentioning it in the second place.

I regret this reversal, and we have to have the Magisterium again state the correct order of the ends of marriage. Every human action, every human institution and society, has to have an objective principal and first end; this is logical. When we don't have this, all our energies and commitments are weakened and confused. We have witnessed in recent decades the negative consequences of this reversal for marriage, family, and sexuality in general. We have to state again that the first end for which God created human sexuality and marriage is to give life, for the spouses to be "one flesh" in order to give new life, to give birth to a possible citizen of heaven. This first end is of course inseparably linked with the unitive end, the aspect of mutual help.

This is the true order established by God: first comes generosity, selflessness, life, i.e., procreation. A couple might ask: "Why have we married?" Not only to have pleasure and emotional closeness with one another, which would close the spouses in an egoistic circle of their being only two. To restate the first procreative end is to restate the generosity of marriage. The explanation of this truth is very important in preparing young people for marriage. We have to tell them: "You will be married in order to be generous, and this implies making sacrifices of yourselves in order to give life."

Can you say more about this?

The primary end of marriage, that is, procreation, represents the first commandment to love God above all, because during the act of procreation it is God who is the first and the most important, since He creates in that moment a new immortal soul, the spouses being His instruments and conscious and loving collaborators in transmitting new human life. The second unitive and subjective end of marriage represents the second commandment to love one's neighbor, and the closest neighbors are actually the spouses to one another. In the process of realizing the marriage, the second end, mutual love, usually comes temporally and psychologically first. However, the objectively higher end, i.e., procreation, comes temporally later, as oftentimes the final end (*causa finalis*) comes to its realization later.

Even for those couples who are not able to conceive, to enter into marriage with the idea that we are getting married to be generous and to give life is still essential...

Yes, this is true. The inability to conceive a child often causes a couple great suffering. As Christians, however, they should accept this situation with faith as a cross. God calls them to be generous in so many other ways.

Despite all of this, efforts have been underway to "reinterpret" Humanae Vitae, even among those appointed to important positions in the Vatican. What's to be done?

We have to restate firmly, publicly, and solemnly the unchanging truth of the teaching of the encyclical, of God's order for human sexuality and for transmitting human life. No interpretation can be given that would weaken the perennial truth of the immorality of contraception, which is intrinsically evil, because it is against the order God Himself established in nature. No circumstances can change this, because it is written into nature by God.

The immorality of contraception is not a teaching that the Church invented, one that depends on the Church or the pope. It is the teaching of God, which the Church only transmits and protects. Therefore, neither the Church nor the pope can give a relativizing reinterpretation of *Humanae Vitae.* The pope has no authority to give an interpretation that would weaken the truth or leave the slightest ambiguity about the intrinsically evil character of contraception. We have to pray that the Holy Father will again restate this teaching with all clarity, without any shadow of ambiguity, and also explain to spouses the beauty and positive nature of human sexuality in marriage.

Catholics and non-Catholics alike often imagine that the Church is simply a naysayer.

Humanae Vitae should not be presented only as a negative prohibition. The divine law of the transmission of human life reflects the love of God and protects the beauty and selflessness of the sexual encounter between husband and wife, protecting them from egoism, which is the greatest enemy of true spousal love. In restating the validity of *Humanae Vitae,* the Church is doing a work with real beneficial and positive effects not only for Catholic couples but for all mankind, contributing an indispensable condition for a true civilization of love.

The bishops of Kazakhstan, on May 13, 2018, the feast of Our Lady of Fatima, issued a pastoral letter, which was read in all churches and chapels in Kazakhstan that day. In the letter, we restated the perennial teaching of the Church, using not our own words, but the words of the Magisterium, which is the voice of Christ, who is the truth and who will give true freedom and happiness to couples.

Six months earlier, on December 31, 2017, you and two of your fellow bishops from Kazakhstan came under fire after issuing a Profession of Immutable Truths about Sacramental Marriage. Some reports characterized the

initiative by saying that the Kazakh bishops, along with at least ten sig-
natories, have detailed the dangers of Pope Francis's summary document
on the Synod on the Family, Amoris Laetitia.

We did not write directly about the dangers of *Amoris Laetitia.* We
did not even mention Pope Francis by name; we spoke of the supreme
authority of the Church. We mentioned *Amoris Laetitia* only once,
saying: "After the publication of *Amoris Laetitia.*" We criticized only
the pastoral norms issued on several levels, which permit unrepentant
adulterers to receive Holy Communion. This is what we criticized. Formally and concretely, we criticized these pastoral norms. This is the
entire issue and therefore we concluded our profession of truth with
quotations from the constant tradition of the Magisterium, in part to
defend ourselves from attacks that we are not faithful to the Magisterium. We then concluded in bold letters, "It is not allowed, *non licet,*
to promote indirectly or directly, or to approve, etc., divorce or sexual
non-marital unions by means of the admission of these people to Holy
Communion." That was basically our statement, so it was in itself not
a formal or direct critique of *Amoris Laetitia.*

How would you respond to those who say this papal document has caused
so many problems that it needs to be retracted, or at least have chapter
8 removed?

I think it will not be done in a direct manner. Otherwise it would
create more rupture in the Church. The same end can be achieved in
another way, as would be necessary for some ambiguous statements of
the Second Vatican Council. Perhaps future popes could simply name the
ambiguous phrases in the Council texts — thanks be to God there are not
so many — and say: "It is not according to the tradition of the Church
to say...," even not quoting formally from the Council documents.
The same could be done with ambiguous and erroneous statements in
Amoris Laetitia.

For example, as we discussed, *Lumen Gentium* n. 16 says that we Catholics and the Muslims adore God together (*"nobiscum Deum adorant"*).
We cannot say this in such a way. Of course, with lengthy explanations
we might be able to affirm it in some way. However, such a plain and
undifferentiated affirmation as the one contained in *Lumen Gentium* n.
16 is problematic. In the future, the Church could take this phrase and
say: "It is wrong to say this," adding the doctrinal reasons for why it is

erroneous. The same could be done with some ambiguous or erroneous statements in other texts of the Council. It would be an indirect, polite rejection not of the entire Council but only of a few statements.

I would do the same with *Amoris Laetitia,* because the whole of chapter 8 from the first letter to the last does not have to be rejected, but only some expressions in this chapter which are objectively theologically wrong. In my opinion, in the future, the Magisterium has to correct and condemn those statements which are wrong, without necessarily formally quoting them.

Unfortunately, Amoris Laetitia *is not the only problem text we are dealing with. Pope Francis has many errors in his daily homilies...*

But this I would leave aside. I would ignore this, because there are some things that we need to ignore and not take too seriously. Otherwise, we also would practice indirectly a form of unhealthy papal-centrism in taking every word of the pope as infallible or too seriously. The authentic papal magisterium regards official documents and not every homily of a pope. The daily homilies and the interviews do not belong in a proper sense to the Magisterium of the Church.

In April 2018, Pope Francis changed no. 2267 of the Catechism of the Catholic Church *on the death penalty. The passage now reads: "The death penalty is inadmissible because it is an attack on the inviolability and dignity of the person." The passage footnotes an address Pope Francis delivered on October 11, 2017, where he said that the death penalty "is* per se *contrary to the Gospel." When the news came out, many people were surprised to learn that the Catholic Church has taught the legitimacy of the death penalty for two thousand years. Pope Francis justified the change by invoking the fifth-century theologian St. Vincent of Lérins, to whom John Henry Newman has recourse in his famous* Essay on the Development of Christian Doctrine. *On what grounds does the Church teach that the death penalty is legitimate, how are we to understand the change to the* Catechism, *and can such a change be seen as an authentic development of doctrine?*

The question of the death penalty touches a relevant aspect of the revealed divine law regarding the fifth commandment of the Decalogue, which says "Thou shalt not kill." The Word of God teaches not only in the Old but also in the New Testament that the principle of the death penalty is in itself legitimate. If this were not so, Our Lord, His Apostles, and subsequently His Church would have revoked the principle of the legitimacy of the death penalty, which however was proclaimed by God Himself in the Old Testament. In the Old Testament, the Word of God identifies several capital offenses calling for execution. Our Lord Jesus Christ never denied that the secular power has the authority to apply capital punishment. He cites with approval the commandment: "He who speaks evil of father or mother, let him surely die" (Mt 15:4; Mk 7:10, referring to Ex 21:17; cf. Lev 20:9). St. Paul says that the ruler who holds authority "does not bear the sword in vain; for he is the servant of God to execute His wrath on the wrongdoer" (Rom 13:4). No passage in the New Testament disapproves of the death penalty. Hence, the constant teaching of the Church throughout two millennia has taught what Our Lord Jesus Christ and His Apostles also taught. The Church could not err in such an important question of the divine law, and in fact she did not err.

God Himself pronounced the first death penalty sentence after Adam and Eve committed the first sin, for through sin death entered the world (Rom 5:12). Consequently, all the children of Adam and Eve are sentenced to capital punishment through bodily death. We all face the death penalty, since we will all die as a consequence of original sin. Therefore, if someone affirms that the death penalty is *in se* contrary to the Gospel, he accuses God Himself of being immoral, since God pronounced against Adam and Eve and He still pronounces the death penalty against every human being by the very fact of bodily death.

But doesn't it seem as if the Church would be contradicting herself by promoting a pro-life ethic while saying that killing is sometimes legitimate?

No one could justify his refusal of the legitimacy of the death penalty by invoking the fifth commandment of the Decalogue, since God's categorical prohibition of killing refers only to innocent persons. Killing a person in self-defense, in defense of the family or homeland, and in a just war, is in principle nothing other than a kind of application of the death penalty in extreme and inevitable situations against an unjust aggressor.[2]

---

2 Usually, the term "death penalty" or "capital punishment" is used only when a criminal is punished by the civil authority in charge of the common good, as private citizens do not have the right to judge and execute in this manner. A private person may, however, defend himself (and, by extension, his family and other bystanders) from a violent attack on the basis of the natural right to life, when no other recourse is possible.

An absolute pacifism represents an illusion and a denial of reality, and substantially also a denial of original sin with its consequences for individual and social life. The Church has never taught an absolute pacifism.

The last logical consequence of the denial of the legitimacy of the principle of the death penalty is the abolition of the armed forces and of military chaplaincies and military dioceses. It would be consistent for people who declare the death penalty an intrinsic evil also to declare immoral the existence of the armed forces and of the principle of a just war, since in such cases the death penalty is also being applied against an unjust aggressor. In the case of the defense of one's own life, or the life of one's own spouse and children and of other innocent persons who are put in imminent danger of death by an unjust aggressor, the natural law, which is given by God, authorizes one to apply the death penalty against such an aggressor, if there is no other means of defense against him.

What's wrong with ruling out the death penalty absolutely?

Those who deny the death penalty in principle implicitly or explicitly absolutize the corporal and temporal life of man. They also deny to some extent the consequences of original sin. Those who deny the legitimacy of the death penalty also implicitly or explicitly deny the need and value of expiation and penance for sins, and especially for monstrous crimes still in this earthly life. The "good thief" who was crucified next to Our Lord is one of the most eloquent witnesses to the expiatory value of the death penalty, since through the acceptance of his own death sentence he gained eternal life and became in some sense the first canonized saint of the Church. Indeed, Our Lord said to him, "Today you will be with Me in paradise" (Lk 23:43).

There are plenty of moving examples of executed evildoers and criminals who, through the acceptance of the death penalty, saved the life of their soul for all eternity. St. Joseph Cafasso is the patron of men condemned to death; his biography provides us with astonishing examples of conversions of such men. All of these examples bore witness to the truth that the short temporal life of the body is disproportionate to eternal life in heaven.

Your mention of the good thief reminds me of a common objection. People say it is cruel to kill a prisoner and more merciful to let him live. Do you think this is true? Would more criminals convert if they lived longer?

We have the example of a "good thief" of the twentieth century in the case of Claude Newman, a murderer who in 1943 was put on death row in Vicksburg, Mississippi. Initially an unbeliever and non-Catholic, he experienced a conversion to the Catholic faith through the power of the Miraculous Medal. He died a holy death as a devout Catholic. He bore witness to the legitimacy and to the expiatory value of the death penalty.[3] One can mention also the case of the Servant of God Jacques Fesch (1930–1957), a murderer who spent more than three years in solitary confinement. He experienced a profound conversion before his execution by guillotine in Paris. He left spiritually edifying notes and letters. Two months before his execution, he wrote: "Here is where the Cross and its mystery of suffering make their appearance. The whole of life has this piece of wood as its center... Don't you think that, whatever you set out to do in the short time that is yours on earth, everything worthwhile is marked with this seal of suffering? There are no more illusions: you know with certainty that all this world has to offer is as false and deceptive as the most fantastic dreams of a six-year-old girl. Then despair invades you, and you try to avoid the suffering that dogs your heels and licks at you with its flames, but every means of doing so is only a rejection of the Cross. We can have no genuine hope of peace and salvation apart from Christ crucified! Happy the man who understands this." On October 1, 1957, at 5:30 am, he climbs to the scaffold. "May my blood that is going to flow be accepted by God as a whole sacrifice, that every drop," he writes, "serves to erase a mortal sin." In his last journal entry, he wrote, "In five hours, I shall look upon Jesus!"[4]

We also know from the life of St. Thérèse of the Child Jesus that, as a young girl, she adopted her "first sinner," the murderer Pranzini, who in 1887 was sentenced to death. The saint writes in her autobiography, *The Story of a Soul*: "The day after his execution I hastily opened the paper and what did I see? Tears betrayed my emotion; I was obliged to run out of the room. Pranzini had mounted the scaffold without

3 See "The True Account of Prisoner Claude Newman (1944)" by John Vennari, *Catholic Family News*, March 2001. This article is taken from the 1960s radio broadcast testimony by Father Robert O'Leary, the priest who baptized Claude Newman on January 16, 1944 in jail with the name "Claude Jude," with Sr. Benna Henken, SSpS standing as his sponsor. See also Ralph Frasca, "The Truth About Claude Newman. Miracles, Medals, and Audiotape," in *New Oxford Review* 82.8 (October 2015), 24ff.

4 See *Light Upon the Scaffold: The Prison Letters of Jacques Fesch*, ed. Augustin-Michel Lemonnier, trans. Matthew J. O'Connell (St. Meinrad, IN: Abbey Press, 1975).

confessing or receiving absolution, and . . . turned around, seized the crucifix which the priest was offering to him, and kissed Our Lord's Sacred Wounds three times. I had obtained the sign I asked for, and to me it was especially sweet. Was it not when I saw the Precious Blood flowing from the Wounds of Jesus that the thirst for souls first took possession of me?"⁵

And meanwhile, in spite of protests about the "barbarity" of capital punishment, modern society treats human life with so much contempt . . .

Today we are witnessing, through the legalization of abortion, a mass application of capital punishment against the most innocent human beings, the unborn children, who are free from any personal guilt. There is also an increasing attempt to legalize the execution of the death penalty against terminally ill persons through so-called euthanasia laws.

I mentioned St. Vincent of Lérins earlier. Do you think there can be a doctrinal "development" on this point?

The invocation of St. Vincent of Lérins's principle of the development of doctrine in order to justify the inadmissibility of the death penalty is objectively wrong and arbitrary. One of the central points in the teaching of St. Vincent is the universal consent, constancy, universality, and antiquity of a particular doctrine. According to St. Vincent, in case of doubt, antiquity must prevail. The legitimacy of the death penalty is a case where all of these aspects, and especially antiquity, have such great theological weight that the denial of the death penalty's legitimacy and the declaration of its contrariness to the Gospel by Pope Francis manifests a kind of papal absolutism which is more like the absolute will of a secular political leader than the behavior of a successor of the Apostles and a custodian of the Church's Magisterium, whose first task consists (according to St. Vincent of Lérins) in keeping, transmitting, and explaining the truths of divine revelation, with the same meaning and in the same sense (*eodem sensu et eadem sententia*) as all their predecessors did. There is no doubt that a future successor of Pope Francis or a future Ecumenical Council will correct this drastic change of the constant teaching of the Church.

---

5 *Story of a Soul: The Autobiography of St. Thérèse of Lisieux* (Washington, DC: Institute of Carmelite Studies, 1975), ch. 5, p. 99.

Your Excellency, we have discussed a number of areas of doctrinal confusion. What in your view is the greatest problem facing the Church today? Is it Modernism? Gnosticism? Freemasonry?

The greatest problem the Church is facing in our days is anthropocentrism and the cult of nature. That is to say, that instead of putting God's revelation in Jesus Christ, His Incarnate Son, at the center, man and his naturalistic and rationalistic views and desires become more important than the unerring commandments and truths of Christ, the only divine teacher of mankind. The world, even a growing number of clergy in the Church, try to bend the clear will of God — as it is clearly expressed in His commandments and in His revealed truths — to their own desires and thoughts. The result of such anthropocentrism is that the historical fact of the Incarnation of God in Jesus Christ has to be denied and in its true sense distorted, because an Incarnate and visible God is disturbing and bothersome to this mentality and attitude. Modern man, even many liberal and Modernist clergy in the Church, want to be free from a God who is so demanding. They want to be free from a God who is so close and real in the Incarnation and in the Eucharist. Instead, they want God and His clear will to be far away, they want God to remain invisible, to remain in a cloud of vagueness and indetermination, so that they might themselves determine what is good and evil and what is right and wrong. All this can be summed up in the motto: "I will do and think what I want!" Such a naturalistic and egoistic anthropocentrism is the core of Modernism, Gnosticism, and Freemasonry and links them together, and it has already conquered vast areas in the life of the Church.

13

Beyond the West

There remains a concern in much of the world about the role of Russia in the future. In your judgment, is Vladimir Putin a man to be trusted, specifically with regard to his apparent enthusiasm for upholding Christian values and identity in an increasingly secular West, or is it perhaps a cover whereby he is tapping into resentments against a post-Christian West?

I cannot judge the heart of any person. In the absence of definitive evidence, we can only judge actions. Some outward actions of Putin are objectively good — for example, the protection of Christians from the extermination carried out by ISIS (Islamic State of Iraq and Syria) during the recent war in Syria. Maybe he had his own particular political interest in doing so. Even the best country always pursues its own political interests and aims. As Otto von Bismarck said, "politics is not an exact science."

There were Christian monarchs in history who employed strategies and tricks and wars simply to establish or preserve a position of hegemony. Catholic France, for example, supported the Protestant King Gustav Adolphus of Sweden in his war against the Holy Roman Emperor and his Catholic allies during the Thirty Years' War. The support that Catholic France gave to Protestant Sweden, while at the same time denying assistance to the Catholic cause, was decisive in Protestantism emerging victorious over Catholicism in Germany at the end of the Thirty Years' War.

Another example is sixteenth-century Catholic France. In 1536, the Catholic and anointed King Francis I of France entered into a political alliance with the worst enemy of Christendom, Sultan Suleiman the Magnificent of the Islamic Ottoman Empire. Such an alliance weakened the political power of the Christian European resistance, and ultimately facilitated the victorious advance of Turkish troops through the Balkans to the gates of Vienna in 1683. Catholic France passively watched the advancing Islamization process of Europe in the sixteenth, seventeenth, and eighteen centuries and declined to assist Christian troops in pushing back militant Islam. Such behavior caused a scandal in the Christian world and was called "the sacrilegious union of the lily and the crescent."

People say that the current Russian leaders, and in particular Putin, in adopting the pro-Christian agenda, are pursuing their own national political goals. How do you see this?

Of course, Putin is doing a great deal to ensure a hegemonic position of Russia, so that Russia continues to be a world power. This was the case even with many Christian monarchs in the past and this is nothing new. Viewing it objectively, it will remain a historic merit that Russia defended the Christians in Syria against the barbarities of ISIS, whereas the European Union and the Obama Administration in the US abandoned the Christians in Syria. Russia also enacted laws against homosexual propaganda, an action which is *in se* good, whereas almost all countries of the Western world — almost all European countries, and North and South America — officially promote the homosexual agenda and enact so-called "homophobia" laws with punitive measures against anyone who dares to say that homosexual acts are against human nature and are a sin. Some people say that Russia issued the anti-homosexual laws with dishonest intentions. However, we do not know the intentions. Maybe Russia does this out of its own conviction or for tactical reasons. To say that it is a tactic of the "crypto-Communist Kremlin regime" would be unreasonable, and simply against common sense. Sometimes I read about opinions which interpret any action of the Russian government as a hidden tactic of a still-existing Communist Russian Kremlin Empire, which intends to establish a Communist world empire. Such statements do not acknowledge the fact that in Russia a new generation has been raised that did not know Communism. Such an approach is reminiscent of the behavior of the Roman senator Cato the Elder, who each time he finished his speeches repeated stereotypically: "Besides, I assert that Carthage must be destroyed" (*"ceterum censeo, Carthaginem esse delendam"*), even though Carthage had been destroyed a long time before. If Russia one day will be converted — and it *will* be converted, according to the words of Our Lady in Fatima — I can imagine some Western liberal and anti-Christian politicians continuing to say, "Russia did not convert but remained the crypto-Communist Kremlin regime, as it was."

Which ideological and political powers in the current historical moment do you consider the most dangerous for Christianity?

There is ever more evidence of the establishment of a One World Government by the United Nations and ultimately by powerful Masonic organizations, which act behind the scenes in order politically to implement the *"novus ordo saeculorum,"* the New World Order, the atheist One World Government. This One World Government reveals a clear ideological program which is essentially atheist, materialist, anti-Christian, and even blasphemous, with the totalitarian imposition of abortion "rights," homosexual indoctrination, the climate change myth and the destruction of national identities through events like the "The Global Compact for Safe, Orderly, and Regular Migration," or the annual meetings of the World Economic Forum of Davos, for instance. In its program, the latter promotes the "global order" — as they call it — of "gender equality" under the acronym of "LGBT." We know from recent history that interference and manipulation of language is part of the repertoire of authoritarian regimes.

Such a recognizably Masonic and atheistic One World Government is in the process of realizing the final stage of the Marxist-Communist plan. Against this real danger of a neo-Marxist and Masonic One World Government, those social and political organizations which have not yet been brought into line with the uniform thinking of the neo-Marxist and Masonic World Ideology, and have therefore retained their freedom of thought and action, should ring the alarm and start to organize a coalition of legitimate resistance, comprising all people with common sense in both East and West and also in Africa and South Asia. The world urgently needs heroic and noble resistance fighters against the world dictatorship which enslaves people through the absurdity of gender ideology, the moral corruption of innocent children, and the genocide of unborn children.

Could there be an ideological connection between the program of the "novus ordo saeculorum" and the classical Marxist-Communist and Soviet-Communist agenda?

The expression *"novus ordo saeculorum"* is the ideological and programmatic code of the One World Government. Freemasonry has as its essential and final aim the establishment of the *"novus ordo saeculorum,"* a new social and political order at the global level for dictatorially imposing upon people religious indifferentism and syncretism, moral perversity and radical anti-Christian and above all anti-Catholic policies. Such a new social order leads ultimately to the worship and adoration of man, which is the most radical form of atheism, more radical than the historical Communist atheism of the Soviet Kremlin Regime. Historical Soviet Communism propagated its ideology under the deceitful and enticing slogan: "Proletarians of the world unite!" The current neo-Marxist and Masonic political powers in Western countries are propagating their ideology under the no less deceitful and enticing slogan "Human Fraternity for World Peace and Living Together" or "Ark of Fraternity." It is quite disquieting to read the statement of the Masonic Grand Lodge of Spain from December 25, 2018, which says that "all Freemasons of the world join with the petition of the pope for fraternity among the diverse religions."

Would you say a link exists between Freemasonry and the Communist founders of the Soviet Union? There seems to be a similar impulse in both.

Freemasonry has been working tenaciously for centuries to achieve the atheistic "*novus ordo saeculorum.*" As we discussed before, we can trace its influence through great social and political revolutions. The so-called French Revolution, for the first time in European history, banished the Social Kingship of Christ, i.e., the presence and the influence of Christendom in public life. Then came the era of a partial restoration of Christian society, after the Congress of Vienna in 1814.

Later, with the help of a new explicitly atheist ideology, the Communism of Karl Marx, Freemasonry was implicated in the second Revolution, the Russian October Communist Revolution in 1917, as powerful Freemasons supported the revolution with their financial, logistic, and political maneuverings. For example, the Russian Prime Minister Alexander Kerensky had been the Secretary General of the Masonic Grand Orient of Russia, and he instructed law enforcement to show only a symbolical resistance to the Communist revolutionaries under the command of Lenin. Kerensky himself was also the leader of the Russian Socialist Revolutionary Party. The Russian Orthodox Churches refused to grant Christian burial to Kerensky — who died in 1970 in the United States — because of his association with Freemasonry and because they saw him as largely responsible for the Bolsheviks seizing power in 1917.[1] Lenin

---

1 See Jüri Lina, *Under the Sign of the Scorpion: The Rise and Fall of the Soviet Empire* (Stockholm: Referent, 2002).

was a member of several Freemasonic lodges in Europe. The first close collaborators of Lenin were members of European Freemasonic lodges, such as for example Trotsky (a Russian Jew and first People's Commissar of Defense of the USSR), Bukharin (who belonged to a group of Russian artists and was General Secretary of the Executive Committee of the Communist International), Sverdlov (a Russian Jew and first Chairman of the Communist Party), Lunacharsky (a Russian Jew and first Commissar for Education of the USSR).[2] Lenin, Zinoviev, Radek and Sverdlov also belonged to B'nai B'rith, a special Masonic lodge for Jews. Researchers who specialize in the activities of B'nai B'rith confirmed this information.[3] Together with Trotsky, Lenin took part in the International Masonic Conference in Copenhagen in 1910.[4]

Were there other important historical events in the twentieth century that, in your view, could be considered a kind of catalyst for the implementation of the One World Government that you mention?

Yes, most notably the two World Wars (1914–1918 and 1939–1945) and the Sexual Revolution of 1968. Currently this process is already very far advanced through the global implementation of gender ideology. Concerning these milestones in the historical revolutionary process, a recommended study is *Revolution and Counter-Revolution*, written by Plinio Corrêa de Oliveira. He was a Brazilian scholar and devout Catholic layman who died in 1995 in São Paulo in Brazil and who devoted his entire life to the defense of Christian tradition, the family, and the natural order of property against the Marxist revolution, which has infiltrated Western countries and even Church organizations.

Therefore, we have to warn all people of good will of the real danger of the One World Government with its official state ideology, i.e., gender ideology. This concrete danger emanates currently not so much from Moscow, but persistently from orchestrated efforts in Brussels (European Union) and New York (United Nations) and lastly from the ongoing efforts of those organizing under Masonic structures. Exactly there, one has to locate the true current neo-Marxist "Kremlin regime."

2 See Nikolai Svitkov's *About Freemasonry in Russian Exile*, published in Paris in 1932.
3 Viktor Ostretsov, *Freemasonry, Culture, and Russian History* (Moscow: Kraft+, 1999), 582–83.
4 Franz Weissin, *Der Weg zum Sozialismus* (München: Ludendorffs, 1930), 9.

Do you think we can speak of a re-Christianization of Russia in our time?

One cannot ignore the historical fact that, since the end of the Soviet Union, approximately one thousand monasteries and twenty thousand churches and chapels have been built in Russia. Never in the history of a country were so many churches built during a period of twenty to thirty years. Of course, the Russian government promotes the status of the Orthodox Church for the sake of enhancing its national hegemony. However, the Orthodox Church is the closest to us: they have the same valid sacraments, the priesthood, they venerate Our Lady and the saints, in all their churches there is the tabernacle with the Blessed Sacrament. Our Lord is sacramentally present in those churches as well, and this is beautiful. A country which, prior to this, over the course of seventy years, systematically destroyed churches and banished from the public square every sign of Christianity now actively helps to put Christian symbols, crosses, icons of Our Lady, of St. Michael the Archangel at wayside shrines and in public places in the cities and countryside. We have to bear in mind that the very presence of a blessed cross and icon in public places has to some extent an exorcising effect, expelling the influence of evil spirits from the people.

Do you see other signs of a re-Christianization of Russia?

Yes, another important sign of the re-Christianization of Russian society is the establishment of regular pastoral care for soldiers and other people serving in the Armed Forces; now there have been established chapels and chaplaincies for the education of the soldiers in the Orthodox faith. Recently I saw a photo of an Orthodox priest hearing the confessions of an entire contingent of parachutists. It is surely better to educate the soldiers in the Orthodox faith, which at least has valid sacraments and a deep Marian devotion, than to let them be educated in Islam, Protestantism, or simply in naturalist ethics, or the "human fraternity for world peace." These public facts are very clear signs of the influence of Christianity in Russian society, which for seventy years was dominated by radical Communist atheism. At the same time, the societies of the Western world do the exact opposite — they are systematically banishing every trace of Christianity from society, e.g., Christmas cribs in public places, even Christmas parties in kindergartens and schools.

Do you find this reversal of roles ironic?

Sometimes Divine Providence uses even our enemies as tools and instruments of the Kingdom of Christ. King Cyrus was one such example; even though he was a pagan and an idolater, he brought the Jews back out of Babylonian captivity to rebuild the temple in Jerusalem. Even if Putin is still a Communist, God can use him to re-Christianize Russian society and to counteract the homosexual agenda and the implementation of the atheistic Masonic One World Government. I don't know his soul. He reportedly has his own confessor, an Orthodox priest. At the same time, we observe before our eyes the political and social implementation of the last, worst, and most radical form of Marxism and Communism, which is the destruction of marriage and the family through the world-wide propagation of homosexuality and gender ideology by the Western European and American countries. History can judge only the exterior acts and facts. Therefore, everyone who loves the advancement of the Social Kingship of Christ and the triumph of the Immaculate Heart of Mary has to rejoice when they observe real and verifiable signs of an awakening and spreading of Christianity.

I will not say that Putin is a new Constantine; rather, I am only making a judgment from common sense, the laws of history, and also from a supernatural point of view. In my opinion, Divine Providence can use the current Russian political leadership to help spread Christianity and prepare the triumph of the Immaculate Heart of Mary.

Constantine, the first Christian Emperor, for instance, did not try to close any of the pagan temples, including in his new capital of Constantinople. Only at the end of his reign did he order the closure of pagan temples. Constantine was the "*Pontifex Maximus*" of the official and pagan religion of the Roman state — the high priest of the pagan god "Invincible Sun" (*sol invictus*) — while at the same time professing to be a Christian. It was the Emperor Gratian who, in 375, severed the official bond linking paganism to the imperial power, by refusing to accept the insignia of the pagan "*Pontifex Maximus*." It was only one hundred years after the edict of Milan that the Christian Emperor Honorius I, in the year 415, definitively proscribed pagan sacrifices and removed temples from public places.

In the United States, President Trump is indirectly helping to spread Christianity through pro-life policies and a strong support for religious liberty.

Yes, I acknowledge all the good actions of President Trump in favor of the defense of human life. Even if President Trump might do this with a strategic and selfish intention — and who can say — I must be honest and just in recognizing and esteeming his actions that are *per se* morally good. I do, however, regret the fact that President Trump publicly promotes the so-called LGBT agenda. Thanks be to God that in Europe new governments are emerging in several countries — Hungary, Poland, Italy — that also promote Christian civilization.

Coming back to Russia, do you think the Russian Orthodox Church is too close to the state?

Yes, of course. The Russian Orthodox Church has never known another kind of life than submission and subservience to the government, no matter which government. I would say this phenomenon belongs, in some way, to the genetic code of the Orthodox Church, precisely because they are not in canonical union with the See of Peter, with the Roman Pontiff. They fill this void of papal primacy with a submission to the government, a submission which is even more servile than the submission of Catholic bishops to the pope. This is the way the Russian Orthodox bishops usually submitted to the Emperors and the Tsars, and then also to Stalin and other Communist rulers, and today they submit to the Russian President. There have been heroic and courageous bishops in the Orthodox Church who protested even against an Emperor or a Christian government for acting against the Law of God. But to be submissive to superiors is an identifying feature of the Russian mentality. We have to keep in mind the Russian mentality and the history of the Orthodox Church.

Governments, even the Western Catholic governments in the Middle Ages, are happy to have the Church submit to them — with the exception of holy emperors and kings, who indeed existed in the Middle Ages and some in modern times. The last was Blessed Emperor Karl of Austria, who died in 1922. Even in the Spanish and Portuguese system of the *padroado*, the government appointed bishops and issued royal norms regarding seminaries and convents. Christian emperors and kings often interfered in Church affairs and wanted the Church to be subservient in some way to their authority. One of the most striking examples of an imperial intervention in Church affairs was that of Emperor Joseph II of Austria (d. 1790), who even prescribed the number of candles to be lit at the altars of the churches. The Protestant Prussian King Frederick II nicknamed Joseph II "arch-sacristan of the Holy Roman Empire" ("*der Erzsakristan des Hei-ligen Römischen Reiches*"). It was like this until just a few centuries ago.

It is not surprising that the Russian government wants the Orthodox Church to be submissive to it. Every political power wants this. Since the Orthodox Church has always been submissive, they go together. I do not agree with this system, and it is harmful to the Church, and I say this to Russian Orthodox clergy whom I know, that it is not good for them to be so dependent on the government.

Are you concerned that the Vatican is pursuing a policy that is putting too much of an emphasis on relations with the Russian Orthodox at the expense of helping Ukrainian Greek Catholics?

Yes, I am concerned about this. Unfortunately, since the Second Vatican Council we have witnessed a wrong method of ecumenism in the Catholic Church. I am not against ecumenism, but rather against a wrong approach which leads to a relativizing of doctrine and ultimately to a denial of our Catholic identity. Concealing one's identity is not honest. In the false ecumenical method which has been implemented since the Council, political reasons play a predominant role. Oftentimes, the Holy See stresses one-sidedly the aspect of harmony in ecumenical relationships, neglecting the central issue of truth. Such an ecumenical method is ultimately worldly and seems to be more a political method than a method according to the Gospel, as is fitting among true Christians. The representatives of the Holy See and the bishops should not be politicians but must, first and foremost, be men of God and apostles of the Truth. We must tell non-Catholics the truth with love, but we must say the truth. We must say honestly to our non-Catholic brothers, "This is what we Catholics believe."

We cannot pursue a cheap ecumenism at the expense of our Ukrainian Greek Catholic brothers who suffered so much for the sake of fidelity to the Apostolic See. It is an injustice to sell our heroic brothers at the market of a politically shaped ecumenism. We have to protect them and, at the same time, say to our Orthodox partners in dialogue, "We must have a very transparent and honest dialogue."

Do you think it is particularly painful for Greek Catholics to see the current confusion in the Church? They suffered under Communism for the sake of the papacy. It seems to me that they would suffer especially through all of this.

They are. In some ways they feel like second-class Catholics — as victims sacrificed on the altar of ecumenism. The Holy See must, in time, change this policy. I hope that the Holy Spirit will guide the Holy See to change this policy, otherwise it is committing a great historical injustice. The manner in which our Greek Catholic brothers, especially in Eastern Europe, are sometimes treated reflects a dishonest and inauthentic method of ecumenism.

Let's turn to China. In September 2018, the Holy See signed a provisional agreement with the Communist Chinese government according to which the future appointment of bishops will be done in consultation with the Chinese authorities. Given your own experience in the underground persecuted Church, what are your thoughts on the agreement, and on the opposition to it expressed by former archbishop of Hong Kong, Cardinal Joseph Zen? Is the Vatican-China deal really good for the Church in China?

We can already see that, as a practical consequence of the agreement between the Vatican and China, the life of the Catholic Church in China has become increasingly controlled by an atheist Communist government. The bishops are now selected by an atheist government. Yet the figure of a bishop is so essential and decisive for the life of the Catholic Church that a bishop who is even a partial collaborator with an atheist regime will bring enormous spiritual damage to the priests and faithful.

One can hardly imagine that St. Peter and his successors in the first three centuries would have conceded to the pagan Roman Emperors a voice in the selection of their successors or of other bishops. With the agreement between the Vatican and China, the liberty of the Catholic Church in China has been more restricted, and the heroic Catholics of the underground Church have been delivered to the full control of an atheist government. The Holy See should have learned a lesson from the so-called "Ostpolitik" with the Communist states in the former Eastern Bloc, which did not strengthen the liberty and the witness of the Church but weakened it. The most famous victim of the Vatican Ostpolitik was Cardinal József Mindszenty (+1975), the Primate of Hungary, who strongly opposed such politics of the Holy See, and whom the Vatican sacrificed on the altar of Ostpolitik, removing him against his will from the office of archbishop of Esztergom and Primate of Hungary and putting in his place a bishop who was essentially a collaborator with the Communist regime. The Holy See recently recognized the heroic degree of the virtues of Cardinal József Mindszenty, but it remains to be seen if they have learned any lessons from history.

How would you explain the basic idea of Ostpolitik?

Ostpolitik was a method used by the Holy See to deal with the Communist countries in Eastern Europe, with the good intention of aiming to improve Church life under Communist rule and to provide episcopal appointments and structures. The aim of the Holy See was good, I suppose, but the method used by the Holy See did not, in my view, achieve the good aim intended. And history has now proven this. In fact, to a certain extent, this policy brought about division and suspicion among the faithful.

Ultimately, the matter centered around the appointment of bishops, as it does with China today. At that time, the Holy See had to make compromises and accept compromise candidates, because the Communist government would never and will never accept a strong courageous successor of the Apostles. Such an episcopal candidate will not be accepted by the worldly governments, even today in the Western world.

Episcopal candidates who were chosen under Ostpolitik were sometimes collaborators with the Communist system. Of course, it is not acceptable for a priest to collaborate or support a Communist system. You can be respectful to authority, but you must not give words and signs that you, as a bishop, support the agenda or the ideology of this government. The bishops in those countries have to distinguish and say to the government, "You are the authority, and I respect authority. I will observe the laws of your country, unless they contradict divine law. But when your laws contradict divine law, I cannot accept them. However, I accept your authority, and I will teach my people to pray for you as the legitimate authority. But I also have to teach my people that, when the authority compels people to do something against the divine law, we cannot collaborate with you." The Holy See must state this.

In some cases, the compromise candidates appointed under the Vatican's Ostpolitik were later revealed to be collaborators with the Communist regime. It is always a matter of shame and harm for a Catholic bishop to be a collaborator with an atheistic system of government or with another totalitarian regime. I repeat: you can be loyal as a citizen, but this does not imply that you have to collaborate. This needs to be carefully distinguished.

But surely the faithful in these countries needed bishops?

It was not always necessary to appoint bishops in the time of Ostpolitik. A Catholic community can survive for some time without bishops. In the Soviet Union, we lived a long time without bishops. We had priests, good priests, clandestine priests. There was also a clandestine bishop, of course, who ordained priests in secret. But these few priests who were ordained clandestinely were real apostles. Even though they were few in number, the effect of their work was far reaching. This was my experience living in the Soviet Union. And the faithful were strong, even without a bishop approved by the government. There were some bishops in the Baltic states who were approved by the Communist government, but they were timid, and in some cases weak, though I understand their situation; perhaps they could not have acted otherwise. But thanks be to God, there were also clandestine bishops and the faith was strong. This is the most important thing, even without a great number of bishops.

Fidelity to Christ, I think, should always be the method and the criterion of the Holy See. For example, in the past there were many countries that did not have a bishop for decades because of persecution. Cardinal Robert Sarah told me that after the imprisonment of Monsignor Tchidimbo, the archbishop of Conakry in Guinea, there was a long period with no active bishop in the country. I repeat: and the life of the Church there was fervent.

A policy of no compromise will actually strengthen the faith and heroism of the people.

We need to apply this to the situation with China. In any case, the Holy See can never accept candidates who live an immoral life or are worldly minded and obvious collaborators with and conformists to the Communist system. It is an offense to the faithful to appoint such candidates.

Unfortunately, such candidates are also appointed nowadays in the Western world: bishops and even cardinals are appointed who are obvious collaborators with the system — in this case not with a formal Communist regime, but with the Western liberal and Masonic regime of the unitary mindset under which we are now suffering throughout the Western world. We are witnessing bishops being appointed in the West who are collaborators with the new politically correct anti-Christian gender system. So, there is a real problem with episcopal nominations not only in China but also in the Western world. The Holy See has to be careful with this situation.

In its relationship with the Chinese government, the Holy See must not make compromises that will weaken or damage the faith. The Holy See under no circumstances should sacrifice the underground bishops. I think that sacrificing the confessor bishops of the underground Church in China would go down in history as a shame and an offense to the martyrs in China, an offense to the bishops and priests who gave their lives for Christ and indirectly for the Holy See, for the pope.

Cardinal Joseph Zen has said that the Vatican Secretary of State Cardinal Pietro Parolin does not understand the Chinese people.[5] They are willing to suffer for their faith, Cardinal Zen said, but what hurts them most is being betrayed by their own family.

Exactly, and Church history shows that all dictatorships were only temporary. They ended. So, the Church has to benefit from this experience and have a longer view. She must not be conditioned by what seems pressing, or seemingly forced to find a technical solution. It would be too human. In my opinion, such a method will be not blessed by God and will not bear fruit, as the Ostpolitik demonstrably bore no fruit in the Eastern Bloc during the Communist era.

We must do the utmost to find a good solution with the Chinese government. However, there should be non-negotiable principles: we must not sacrifice the confessor bishops under any circumstances. This should be a condition *sine qua non*. And we must not accept candidates with a dubious moral life or a dubious attitude towards a Communist system itself. Better not to have bishops and wait for the intervention of Divine Providence, which will put an end to the dictatorship.

Even among the official bishops, I assume there are good spiritual men. They are not all collaborators, and the faithful are also under their leadership. It is a complex situation and we have to state this out of justice. A fervent faith can also be found among those who belong to the patriotic church. The problem is the clergy, not the faithful. I think that the clergy in the official patriotic Church, as compared with the clergy in the underground Church, are less courageous in faith,

---

5 Diane Montagna, "Cardinal Zen: 'A schismatic church with the Pope's blessing will be horrible!,'" *LifeSiteNews*, February 13, 2018; cf. Cardinal Zen's blog, "Non sono ancora riuscito a capire per che cosa dialogano con la Cina," available at https://oldyosef.hkdavc.com/?p=987.

because they are collaborating to various degrees with the regime, and when you are a collaborator and a conformist you cannot be fervent in faith. From this point of view, all non-Christian governments always want a clergy that is not fervent and zealous. They fear fervent and zealous bishops and clergy.

Therefore, it could be a tactic of the enemies of the Church to promote a less fervent Church with compromise candidates and to make a deal with the Chinese government to temporarily and technically resolve the problem. This is too worldly a view and will not bear fruit.

Let's move to South America. Given your own experience in Brazil, how concerned are you about the spread of Pentecostalism in South America?

Pentecostalism is a new phenomenon — in a sense, even a new religion. The Pentecostal, charismatic, sentimentalist, and irrational religious experience has penetrated many Christian confessions and even non-Christian religions and presents a real spiritual danger. We have two main branches of Christianity: Catholic-Orthodox Christianity, which is sacramental and has a priesthood and episcopal hierarchy; and the Protestants, who lack this. And now, we have a new Christian branch — the Pentecostal — which equates the essence of religion with feeling and irrationalism, even though these principles were anticipated in some ways by Martin Luther. The new Pentecostal Christian religion is dangerous and leads to the destruction of the virtue of religion, the authentic relationship to God. Pentecostalism ends in subjectivism and arbitrariness. Experience and feeling become the measure of all things. There is a lack of reason, of truth, and of the necessary creaturely awe before the majesty of God. However, divine revelation is essentially bound to reason and truth. Jesus Christ, the Incarnate Son of God, is the Word, the *Logos*, the Truth, the Second Person of the Most Holy Trinity.

When my religious feeling disappears, my faith disappears.

Exactly. Pentecostalism, in the long run, damages faith and truth. Unfortunately, the Pentecostal phenomenon has already deeply penetrated the Catholic Church through the so-called Charismatic Renewal. Neither the Old or New Testament, nor the Apostles, nor the Church Fathers approved of a sentimentally irrational religious or liturgical practice, where feelings are central. The religion of the Old Testament came through divine revelation and was essentially characterized by the Law (liturgical and moral commandments) and the Prophets (the teaching of doctrine), which were represented by Moses and Elijah at the Transfiguration of Our Lord on Mount Tabor. Our reason is illumined by the light of faith, remaining however always faith and not pure rationalism. This is the aspect of Christianity that especially Cardinal Ratzinger and then Pope Benedict XVI stressed so often: it is the *Logos*, the Incarnate Word, who is Divine Reason, who grants us His illumination by the gift of supernatural faith. Therefore, the Christian Religion is essentially a doctrine, and Christ calls Himself "master, teacher" (*rabbi* in Hebrew, *didáskalos* in Greek, *magister* in Latin). He told His disciples: "You have only one teacher, Christ" (Mt 23:10), "You call me Teacher and Lord, and you are right, for so I am" (Jn 13:13).

So you think the main emphasis in Christianity is on learning, by way of the intellect?

The original name of Christians, of the followers of Jesus Christ, was "disciples" ("pupils," "learners"), those who were instructed in a doctrine, in the revealed doctrine of God. Besides the act of offering the sacrifice of His Body and Blood on the Cross for the salvation of all mankind, the main work of Jesus Christ on earth was teaching the doctrine of God the Father, although this latter work was subordinated to the salvific act of His Sacrifice on the Cross. Christ said, "My teaching is not mine, but his who sent me" (Jn 7:16).

The solemn divine command which Christ gave to His Apostles and to His Church for all times consists primarily in teaching, in delivering a *doctrine of truths*: "Go, therefore, and instruct (*matheteúsate, docete*) all nations, teaching (*didáskontes, docentes*) them to observe all that I have commanded you" (Mt 28:19–20). Christianity is therefore essentially a supernatural faith and belief in a divinely revealed doctrine with the inseparable implementation of the doctrine in the moral life through good works with the help of God's grace. According to Acts 2:42, the first Christians in Jerusalem were characterized by the following four characteristics: "persevering in the doctrine of the apostles" (*doctrina fidei, veritatis*), "communion" (*koinonia*, hierarchical communion), "breaking of bread" (*fractio panis*, Holy Eucharist), and "prayers" (*orationes*, especially the liturgy). It is significant that a faithful attachment to doctrine and truth is mentioned as the first characteristic of the Christians. The suggestion that being a Christian is not about adhering to doctrine is a direct contradiction and denial of the divine teaching, which says that a Christian must "persevere in the doctrine of the apostles."

Why such an emphasis on handing down and taking hold of truth?

The importance of reason illumined by faith reflects the principle of the objectivity of the Christian religion. The incarnational path, the incarnational "method" which God chose to save humanity, signifies objectivity, as St. John states so strikingly: "That which was from the beginning, which we have heard, which we have seen with our eyes, which we looked upon and have touched with our hands, concerning the word of life — the life was made manifest, and we have seen it, and testify to it and proclaim to you the eternal life, which was with the Father and was made manifest to us" (1 Jn 1:1–2). I have always been struck by the comment of Pope St. Gregory the Great, found in the Breviary, about the doubting Apostle Thomas. In his brief and concise formulation, he aptly summarizes the incarnational path and method of the Christian faith: *ad fidem Thomas palpando reducitur*, "by touching [Christ], Thomas was led back to faith" (*Hom. 26 in Ev.*).

Divine revelation in the Old Testament already manifested incarnational and objective characteristics, since it led to its fulfillment in Christ. It is the incarnational, sacramental, visible, objective way to God. God also willed to give us the Holy Spirit in a visible and objective manner, in the first place through the seven sacraments — particularly through the sacrament of confirmation.

On the day of Pentecost, when the Holy Spirit descended on the Blessed Virgin Mary, the Apostles, and the disciples of Christ, they did not speak in unintelligible words but in a well-articulated language which everyone could understand. On Pentecost, Our Lady and the Apostles did not fall to the floor and "rest in the spirit," as happens at many Charismatic Renewal events in our days. On the day of Pentecost, the Blessed Virgin Mary and the Apostles did not practice glossolalia by speaking unintelligible and incoherent words, they did not cry, they were not clapping their hands or jumping or dancing, as so characteristically happens today even in many Catholic charismatic events and liturgies. The sacred liturgy uses the expression *sobria ebrietas Spiritus*, which means a "sober inebriation" with the Holy Spirit. This means having an ardent heart and nevertheless remaining sober, orderly, guided by reason, supernatural wonder, and faith.

Why do you think Pentecostalism has made such inroads in South America?

I think there are several factors. For one, because Liberation Theology, Modernism, and liberalism in the liturgy and in the practice of the faith emptied Catholic life of its richness for so many people, and they are seeking something which appeals to their emotions, to their experience of God. Simple everyday Latin American Catholics were betrayed and robbed of the faith-filled devotions of the Catholic faith, such as festivals in honor of saints, processions for Our Lady, and so on. Given the intellectual, abstract method of Modernism and Liberation Theology, with its sociology and empty naturalism, people desire something that expresses real devotion and the supernatural. Simple people thirst for the supernatural, and the Pentecostal and charismatic communities appeal to the senses and speak of supernatural realities, of the Holy Spirit. Charismatics perform gestures and prayers that touch the soul, the emotions. They do this, however, in an eccentric way, which is alien to the entire Catholic tradition.

Catholic tradition appeals to the senses, ignites devotion, and communicates the supernatural in a much more moderate and balanced manner, in the first place in the traditional liturgy: there is beauty that also touches the senses, the feelings, very much. We had this in the traditional liturgy and in traditional devotions. But when this was taken away from the people, especially in Latin America, the charismatic Protestant sects took advantage of this spiritual vacuum, especially as the temperament of the Latin American people predisposes them to emotion and feeling in religion. The ultimate guilt and responsibility, in my opinion, lies with the bishops of Latin America and the priests who created this spiritual void, spreading the new sociological and naturalistic religion of a Liberation Theology that was "Catholic" in name only and merely had a Catholic veneer.

When we begin to improve the liturgy in Latin America and to make the liturgy more sacred and venerable, when we begin to give the people sound devotions and especially sound doctrinal and catechetical formation, the sects will not have so much power — especially when the priests themselves give a good example and radiate holiness in their lives. Then the Protestants, the Pentecostals, and the charismatics will not have so much power in Latin America.

Let's turn to the continent of Africa. How can the orthodoxy of so much of the Church in Africa be better communicated to the West, which has fallen away?

I had some experience visiting a community of religious sisters and priests in an African country as an Apostolic Visitor, and I was very impressed by the fervor and simplicity and purity of the faith of the African people. I was edified and moved by the African Catholics — more the lay people than the clergy, I have to say. Even so, I met good bishops and had many meetings with them, and I admired in them a fresh Catholic faith, an unspoiled and, in some way, pure Catholic faith of a child. It is so beautiful to see in an adult man, in a bishop, the soul of a child who believes in God, who believes the truths of the catechism. The Apostles must have been like this. They ought to have the pure faith of a child, a faith which is not spoiled by the doubts or distortions of adult infidelity towards the truths which God so clearly and simply revealed in the Gospel.

The Lord said, "unless you be converted, and become as little children, you shall not enter the kingdom of heaven" (Mt 18:3).

Exactly, and so I think the Catholic bishops of Africa can give to the world, especially in the West, this fresh air of a pure childlike faith and a deep reverence for the sacred. Yes, a deep reverence for the laws of God, even though, as everywhere, people in Africa also commit sins. While there is sin in Africa, the difference is that the people there recognize that it is wrong, that it is against God, and they have true repentance. And repentance is hope. Even though there are many sins and immoral situations in Africa, the African people still have a repentant and contrite soul. In the Western world, even inside the Church, people try to justify their sins. They try to justify their offenses against God in order to justify themselves; there is no hope in this attitude. It is the same issue we saw in the debate on Communion for the divorced and remarried, and now in the homosexual agenda. An increasing number of priests and even bishops and cardinals seek to legitimize the so-called "LGBT" community, and with this they want to legitimize homosexual activity itself.

The second thing the Church in Africa can give to the Western world is a deep sense of family. I once met an Englishman who worked in Africa. The Africans would say to him: "Oh, you are from England, you have a car, you have a watch, and so on. We don't have these things." And this Englishman, who was a Catholic and a believer, said to them, "But you have better values and richer values that we do in Europe. We have cars and watches and good apartments and everything we need, but you have the family, and you love the family, and you cherish the family. And this makes you wealthier than us."

In Europe, when a parent or grandparents dies, they gather and cremate him to find a quick solution, or when there are relatives that live far away, they have the funeral before they all arrive. But it is impossible for African people to do this. It would be a sign of irreverence and ingratitude toward the deceased father or mother or grandfather or grandmother. They wait until all the relatives have come. They wait, they will not bury him or burn him; this is so beautiful. It is a small example, but an important one, about how to care for the elderly in your family. The issue of euthanasia is unthinkable for an African person. Even to put one's parents in a nursing home is impossible for the African people. They remain together. The parents live with the adult children who care for them. And so, I think that these values of the fresh, pure faith of a child, the attitude of repentance of a sinner, the deep sense of family, and respect and love for the parents, will enrich Western people and the Church in Western countries.

And to see every child as a gift...

Exactly, to welcome life, to always welcome life. I spoke with a lot of humble people in Africa, including couples. For them, even for non-Christians, contraception is unthinkable. They have the natural instinct that contraception is against nature. It is an issue of natural law.

Of course, in Africa evil practices exist among non-Christians in pagan environments, such as human sacrifices, cruelty, vengeance, and so on, because they are not Christians. It is because of the lack of the Christian spirit that there are such cruel and inhuman phenomena among pagans in Africa. That is why there is a need to evangelize Africa, to penetrate Africa with the spirit of the Gospel, and to eliminate those cruel situations where people are without belief in the true God, in Christ. But Western society itself is once again becoming barbaric, with barbarian cruelties. The number of abortions perpetrated in the Western world is barbaric and is worse than the cruelest pagan practices in Africa. Abortion is crueler, because people are killing their own babies on a mass scale and justifying this with laws. And now with euthanasia they are killing the sick and elderly, with the so-called brain-death theory they are harvesting organs, and they are killing terminally ill persons.

When a society abandons the true faith — faith in Jesus Christ — it slowly becomes barbaric. They may have sophisticated technology but morally they are barbarians, even in some ways worse than cannibals — as the macabre business of selling the organs and body parts of aborted children demonstrates.

Cannibals?

Yes, to dismember a child in his or her mother's womb with abortion technology and then to sell the body parts is, in my view, crueler than cannibalism. To sell aborted baby body parts for medical research or to make from them vaccines and vaccinate children and adults with such a "medicine," this represents a crueler form of cannibalism than existed among uncivilized barbarians. We have to say this.

The only solution is to return to Christ, the only true God. To return to the only true religion, to the Gospel. And, once again, the African Church can be a means for the whole Catholic world to regain these good values which I mentioned, especially the pure faith of a child and family values.

Western nations are introducing "reproductive rights" in Africa. The United Nations and other international and private organizations are flooding the continent with contraceptives and abortion in the name of alleviating poverty.

Yes, this as you mentioned is one of the cruelest methods of colonization carried out by the Western world. Colonization is a historical phenomenon. However, we have to recognize that, in those times, although they perpetrated many injustices, the colonial powers brought some real benefits and advancements to social life. Roads, hospitals, and schools were built. But the current colonization of Africa by the European Union, the United Nations, and other heavily funded international and private organizations is the worst method of colonization. They want to kill African people through the introduction of contraception and abortion. It's meant in some way to reduce the African population.

It has been called "ideological colonization," but it is more than ideological, because the secularists are not just spreading ideas but preventing children from being born. It is therefore also a new kind of slavery, the worst kind: that which prevents life from the very beginning by enslaving people's passions to conform to the secularist-consumerist mentality.

It is also a form of racism, because the white people who are carrying this out don't want there to be so many black people. White people in

Europe and the United States who are ideologically colonizing Africa introduce contraception in Africa, so that the African population will not grow. White people do this under the cynical pretext of reducing poverty.

Ordinary African people believe that their children are their true wealth. They are happy to live in the countryside and do not need so much technology. They live happily and peacefully. I observed this during the several journeys I have made through African rural areas. I observed some African farmers. They live quietly and happily with many children. Of course, sometimes they suffer calamities when there is no rain and even moments of famine and drought. That is when the Western world should help them, with food and by improving the water systems and financing water-well drilling. This would provide real help for them and promote development — not killing their babies through contraception and abortion. The Western world is showing its cruelty and inhumanity towards the African peoples. One day, human history will judge severely this modern colonization and slavery which has killed so many people in Africa and has sought to import its own morally corrupt ways to African populations. I also observed that life in the big cities in Africa brings African people a more hectic and chaotic lifestyle than rural life. Building up urban life in a way that is both morally healthy and culturally and economically beneficent requires time and a true Christian spirit. This was the case, for instance, when Christianity modelled and created medieval urban life.

Unfortunately, some of these international bodies and individuals are trying through the Pontifical Academy of Social Sciences to use the Church's moral authority to promote this agenda.

I have to say that the bishops of Africa are aware of this, at least those whom I visited, and they are trying to resist, thanks be to God. The Holy See has to help the African bishops to resist this new inhuman colonization and to support those African governments that still resist the new "ideological colonization." I hope that African Catholicism will give to the Catholic world and to the Western world a new impulse to regain those beautiful values which the Western Church, to a considerable extent, has lost and which the African Catholics still hold.

Today throughout the world — especially in the Middle East, in China, and in nations in Africa and Asia — Christians are being persecuted and

*martyred for their faith in Jesus Christ. What is your message to them
and to the wider Church?*

I would like to say to all of our heroic brothers and sisters in Christ
that their suffering and sacrifices are one of the most powerful spiritual
forces for the growth of the Church in our days. Their tears, their pain,
and their blood are collected in the crystal-clear chalice by the angel, as
we see it described in the third part of the secret of Fatima, and the spiritual field of the Church of our day is being watered with their sacrifices.
Our persecuted brothers and sisters demonstrate to the entire world the
validity and spiritual fecundity of the Gospel's beatitude: "Blessed are
you when men revile you and persecute you and utter all kinds of evil
against you falsely on my account. Rejoice, and be glad, for your reward
is great in heaven, for so men persecuted the prophets who were before
you" (Mt 5:11–12).

On the other side, the Holy See and the entire Catholic Church have
the duty to defend our brothers and sisters by clear words of protest
and appropriate action. The authorities of the Catholic Church should
resist the temptation, from political correctness, to keep silent about or
belittle the persecution of Christians in our day.

The true Catholics in the so-called free world in the West are being
persecuted as well, but through extremely sophisticated and cynical
forms of psychological, bureaucratic, and social marginalization and
repression. The physically and psychologically persecuted Catholics
in our day represent the true honor and the crown of our Mother the
Church. I would say to them, "You are the darlings of Our Lord," "We
are proud of you," "We don't forget you!," and "Be faithful unto death
and the Lord will give you the crown of life" (cf. Rev 2:10).

*Do you think the near extinction of Christians in the Middle East is an
ominous sign of a much greater age of tribulation to come?*

I think we have every reason to see in the dramatic situation in the
Middle East a prophetic sign of a future great persecution of Christians
on a broader level. In the meantime, we are already witnessing in the
Western world signs of a discrimination and marginalization of those
Christians who do not accept the reigning gender ideology, the new
climate religion, and the worship of the earth, the so-called "Mother
Earth." The mass immigration to Europe of a predominantly Muslim
population will in time naturally lead to Muslim people gaining political

power in Europe. One cannot exclude the possibility of a future alliance between Freemasonic political powers and radical political Islam united in the aim of persecuting and repressing Christians. Since the French Revolution, Freemasonry has always acted to persecute Christians behind the scenes by means of political powers and systems, e.g., the persecution of the Church in Portugal in the beginning of the twentieth century, of the Church in Mexico in the 1920s, and of the Church in Spain in the 1930s, even before the Civil War.

As true Christians, however, we should not be fearful, but confident in the victory of Christ and His Church over all persecutors and persecutions. Pope Pius XI reminded us of this truth: "Unbelievers and enemies of the Catholic faith, blinded by presumption, may indeed constantly renew their violent attacks against the Christian name, but in wresting from the bosom of the militant Church those whom they put to death, they become the instruments of their martyrdom and of their heavenly glory. No less beautiful than true are the words of St. Leo the Great: 'The religion of Christ, founded on the mystery of the Cross, cannot be destroyed by any sort of cruelty; persecutions do not weaken, they strengthen the Church. The field of the Lord is ever ripening with new harvests, while the grains shaken loose by the tempest take root and are multiplied'" (*Homily at the Canonization of John Fisher and Thomas More*, May 19, 1935).

We possess an impressive text from the third century, which makes an ardent appeal to remain always a good soldier of Christ and not to fear persecution. It reads: "Consider this fairly with me: When has Christ need of your aid? Now, when the wicked one has sworn war against His bride; or in the time to come, when He shall reign victorious, having no need of further help? Is it not evident to anyone who has even the least understanding, that it is now? Therefore, with all good will, hasten in the time of the present necessity to do battle on the side of this good King, whose character it is to give great rewards after victory" (*Epistola Clementis ad Iacobum* 4).

IV

The Stars Shall Fall from Heaven

14

The Eucharist and Holy Communion

Your Excellency, you said earlier that the way out of the current crisis in the Church is to "rediscover the supernatural" and to "give primacy to the supernatural in the life of the Church" through a renewed focus on prayer and the Holy Eucharist. Can we now return to the mystery of the Real Presence, and discuss its importance?

When we speak about the Eucharist, we have to focus on the essence of the liturgy, on the mystery of the Eucharist, and this is Christ—the living Christ, our Incarnate God, who is really living with His mind, His heart, His soul, and His divinity in the sacrament of the Most Holy Eucharist. But in this mystery, He is veiled, as His divinity was veiled when He walked on the earth with His people, teaching and speaking with them. Since He was so simple and looked like an ordinary man—though the fullness of divinity was present in Him—many people did not recognize Him and rejected Him—the Pharisees, and scribes, and others—because of His humble appearance. St. Paul says of Our Lord Jesus Christ, "He took the form of a servant, being made in the likeness of men, and in habit found as a man" (Phil 2:7).

In a deeper and more radical manner, the same happens in the mystery of the Eucharist, which is an extension of the Incarnation. The Incarnation is continued because now not only is Christ's divinity veiled by His humanity, but the Eucharistic species of bread and wine veil both the humanity and the divinity of Christ. Christ is veiled, but He continues to be the same; He lives here on earth in the same reality of His Incarnation, but in a different mode. It is now a sacramental mode. His humanity in the Eucharistic is already a glorified humanity, but the glorified humanity is real and can be touched. When Jesus rose from the dead He could be touched; He had a real but transfigured Body. The same is true of the Eucharist: His real body, real soul, and the whole plenitude of His divinity are veiled under the appearance of a small piece of bread.

This presents a continuous challenge to our faith, our love. We are challenged to renew our love for the Incarnation, by continually exercising our faith when we see the consecrated Host. This is our Incarnate God: *et Verbum caro factum est: et habitavit in nobis,* "and the Word was made flesh and dwelt among us" (Jn 1:14). And now He dwells among us even more deeply and more humbly and more mysteriously — really, in the same realistic way that He walked on the earth, but in another mode. It is real; that is why we speak of the Real Presence — I want to stress this point. This is our faith: that under the veil of the Eucharistic species of bread and wine, the plenitude of Our Lord's humanity and divinity is present. It should touch the deepest depths of our soul and provoke in us a corresponding attitude of soul *and* body, because this is the Incarnation. We cannot dispense with bodily signs of reverence and respect, because He is bodily present; the God-man is truly present. Concrete gestures of worship, adoration, and awe are the logical consequence of our faith.

And when we dispense with these gestures, faith in the mystery is weakened?

Yes. When we diminish the exterior signs of awe, sacredness, and reverence, in time it quasi-necessarily diminishes our faith in the Real Presence of Our Lord and in His Incarnation. These are connected. Every time we diminish our respect and our awareness of the presence of Christ in the sacrament of the Eucharist — the real, full, substantial, and divine Presence — we diminish at the same time our faith in the Incarnation itself. Faith in the Eucharist and faith in the Incarnation are inseparably linked. Thus, it is a continuous act of faith in the Incarnation and in the supernatural because it *is* supernatural, because the divinity is so close to us. In the sacrament of the Eucharist Our Lord deigned to veil Himself beneath these external, weak elements of matter. There is nowhere in the entire world, in the entire history of the world, in the entire universe, where God is so close, where the divinity is as close to His creatures, as in the mystery of the Eucharist.

In the Eucharist, only the external elements of the matter, which are called the "accidents," persist, while the substance of the elements is transformed into the substance of the Body and Blood of the sacred humanity of Christ and, through the humanity, the divinity of Christ is also present. In the Incarnation, God inseparably united His divinity to our human nature: both natures are united in the Son, the Second

Person of the Holy Trinity; we call this the hypostatic union. In the Eucharist, this hypostatic union receives a new aspect. The accidents of bread and wine are associated with the substance of Christ's Body and Blood and thus are related to His Divinity in a mysterious and unspeakable manner. St. Thomas Aquinas says that the Godhead of Christ is in this sacrament from real concomitance, "for since the Godhead never set aside the assumed body, wherever the body of Christ is, there, of necessity, must the Godhead be; and therefore it is necessary for the Godhead to be in this sacrament concomitantly with His body. Hence we read in the profession of faith at Ephesus (p. 1, ch. 26): 'We are made partakers of the body and blood of Christ, not as taking common flesh, nor as of a holy man united to the Word in dignity, but the truly life-giving flesh of the Word Himself'" (*Summa theologiae* III, q. 76, a. 1, ad 1). And the Council of Trent taught: "under the species of bread and wine is the divinity, on account of the admirable hypostatical union thereof with His body and soul" (sess. 13, ch. 3).

Why do you think Love invented this particular way?

This could only have been invented by Love. The Eucharist is a divine invention. It could not have been invented by a creature, by anyone. He reserved this to Himself because of His unending love for us, and therefore this is the *sacramentum caritatis*; and at the same time the Eucharist is the *sacramentum fidei*, the *mysterium fidei*. Love desires to be close to the beloved. There is no way to be closer to us, there is no more humble, fragile, vulnerable, and defenseless way than the Eucharist. It can only be an invention and a maximum expression of divine Love towards us.

Through the sacrament of the Eucharist, Jesus Christ says to us, "I love you. Not only do I want to be close to you, I want to enter into you through the Eucharist, into your body, into your soul, in the most profound way possible. I want to be united to your soul by my divinity, to visit you, to enter even into your body, and to sanctify you, to dwell in you." The Incarnate God not only dwelt *among* us on earth. He is now dwelling on our altars at the moment of consecration in the Mass and He is dwelling in the tabernacle. He descends always onto the altar. It was St. Thérèse of the Child Jesus who said: "Jesus does not descend in order to live and dwell in the golden chalice, in the tabernacle, but He wants to dwell in our souls." This is the Eucharist. This is Love. There could not be a mode that was closer to us, more real and more "incarnational," than the Eucharist. Christ does this for our sake even to the extent that He allows Himself to be despised in the Sacrament, dishonored, rejected, profaned in the most horrible way. Despite this, He invented and instituted this sacrament of the tremendous majesty of divine Love. He did this all for us.

Indeed, would not the foreknowledge of how He would be dishonored and rejected by the ones He loves have been part of His suffering in His Sacred Passion?

I think that during His suffering in the Garden of Gethsemane, He foresaw these incredible and horrendous sacrileges against His Eucharistic Presence. I think, especially, that the most horrible sacrileges are perpetrated by priests, who are His "friends." When you love someone, when someone is your friend or very close to you, and he hurts you, you suffer more than when a stranger does this. When the Communists and the pagans profaned the Eucharist, Christ did not suffer so much as when He is profaned by His own children, by His priests and bishops. This has been happening now on a large scale, over the period of the past fifty years. There has never been a time in history when, inside the Church, our Eucharistic Lord has been treated in such a horrific manner and been so profaned and outraged by His own faithful and priests, as in our times.

This situation is mainly caused by Communion in the hand. There is a myth which liberal clerics are spreading, and perhaps intentionally, which says that in the first centuries there was also Communion in the hand, and so we need to get back to the early practice of the Church. This is a lie, this is a myth, this is propaganda in disguise. Why? The intent to return to a particular and not yet fully developed ancient liturgical practice is called "liturgical antiquarianism." Pope Pius XII condemned this mentality in his Encyclical *Mediator Dei*, as being contrary to the perennial sense of the Church. Liturgical archaeologism is one of the basic errors of the Modernists in the Church, and of Protestants. To go back, as they say, to an "ideal" time in the Church, to jump back over millennia. This is an expression of radical rupture, of the 1,700-year parenthesis we discussed before. Rupture and revolution contradict the essence of the Church and the Christian faith because the Church is an organism and lives in organic growth. One cannot simply cut out a considerable segment of history and jump back in time.

You cannot tell the branches and blossoms to return to the root and just cut the trunk off . . .

That is a good expression. We as adults cannot say, "I want to go back to the beautiful and romantic time of my childhood, because it was an ideal time and I would very much like to dress in the clothes I wore when I was seven or eight years old." No: now I am a man, and you are an adult woman. You cannot put on the dress you were so fond of when you were an eight-year-old girl. It would be funny and bizarre. It would not fit you and you would create a comedy.

And a tragedy . . .

Indeed. This is the error of the liturgists: they want to go back to the fourth or fifth century. But fifteen centuries have passed since then!

But even concretely, there was an error in the myth they were circulating, because the practice had a different form in ancient times than it does today: the Holy Eucharist was received on the palm of the right hand and the faithful were not allowed to touch the Holy Host with their fingers, but they had to bow down their head to the palm of the hand and take the Sacrament directly with their mouth, thus, in a position of a profound bow and not standing upright. The common practice today is to receive the Eucharist standing upright, taking it with the left hand. This is something which, symbolically, the Church Fathers would find horrific — how can the Holy of Holies be taken with the left hand? Then, today the faithful take and touch the Host directly with their fingers and then put the Host in the mouth: this gesture has never been known in the entire history of the Catholic Church but was invented by Calvin — not even by Martin Luther. The Lutherans have typically received the Eucharist kneeling and on the tongue, although of course they do not have the Real Presence because they do not have a valid priesthood. The Calvinists and other Protestant free churches, who do not believe at all in the Real Presence of Christ in the Eucharist, invented a rite which is void of almost all gestures of sacredness and of exterior adoration, i.e., receiving "Communion" standing upright, and touching the bread "host" with their fingers and putting it in their mouth in the way people treat ordinary bread. The Anglicans, however, though being doctrinally influenced by Calvinism, received Holy Communion usually kneeling, yet they were allowed to touch the Host with their fingers and put it themselves in their mouth.

Of course, the Anglicans, whose ordinations are invalid, also lack the Real Presence and the priesthood.

Most Protestants don't believe in the Real Presence. For them, Communion is ordinary bread and only has a symbolic value.

For them, this was just a symbol, so their exterior behavior towards Communion was similar to behavior towards a symbol. During the Second Vatican Council, Catholic Modernists — especially in the Netherlands — took this Calvinist Communion rite and wrongly attributed it to the Early Church, in order to spread it more easily throughout the Church. We have to dismantle this myth and these insidious tactics, which started in the Catholic Church more than fifty years ago, and which like an avalanche have now rolled through, crushing almost all Catholic churches in the entire world, with the exception of some Catholic countries in Eastern Europe and a few places in Asia and Africa.

There is another aspect to this error. In the Early Church, women could not receive the holy Host directly on the palm of their hand; they had to use a white linen cloth. And men had to wash their hands before presenting themselves for Communion: it was impossible to receive the Holy of Holies with unwashed hands because people had touched doors and coins beforehand.

Today people go and receive the Holy of Holies even though they have touched doors and coins and money and who knows what else with unwashed hands. I know the counterargument would be that you need a clean soul, not a clean hand. But, again, to reject the corporeal and natural as unimportant is a Gnostic argument. The exterior and corporeal side *is* important! A person with a good education and common sense would surely greet an extraordinarily important person with washed hands.

As you mentioned, people say: "But it's the heart that counts. It's my intention that counts. The bishop and priests allow me to receive the Lord on the hand, and I do love Him. In fact, I feel closer to Him when I receive in the hand."

That is subjectivism and it is wrong, because it denies the way of the Incarnation. The Lord could also say, "I am in Heaven. I sent you a prophet and I love you with all my heart and it is enough for me. I don't have to come among you so that you can approach me or shed my blood for you on the Cross. I love you in my heart and I am close to you." The

Lord could have said this to us. But He didn't. He loved us to the end, concretely, not only interiorly, but also exteriorly: He loved us to the shedding of the last drop of His Blood, and after His Resurrection He emphasized the visible reality of His Body.

I would also offer this analogy: there is a young man who has fallen in love with a girl and he says, "I love you in my heart and I am very close to you." But he never gives her a flower, he never touches her hand. She would not believe his profession of love were he never to show an exterior sign of his heartfelt love for her. Such behavior would be inhuman. It would not correspond to our nature. It is the same with the Eucharist. It is an illusion for a believing Catholic to say, "I love Jesus and I am close to Him when I am receiving Him in the Eucharist, and so the minimum of exterior signs of faith and reverence are fine."

The Catholic view is *et . . . et*, "both . . . and" — a synthesis. I love the Lord in my heart *and* show this exteriorly with clear, unambiguous signs of adoration, reverence, and sacredness that point to the supernatural. Over the centuries the Church instinctively, by the guidance of the Holy Spirit, has felt the need to use more expressive signs of adoration and more expressive ways to protect the Holy of Holies, because the Host could fall on the ground or be stolen. Therefore, since at least the sixth and seventh century, the Church in East and West distributed Holy Communion exclusively and directly into the mouth, to avoid any possible danger of profanation of the Sacrament. We also have to bear in mind the fact that the praxis of Communion given in the palm of the right hand is attested only in specific places in the first centuries — mainly in Syria, South Gallia, and North Africa. Thus, we do not possess a clear testimony of a universal praxis.

In your experience, have you heard any other common counterarguments?

The other counterargument is that Jesus said, "Take this, all of you." But this is a manifest error, because this word was not addressed to the laity, but directly to the Apostles only, and He consecrated them as priests of the new covenant. At the Last Supper, there were no laypeople present; even Our Lady was not present. "Take this all of you and do this in memory of Me." To whom were these words directed? They were directed to the Apostles. Otherwise, every member of the faithful could celebrate Mass because Jesus said, "Do this in memory of Me." The Council of Trent taught that by the words "Do this in memory of Me," the Lord constituted the Apostles priests of the new covenant. As these words refer to the Apostles, so also the words "Take and eat of it" refer primarily to the Apostles. The command was given first to the Apostles and they had the right to touch the Eucharistic Body of the Lord, and then they had to distribute the Eucharist to the faithful. This is shown also in the Gospel account of the multiplication of the loaves. It was the Apostles who distributed the loaves to the people.

The Vulgate translates the Greek term *lambanein* with the Latin word *accipere*. It is commonly used in the Holy Scripture in the sense of receiving, not taking. For example, when Our Lord breathed on the Apostles, saying "Receive ye the Holy Spirit," it is the same word *accipere* (Greek: *lambanein*). Nobody would translate it as "take the Holy Spirit." *Accipite Spiritum Sanctum* means "receive the Holy Spirit." Therefore, the translation "take" in the words of the institution of the Eucharist is incorrect in English, in German (*nehmet*), and in some other languages. The translation ought to be "Receive ye, all" because the Greek and Latin word is "receive." Sometimes, it could be meant as "take," but in most places in the New Testament, this word is used in the sense of "receiving" — whether a gift of God, the Holy Spirit, etc. This is an incorrect translation, which needs to be corrected. In the Slavonic languages, it is translated correctly as "receive" (*priimite*). So, we are saying in Russian, Polish, and other Slavonic languages — "Receive, all of you, and eat."

We have to recognize *who* is in the sacrament of the Eucharist, not only *what* the Eucharist is. There is a short phrase that summarizes the entire Eucharistic mystery and says it all: "This is the Lord," or "It is the Lord." In the Gospel of St. John, on the morning of the Resurrection, Our Lord was standing on the shore of the sea, and no one recognized Him (cf. Jn 21:7) — only the Apostle John, who loved the Lord more than the others. Love sees. "It is the Lord." *Dominus est!* That is why I titled my first book *Dominus Est*. This phrase explains everything. If this is the Lord, this small, fragile Host; if this is the Lord, then I have to fall down on my knees. I cannot stand. I have to open my mouth like a child, in the spirit of childhood, as Jesus said: "Whoever does not receive the Kingdom of God like a child . . ." (Lk 18:17). If you do not receive the Kingdom of God like a child, you will not enter the Kingdom of God. As St. Peter writes in his epistle: like newborn babes, long for pure spiritual milk (cf. 1 Peter 2:2). Since the first centuries of the Church, the Lord's Eucharistic Body and Blood has been compared to mother's milk. The newborn child cannot take food and put it in his mouth—it's impossible. A newborn can only open his mouth and receive the milk. We have to be like newborn children toward the Eucharist. It is so logical that we open our mouth as babes and that the priest, who is another Christ, puts the Host in our mouth.

Some people will not want to do that because it's a position of vulnerability and littleness. Could we say that in some sense—not in the human sense—God is vulnerable? His "divine vulnerability" is unexpected, but this is the way of love.

That is correct. We spoke earlier about this: the mode of this presence in the Eucharist itself is vulnerable, fragile, defenseless, and this is a sign of love; God so loves us that He made Himself vulnerable and defenseless on the Cross, and beginning even in the crib. The mysteries of the crib, the Cross, and the Eucharist form a unity. The Eucharist is even more deeply vulnerable and defenseless because everyone can take Him and do what they want with Him.

But on His part, this is not truly weakness.

No. It is not weakness. Rather, it is the almighty power of Love in the Eucharist, in this littleness. There is a story I once read of a little girl who was preparing for First Holy Communion and she had an uncle who was an atheist, who wanted to trouble this child in her faith, to shake her. He asked her, "Do you believe that this little piece of bread is Christ?" "Yes, I learned this in catechism," she said. "But you learned in catechism that God is infinite. Nothing can contain God." "Yes, I learned this also: God is immense and almighty, so God is great," she responded. "But how, if God is immense, can He be contained in this little host, as you have said?" And she looked upon him and said, "God is so great that He has a place in my little heart and He is so great that He cannot be contained in your mind." It was a beautiful answer of a little girl. Truly, this reminds us of the words of the Lord, "Thou hast hid these things from the wise and prudent, and hast revealed them to the little ones" (Mt 11:25). The Eucharist is Our Lord, and I think that the Church can be restored once again only with the restoration of an awe-inspiring and reverent Eucharistic worship, regarding especially the rite of Holy Communion with its necessary spiritual as well as exterior preparation.

I am from the United States, and in many dioceses we have the particular problem of the multiplication of extraordinary ministers of Holy Communion, mainly because the Eucharist is distributed under both species. At any given Sunday Mass, as many as twelve laypeople might descend upon the altar before Communion to distribute the Holy Sacrament. How can the Church be restored when you have so many people who have not been formed in authentic piety and perhaps even unconsciously assume that this is "tradition"? The argument would go something like: "We've always received the Eucharist under both species. It would take far too long to distribute the Eucharist otherwise. And besides, the Church allows this. The bishop allows it." Laymen and women are allowed and encouraged to be extraordinary ministers of Holy Communion at Sunday Mass and even daily Mass.

It's difficult to turn this around suddenly. We have to go slowly, step-by-step, and with good catechesis we have to show the greatness of the Lord. Who is the Eucharist? Often the Masses with so-called extraordinary ministers of Holy Communion resemble a cafeteria service and are done quickly. This destroys the supernatural meaning and faith in the sublimity and divinity of the Eucharist and also the essential difference between laypeople and ordained priests. I am not denying that a lot of the so-called extraordinary ministers of Holy Communion have real faith in Jesus and love for Him.

I believe that's what most would say, that they do it because they love Jesus, or they want to serve, or they do it because their priest asked them to —

But they don't know what they are doing. If they knew, they would never do this. Because with this service, they are helping to decrease the sanctity, the sacredness, the supernatural reality of the mystery of the Eucharist and the essential difference between the lay state and the sacramental priesthood itself. In this way, there is a blurring of the distinctions between the sacramental priesthood and the common priesthood, visibly, and the scene itself is more like a Protestant Communion service or a cafeteria.

When I was a girl, I vividly remember the Sunday we no longer received Holy Communion kneeling at the altar rail, and instead everyone stood in line. I can remember at the time thinking that it reminded me of the McDonald's drive-thru.

We have to take time for the Lord. We cannot be in a hurry during Holy Communion. The priest says, "I have no time. I have to celebrate other Masses and so I need extraordinary ministers of Holy Communion." Oftentimes this is only a pretext. Usually the same priest calmly spends fifteen minutes or more after Mass chatting, on the internet, and so on. He could spare these fifteen minutes and distribute Holy Communion without the lay ministers. Again, it would be better for the priest to shorten the homily by five minutes and distribute Holy Communion himself without the help of laypeople.

In ancient times, and in the persecuted Church, people travelled entire days on foot to get to Mass and sometimes went several years without Holy Communion, and they took time to prepare themselves to receive Holy Communion. Today, in the United States and Europe, it is so easy to reach Catholic churches — we are mobile, we have cars.

Never before in Church history did laypeople distribute Holy Communion during Mass. This was only permitted in exceptional cases and was *always outside of Mass*. In times of persecution, when Catholics were dying or in the prisons and wanted to receive the Lord, the Church permitted laypeople to give Holy Communion. In extreme exceptional cases, but, I repeat, never during Holy Mass. During the Mass, there is always a priest and there is no reason to enlist laypeople to distribute Holy Communion. Even deacons never distributed the Holy Host during Mass, but only the chalice. Therefore, in the tradition of the Latin Church, they (the deacons) were later called extraordinary ministers of Holy Communion. Nowadays deacons are called ordinary ministers of Holy Communion. In the Orthodox Church, however, the deacons are still not allowed to distribute Holy Communion.

One of the counterarguments in the United States would be: "Our tradition is to receive the Sacrament under both species, so we need a Eucharistic minister for the Precious Blood."

This is not a tradition going back even a hundred years — maybe just forty years. It is not a long tradition.

Maronite Catholics use intinction.

I had wanted to mention this. In many Catholic churches in Kazakhstan, intinction is used at the Communion rite. It is not so complicated. There are ciboria made in such a way that they contain a small chalice

inside for the Precious Blood and another space around for the Sacred
Hosts and the priest can hold such a ciborium easily distributing Holy
Communion by intinction, with the altar server holding the paten. It
is better for a priest to use intinction than to give to people the chalice
directly. It is very dangerous to give people the chalice to drink from. A
drop of the Precious Blood can easily drop down, because sometimes people are nervous, have trembling hands, are distracted, inattentive, and so on.

*Sometimes elderly people serve as Eucharistic ministers. With the deepest
respect for the elderly, one can still acknowledge that sometimes their hands
might be trembling, or become weak . . .*

     This is very dangerous, indeed. For the Eucharist, which is most holy
and our greatest divine treasure on earth, we have to use not only signs
of reverence but also signs of security and care. The same people, when
they have a precious treasure in their house, will secure it and defend
it. But as regards Our Lord in the Eucharist, bishops, priests, and faithful in the Church are often very superficial and do not care and worry
about Him in the way they would care and worry about their personal
material treasures. I think we have to stop the practice of directly giving
the chalice to the faithful. A transitional solution would be to say, "You
can continue to receive under both species, but by intinction." When the
Roman Church many centuries ago stopped the custom of the faithful
drinking directly from the chalice, it was a well-founded decision based
on undeniable and proven negative experiences.

You chose to dedicate the subject of your first book, Dominus Est, *to the
proper reception of the Eucharist. Would you say more about why you wrote
it, and how it was received?*

     There is the grievous fact of the loss of Eucharistic fragments because
of Communion in the hand. No one can deny this. Fragments of the
consecrated host fall to the floor and are subsequently crushed by feet.
This is horrible! Our God is trampled on in our churches! No one can
deny it. This is happening on a large scale. We cannot continue as if Jesus
our God is not really present, as though the Eucharist is only bread. As I
said before, the modern practice of Communion in the hand has nothing
to do with the practice in the ancient Church. The modern practice of
receiving Communion in the hand contributes gradually to the loss of
the Catholic faith in the Real Presence and in Transubstantiation.

A priest and a bishop cannot say this practice is all right. Of course, there are people who receive Holy Communion in the hand with much devotion and faith, but they are a minority. The vast majority are losing the faith through this very banal practice of taking Holy Communion like common food, like a chip or a piece of cake. Such a manner of receiving the Holy of Holies here on earth destroys over time the deep awareness of the Real Presence and Transubstantiation. Christ is not only "God with us." He is God who, in the little sacred Host, has delivered Himself into the hands of men, entirely renouncing his own defense. The Eucharistic Jesus in the sacred Host is truly the poorest and most defenseless in the Church, and this He is especially during the distribution of Communion.

At the end of 2005, I wrote a letter to Pope Benedict XVI and enclosed the manuscript of my book *Dominus Est.* In that letter, I implored the pope in the name of Jesus Christ to stop distributing Holy Communion in the hand but instead to give Holy Communion to the faithful kneeling and on the tongue. Pope Benedict XVI answered me in a personally signed letter, in which he said that my arguments were convincing. Then, beginning with the Feast of Corpus Christi and until the end of his pontificate, Pope Benedict XVI distributed Holy Communion exclusively in this manner: the faithful knelt on a prie-dieu and received the Body of Christ directly on the tongue. For me this was a miracle and I was filled with a deep joy. I believe that my letter and the manuscript of my book *Dominus Est* did influence Pope Benedict XVI.

The irony seems to be that "High Church" Protestants have more reverence during their communion services, which are only symbolic, whereas we Catholics have been given the Real Presence of Jesus Christ in the Holy Eucharist, but our manner of receiving Him undermines what we actually believe.

The way to receive Holy Communion that has proved for centuries to be the safer and more sacred manner is to receive Our Lord kneeling and on the tongue.

Once I spoke with a Norwegian Lutheran clergyman and asked him how the Lutherans in Norway receive Communion. He answered: "Until about fifteen years ago people received Communion kneeling and on the tongue. But now they receive standing, and in the hand." I asked the reason for the change, and he answered: "We changed because of the influence of our Catholic brothers."

During an interreligious meeting in Kazakhstan, in which I participated, we spoke about the most holy realities of each religion. An Imam
said that, for Muslims, the holiest thing is the book of the Koran in Arabic letters, and he stressed this by saying it would be an act of sacrilege
were someone to dare to touch the Arabic Koran with unwashed hands.
Hearing this statement, I suddenly thought about scenes of the reception
of Holy Communion in the hand, lacking almost any clear sacral sign
and surely without washing hands immediately before. Such scenes do
occur in the vast majority of the Catholic churches all around the world.

I then imagined a hypothetical scene. If one day this Imam were to
visit a Catholic Church, and Holy Communion was being distributed in
the hand to faithful who are approaching the altar in a quickly moving
queue, he would ask: "What is this little piece of white bread?" The
Catholic would answer him: "It is Christ." The Muslim would say: "This
is surely only a sign or a symbol of Christ." The Catholic would answer
him: "No, it is not a symbol or a sacred object. The Lord Jesus Christ is
really present there." The Muslim will continue to say: "That can't be.
Christ must be only spiritually or symbolically present." The Catholic will
answer: "No, Christ is really, truly present with the substance of His Body,
Blood, Soul, and Divinity." The Muslim will respond: "Then this little
piece of bread must be, according to your faith, your God and the Holy
of Holies for you." The Catholic would answer: "Yes, what looks like a
little piece of bread is really our living God personally in His human Body
and Blood, and not an object like your Koran." Finally, the Muslim would
say: "The fact that you treat your God and the Holy of Holies in such a
banal manner tells me that you don't believe He is really present there. I
am unable to agree with you that you really believe what you are saying."

Should we wait for the bishops to change this, to eliminate the reception of
Holy Communion in the hand? Or should it come from the laity? It can
often be a struggle for the laity to discern how to act.

Our time is a special time for the laity, as the Second Vatican Council
stressed. The laity are called to start catechizing and showing forth the
beauty and greatness and uniqueness of the Eucharist. Certainly, individual lay men and women, Catholic families, and even parish groups
can choose to begin receiving Holy Communion kneeling and on the
tongue. They can also encourage their priest to preach on the truths of
the Holy Eucharist.

Ultimately, though, a true renewal of the Eucharistic cult has to come from the clergy and from the Holy See. The pope is the defender of Jesus Christ and, in this case, he has to use his authority to defend unambiguously and strenuously the sacredness of the Holy Eucharist, even at the cost of some personal disadvantage. The pope has to say, "I have to defend the Lord. I cannot allow such doubtful and dangerous practices in the reception of Holy Communion." Unfortunately, Rome allowed Communion in the hand, Communion from the chalice, and so-called extraordinary ministers. From Rome, therefore, must come the correction of these clearly detrimental liturgical customs. It was the Holy See which unleashed the avalanche of massive trivializations, outrages, and sacrileges towards our Eucharistic Lord. One day history will state this.

We must put an end to Communion in the hand, and we need also to kneel down before Our Lord with the angels, who fall on their faces before the throne worshiping God (cf. Rev 7:11). As St. Paul says, "at the name of Jesus every knee should bow, in heaven and on earth" (Phil 2:10). During Holy Communion it is not only the name of Jesus, but Jesus Himself, who is present: *Dominus est!* We are called to be on bended knee. The entire Church has to kneel down again before Our Eucharistic Lord, to love Him, to venerate Him. Only then will her heart be healed. Only after this healing will she have true spiritual energy with which to glorify God, to save souls, and once gain to vigorously spread the Gospel.

She needs to return to her First Love.

To Eucharistic love. To true incarnational love, not only to invisible sentiment, saying, "I love Jesus in my heart, and gestures are not so important." This is wrong, it is not Christian; in the end, this is Gnostic and Protestant. We have to help people with patience, with catechesis, but ultimately the correction must come from Rome. The pope has to be a *Confessor Eucharisticus*, a defender and outstanding lover of the Eucharistic Christ. He is the visible head, and so, from the head, this love and defense of the Eucharistic Christ has to spread to the bishops and then to the priests. It is consoling that the laypeople — the "little ones" — are already laying the groundwork for this Eucharistic renewal in the Church. This is so beautiful and gives us hope.

15

"Reform of the Reform"

Now that we have discussed the reception of the Holy Eucharist, perhaps we may turn to the liturgy more generally. Your Excellency, what is the Holy Mass?

The sacred liturgy is first and foremost the glorification of the Most Holy Trinity, which the Incarnate Son of God offered in the name of all mankind and the entire creation to His divine Father in the Holy Spirit through His Sacrifice on the Cross, as a sweet fragrance for all eternity. The Holy Mass renders present in a sacramental way the same liturgy of the Sacrifice of the Cross, with the same priest (Jesus Christ) and the same victim (Christ in His sacred humanity) present at Mass as was present in the Sacrifice of the Cross. Hence, the sacred liturgy is primarily and essentially the glorification of the Triune God. Such a perfect glorification of God secondarily brings graces and eternal salvation to all who celebrate it, who participate in it, and for whom it is specifically offered.

Did the fathers of the Second Vatican Council intend that Holy Mass should be celebrated as we see it done in Latin rite churches throughout the world today?

Without a doubt, the way Holy Mass is celebrated in most cases around the world in the Roman rite is not what the fathers of the Council intended, even if the Mass is celebrated according to the new liturgical books. One need only read the debates about the liturgy in the conciliar Acts to discover that the Council fathers could hardly imagine a celebration of Holy Mass where the celebrant is continuously facing the people; a Mass where the traditional offertory prayers were replaced by prayers from the Jewish Sabbath supper, diluting thereby the sacrificial character of the Eucharistic liturgy and adapting it more to the Protestant meaning of a banquet; a Mass where numerous other and often newly-invented Eucharistic prayers can be substituted for the Roman Canon; a Mass where the vernacular is used exclusively; a Mass where Holy Communion is received standing and in the hand; a Mass where there are lay people distributing Holy Communion; a Mass where women and men in civil clothes function as lectors and where girls and women serve as acolytes, sometimes clothed in clerical vestments (cassock and surplice). When one takes into account all of these elements, approved unfortunately by the Holy See for the celebration of the new rite of the Mass, the need of a Reform of the Reform of the sacred liturgy becomes an evident and urgent demand.

The so-called "extraordinary" form of the Mass — which I, however, would call the "constant" form of the Roman liturgy of the Mass — is, in its prayers and rites, without any doubt objectively theologically and spiritually richer, for it expresses more clearly the essence of the Holy Mass, i.e., the sacrifice of Our Lord on the Cross and the sacredness and sublimity of the heavenly liturgy. I think that, in the future, the new order of Mass should be reformed in such a way that it becomes closer and more similar to the constant or more ancient form of the Roman rite of the Mass, called today the "extraordinary" form. In this way, it will reflect more faithfully the perennial sense of the liturgical spirit of the Church, which was the true intention of the fathers of the Second Vatican Council.

There is certainly a lot to unpack here.
Yes. The expression "Reform of the Reform" already demonstrates that the liturgical reform contains problems and defects which cannot remain as they are, hence the need for reform. Pope Benedict XVI, in his writings as a cardinal — especially in his famous book *The Feast of Faith* and in other famous works such as *The Spirit of the Liturgy* — spoke in detail about what a Reform of the Reform would look like. As we know from his writings and his words, the main point he stressed was that, beyond the need to reform some of the aspects of the new rite of the Mass, we need to turn again toward the Lord. The entire Church with the celebrant has to turn toward the Lord, i.e., the orientation of the celebrant towards the Lord in the apse, in the tabernacle.

This is connected with the theme about which we spoke earlier — i.e., the supernatural — because the loss of the supernatural is a turning of man toward himself, a focus on self. This is the core of naturalism. And this is reflected very visibly in the manner of celebrating Mass facing the people (*versus populum*) introduced after the Council and still unfortunately the norm. We see this manner being used throughout almost the entire Church today. We have before our eyes this man-focused shape

Isn't St. Peter's Basilica one example of a Roman basilica whose apse was geographically not oriented toward the East?

Yes, because the geological structure of the hill in the Vatican made it impossible to build the Church in another way. The Roman Church was always very conservative and kept literally the rule to pray toward the East. From historical and archeological studies, we have evidence that the churches of the first millennium had their apses facing East in almost ninety-eight percent of cases. All were turned toward the East, even when the altar was not up against the wall. A freestanding altar is not an argument against facing East, since the priest was in front of the altar facing East nevertheless, just as the Oriental Church still does today.

In St. Peter's Basilica, there was no way to make the apse face East but only West because of the topological structure. The popes were aware that they had to pray toward the East, and so, when they turned toward the nave, it was for the sake of turning eastwards. Hence, this is not an argument for celebration toward the people. In addition, until the ninth century, during the Eucharistic prayer, the papal altar was curtained, as even today the Eastern Churches have curtains. The people did not see the face of the pope. Then, when curtains were no longer used, they put large candlesticks and a large crucifix on the altar. We have pictures of the liturgies before the Council; the pope's face was really not seen, even though the Mass was celebrated, in a certain sense, towards the people.

The prime concern, then, was facing East?

Yes. There was a very traditional, conservative mentality in Rome. Even today, the Orthodox Churches observe the law of the orientation of the apse of a church. The Latin Church started in the sixteenth century to allow exceptions regarding the orientation of the apse of a new church. The attitude of being turned together toward the crucifix always remained, with the apse ordered to the crucifix on the altar, and the crucifix standing in the place of geographical East.

We have to turn to the Lord, to convert to the Lord. The entire Church has to turn away from secularism, from being immersed in naturalism, from the loss of the sense of supernatural, from the anthropocentric attitude. The entire Church has to convert once again and turn herself toward the Lord in the liturgy, even in a visible manner. The celebration of the Mass *ad Deum* (we can also say *ad orientem, ad crucem, ad apsidem*) would be the first and indispensable step in the process of the Reform of the Reform. It would essentially reshape the thinking of the clergy and laypeople in terms of what true prayer is and what the meaning of the Mass is — that it is a sacrifice, the divine sacrifice of our Redeemer on the Cross, and not simply a religious banquet event or a Protestant-style religious instructional event.

Celebration towards the people destroys over time the central truth that the Mass is substantially the same as the Sacrifice of Calvary. The Holy Mass is *not* the perpetuation of the Last Supper. It is the sacramental perpetuation of the mystery of the Cross. This truth has to shape our attitude and our exterior position. It was Martin Luther who started to spread the Eucharistic heresy that the Mass is a kind of repetition and commemoration of the Last Supper and not the sacrament of the Sacrifice on the Cross. The Eucharistic heresy of Luther, which denies the primarily sacrificial character of the Holy Mass, has entered into the teaching of theological faculties and seminaries and into the preaching of a large number of priests and bishops.

*We could say that turning in the same direction during prayer is an example of a "good or truth" found in other religions, as Vatican II says (*Lumen Gentium, *n. 16).*

God has written His law in the conscience of man on the natural level, and some elements of the psychology of prayer are also written on the heart of man. In all religions, when people pray, they turn together in the same direction to a concrete sign, which represents the divine, as all Muslims face Mecca on their knees. Therefore, we cannot turn away from this principle; it would be against even our natural sense. With our current circular shape of celebration, we go against even the natural religious sense of man.

Why do you think there such a strong pushback against the priest and faithful together turning to the Lord?

This is a sign, to me, that those clergy who oppose it love to be at the center of attention. They are already so deeply imbued with the temporal human sphere that they are blinded with self-love. They have lost the sense and the longing for eternity, for the supernatural, and are happy in the natural, in the anthropocentric circle. These clergy have lost the sense of true adoration and worship. The circle-shape celebrations (*versus populum*) are ultimately not a prayer, but rather an inter-human gathering. So, these clergy and their communities simply celebrate themselves, even if they do not want to admit it.

But surely you would find many good and faithful priests who do spend time in adoration before the Blessed Sacrament but who are also celebrating the Mass versus populum.

Yes. But not all of those priests who pray devoutly and celebrate towards the people endorse or advocate this shape of the liturgy; they simply have to obey the policy of the bishop or the diocese which makes this form compulsory. Unfortunately, many of them who would prefer *ad orientem* in the celebration of the Mass cannot introduce it on their own.

Or perhaps they haven't had the experience of celebrating the Mass ad orientem *with the people, and so have not had their eyes opened to its fittingness.*

Perhaps they have not experienced it and are unconsciously accustomed to celebrating the Mass *versus populum* and have lost the sensibility for exterior signs. So, even if they spend time in adoration and are pious, we have to state objectively, without judging their interior attitude, that they and their piety and devotion have an objective defect because they have lost the sensibility even for the natural religious law of the common direction of a worshipping assembly in public prayer.

Or they never acquired it in seminary . . .

Or they never acquired it, or they lost it, or they never developed in themselves the sense of this necessary correspondence between the inner truth of being turned towards the Lord and being Christ-centered, and the external expression of this truth in the liturgy. They may believe and adore, and may be pious, but in their exterior comportment, they do the opposite: they worship during the Mass in a man-centered manner. Their outward actions and interior piety do not correspond, since they are happy to celebrate *versus populum* and do not feel that something is spiritually and theologically awkward or uncomfortable. So, they have either lost this sensibility for the exterior laws of prayer or have insufficiently cultivated them.

Of course, the majority of the priests in our days never had a healthy traditional liturgical formation in seminary or in their parishes when they were young people, and then later they became priests. So the natural sense of this necessary correspondence between the inner truth and the external expression is evidently not there. We see a contradiction. This sense has atrophied even in pious people. It has to be restored once again, reawakened, revived, so that they might discover the contradiction they lived unconsciously. The true liturgical sense was repressed in them from a false formation or simply through habit.

Your Excellency, I think a lot of priests are terrified that the people (or many of them) will be furious and the bishop will kick them out of the parish and they will never be given a ministry again or they will be ordered not to do it by the bishop and then, even if he hasn't the authority to make the command, he will consider that he is being defied if the priest does not obey. Perhaps thoughts like these flash through the priest's mind, and he is too afraid, but he is ashamed at his fear and so he becomes angry at any suggestion that he celebrate Mass ad orientem, *because he knows it is right and he does not wish to admit his cowardice to himself. Also, offering Mass* ad orientem *might feel like a final definitive acceptance that the Holy See has erred prudentially in the most serious way for many decades and so it would amount to a renunciation of ultramontanism, and this is a frightening step — especially when the authority of the pope has hitherto been the shield of the faithful lower clergy against other heterodox clerics and hierarchs.*

Such fears and ways of behaving for a priest are understandable, since they are very human. It requires in a priest a strong supernatural perspective to look at things *sub specie aeternitatis,* that is, under the aspect of eternity, and always also under the aspect of the truth. More than other people, a priest has to live principally for these two aims: for the truth and for eternity. For the sake of these aims, he must be ready to lose temporal advantages, even in his ecclesiastical career, to lose friends, to be ready for humiliation and marginalization, but also to be so honest and humble that he recognizes his own errors and faults.

In July 2016, Cardinal Sarah, at the Sacra Liturgia Conference in London, invited priests to begin celebrating the Mass ad orientem, *beginning the following Advent, after preparing the faithful through good catechesis. The Vatican does not often speak quickly about issues but within a few days a correction was issued. Given the swiftness of the Vatican's response, it seems that someone is very concerned about priests celebrating* ad orientem. *My sense is that it's precisely on the level of experience, because most of the faithful have not experienced worship* ad orientem, *and most priests have not done it either. My guess is that, were priests and faithful to experience it consistently over a somewhat prolonged period, it would awaken in them the sense of how we should be worshipping—and they wouldn't want to go back. I think certain forces in the Church know that experiencing the Mass celebrated* ad orientem *opens the way to losing the battle against tradition that they have been fighting for decades. Once people turn to the Lord in earnest, it's over for the "progressives."*

I completely agree with you, and I thank you for this observation. In my mind, it is exactly this way.

When the Three Magi came to Jerusalem, they asked: "Where is he who has been born king of the Jews? For we have seen his star in the East and have come to worship him" (Mt 2:2). And what was the immediate consequence? Herod and all of Jerusalem were "troubled." They were afraid and uncomfortable: you have to give worship and adoration to a king? When those bishops and priests—and even some key persons in the Vatican—reacted swiftly against the proposal of Cardinal Sarah, I was suddenly reminded of the similar reaction of Herod and of the priests and scribes in Jerusalem. "They were troubled" (cf. Mt 2:3).

And so it is. These prelates in high positions were troubled, because they would lose the element of anthropocentrism. Man likes to be adored, to be paid homage, instead of Christ. Unfortunately, bishops and cardinals have grown accustomed over the past fifty or sixty years to being the center of attention in the liturgy, in the worldly sense of the position of a showman. Therefore, when they have to turn towards the Lord, their face will only rarely be seen during the Mass, and this troubles them, because the clerical showman loses his joy when he is not continuously seen and admired by the audience. During the celebration *versus Deum*, the priest's face is not seen, it is veiled, and the main attention has to be given not to him, but to another, namely to Christ.

They say, "Well, I speak about Christ and the priest is a second Christ, an *alter Christus*." Here they introduce yet another counterargument, a cunning and deceitful abuse of the theological truth that the priest is an *alter Christus*. They claim that in the Mass people have to see continuously the face of the priest and therefore he has to celebrate towards the people. This is a lie because he is not "another Christ" always and in each of his liturgical acts and words—even though he has in his soul the indelible character of the priesthood, which he received in his ordination. The priest acts *in persona Christi* in the strict sense of the phrase only when he pronounces the sacramental words (*forma sacramenti*), particularly the words of absolution of sins in the sacrament of penance and the words of consecration in the Mass. When a priest preaches, for example, he is not speaking *in persona Christi*, otherwise each of his words would be Christ's words and therefore would be infallible.

Only in those limited moments.

Yes, in those limited moments. Otherwise, he could go through the streets and say, "I am another Christ; please, kneel down! Everything I do throughout my day is done as an *alter Christus*." But this would be nonsensical and bizarre. By saying that the priest has to celebrate *versus populum*—because the people have to see him, since he is an *alter Christus*—we implicitly make the priest to be a kind of Eucharistic species that veils Christ. We compare him in some way to the Eucharistic species, which we expose for veneration. But the Real Presence of Christ under the veil of the Eucharistic species is not the same as the theological truth of the priest being "another Christ." The priest's face is not the Eucharistic veil and therefore it does not have to be continuously seen during Mass. Some advocates of the *versus populum* celebration use this theologically specious argument, and they behave unconsciously as if they themselves are a perpetual exposition of the Blessed Sacrament. "Look at me: I am here as Christ."

This is theologically incorrect and is pastorally, liturgically, and practically misleading, making the priest a kind of guru.

Many people who have grown accustomed to the Mass ad orientem, *when they again attend a Mass* versus populum, *have the sense that the priest always facing them becomes a distraction.*

This is true. We are corporeal, bodily. The priest is only a channel, only a voice, and he has to behave like John the Baptist: "I must decrease, that Christ may increase." Or: "I am only the friend of the Bridegroom." The priest has to be like John the Baptist, and not take the place of Christ, the Bridegroom, as the source of the liturgy.

I remember a very wise old lady in Kazakhstan who suffered persecution during the time of the underground Church. Afterwards, when freedom had come, many priests came from abroad to Kazakhstan, bringing with them their own style of celebration. Unfortunately, some of them introduced a style of placing themselves at the center. One day this old lady said in a conversation with the bishop, "I see three kinds of priests: the one, who is in front and hiding Christ in the liturgy with his own face and with his personality, and this is not a true priest; the other, who stands with Jesus at his side, placing himself on the same level, and this too is not correct; but the true priest stands hidden behind Christ and hides his own face, such that Christ is the center." This is the law of the liturgy, and this is a very wise observation of a simple woman who lived during the persecution and perceived with the instinct of faith that, with a *versus populum* celebration, something is going wrong.

To celebrate the Holy Mass *versus Deum*, as it is celebrated in the old liturgy, is exactly as the old woman said — the priest has to be behind Christ and in some way hidden. In the old liturgy, when the priest veils his face by turning toward the altar, toward the crucifix, during the entirety of the Eucharistic prayer, the people do not see his face. Rather, they see the "sign" of the priest, which conveys the truth that he is the *representative* of Christ. He is vested not in ordinary vestments, but in beautiful vestments, and these are all signs of the supernatural.

I think that since even the angels veil their faces, we should imitate the angels (e.g., Isaiah 6:2).

All of this reinforces the centrality of Christ and the love and worship we owe Him.

When we prostrate ourselves in the liturgy ... even these gestures were observed in the Gospel: people came and prostrated themselves before Christ. In the heavenly liturgy portrayed in the Apocalypse of St. John, the angels and the twenty-four elders prostrate themselves, they lower themselves and, in some way, disappear in order to give honor to God and to the Lamb (Rev 7:11). The same gesture appeared in the first centuries in the liturgy.

In the Latin liturgy, we have kept the gesture of the total bodily prostration in the Good Friday liturgy, at the beginning of the liturgy when the priest, deacon, and subdeacon prostrate themselves. Prior to the 1955 reform of the liturgy of Holy Week, the sacred ministers also prostrated themselves during the first part of the Litany of the Saints in the Easter and Pentecost Vigils. This gesture is also observed during ordinations and solemn religious profession while the Litany of Saints is sung. This is a profound gesture, a gesture of the New Testament and of the liturgy of the heavenly Jerusalem, the final liturgy. We have to imitate this attitude. Celebration towards the Lord is in some way an expression of this prostrating attitude, as the priest's face is not seen. This is true not only, as we discussed, from the point of view of a gesture that expresses the theological truth of being towards the Lord, but it is the law of prayer, which, I repeat, was already present in the Old Testament and even in natural religion.

Our Lady prayed in this way in the temple when she visited it with St. Joseph and the Child Jesus every year. All were turned toward the Holy of Holies. It would be unimaginable for the Holy Family and for the Apostles to be turned in a circle while praying in the temple or in the synagogue. It would have been a blasphemy to turn their backs to the Torah scrolls in the synagogue. The Jews in their houses, when they prayed together, turned toward the Temple in Jerusalem and so did the Holy Family in Nazareth. The Holy Family prayed the Psalms as a family, turning together in the same direction toward the Temple. We have God's own example of how to pray, and the Church kept this throughout two millennia.

What other elements would you see as essential to implementing the Reform of the Reform?

As a second step in the process of the Reform of the Reform, we have to restore the reception of Holy Communion kneeling and on the tongue, as we have discussed. Elements of the traditional Mass should be introduced into the *Novus Ordo*, initially *ad libitum* — for example, the prayers at the foot of the altar, which help the priest and the faithful to enter the sanctuary of the Holy Mass in the right spirit. The double *Confiteor* at the beginning of the traditional form of the Mass is also very pedagogical and spiritually helpful. A few years ago, I visited a Congregation of religious sisters and religious priests in Africa, who were under the Pontifical Commission *Ecclesia Dei* and hence used the traditional form of the liturgy. The Sisters run a boarding school for girls and the priests have a minor seminary. I celebrated Holy Mass for each of the communities. At the Mass, the entire school of girls participated, and in the other Mass the entire minor seminary of boys. The Holy Mass was celebrated in the form of a *Missa dialogata* (dialogue Mass), which is more fitting to the mentality of the African people. I was moved when the entire assembly recited loudly and intelligibly the words, "*Misereatur tui omnipotens Deus et dimissis peccatis tuis . . .*"— *tuis*, "may God forgive *you* your sins." I heard the loud voices of the children, praying for me in Latin, "May God forgive *you* your sins." I was moved to tears hearing the voices of these innocent children as they were publicly and solemnly praying for me, a sinner.

"Out of the mouths of babes..." (Mt 21:16).

Yes, I remembered these words of Our Lord in the Gospel. First, I confessed to the children, calling them brothers, and saying "I confess to you," *vobis fratres, quia peccavi nimis,* "that I have sinned grievously." Then they confessed to me and said, "I confess to you, Father," *et tibi, Pater.* This has to move anyone who still has even a little religious or supernatural sense. Why not reintroduce the double *Confiteor* at the beginning into the Holy Mass in all Catholic churches? I think that in the future the double *Confiteor*, i.e., the *Confiteor* recited first by the celebrant alone and then by the altar servers or the entire community of the faithful, must be compulsory because it is so profoundly pedagogical and spiritually rich. This is the spirit of a family, where the father confesses his sins, publicly — I do not mean in detail — before his children and then the children to their father. This is an expression of the truth that the Church is at the same time a community and a hierarchy, as St. Paul said, "You are all one in Christ" (Gal 3:28) and "Just as the body is one and has many members, and all the members of the body, though many, are one body, so it is with Christ" (1 Cor 12:12). The double *Confiteor* also reminds us of the words of the Apostle St. James: "Confess your sins one to another" (Jas 5:16).

The new rite of the Mass partly obfuscated the truth of the hierarchically structured Mystical Body of Christ, which has to be reflected in the rite of the Mass. In the new Mass, the priest and the faithful pray the *Confiteor* together without distinction. To put the priest and the faithful on the same level is a kind of Protestant way of thinking and does not correspond to apostolic, hierarchical, Catholic thinking.

And the Offertory prayers from the traditional Mass: would you reintroduce these into the Novus Ordo?

Absolutely. The Reform of the Reform has to reintroduce all the theologically profound and beautiful prayers of the Offertory, which have been used in the Roman rite for more or less a thousand years. Their use became compulsory with the Missal of Pius V in 1570. The traditional Offertory prayers were contained in several missals already at the end of the first millennium, as attested to in manuscripts, with various formulations but all with the same spirit. These beautiful old prayers of the Offertory are a kind of foretaste and anticipation — in a symbolic manner — of the unspeakably great moment of the "wonder of wonders" (*miraculum miraculorum*) of the Eucharistic consecration. All Oriental liturgies have this form of anticipation in the Offertory prayers. It is a common tradition of all rites and we must restore this in the new Mass. We cannot remain with the new Offertory prayers, which are alien to the entire tradition of the Catholic liturgy.

The new Offertory prayers are alien? In what sense?

They are alien. They were invented at the table of Father Annibale Bugnini's commission. They were taken from the rite of the Jewish Shabbat supper. However, in Holy Mass we are not celebrating a Jewish Shabbat supper. We are not even perpetuating the Last Supper. No! During Holy Mass, and concretely during the double consecration, Golgotha is sacramentally and really present. Therefore, the Offertory prayers have to express already in an anticipatory manner the mystery of the Sacrifice of Calvary. The Church was always aware of celebrating the Sacrifice of the Cross in the liturgy of the Mass.

Also, as Cardinal Ratzinger and Cardinal Sarah stressed, the Eucharistic prayer, the *Canon Missae*, has to be recited or prayed silently, or at least in a low tone of voice, in order to give an atmosphere of contemplation and adoration during the most holy moments of the sacramental actualization of the supreme Sacrifice. These are truly the most holy moments man can experience here on earth.

If all of these elements of the traditional Mass — celebration *ad Deum*, Communion received kneeling and on the tongue, the prayers at the foot of the altar with the double *Confiteor*, the traditional Offertory prayers, the Canon in silence — were inserted into the new Mass, we would have already restored the liturgy of all ages to a large extent.

In future, the restored liturgy of the Roman rite should, of course, have only one Eucharistic Prayer, i.e., the Roman Canon.

And the sign of peace? In 2008, it was reported that Pope Benedict was considering placing it before the Offertory in order to "create a moment of reflection while we prepare for communion."

The sign of peace, in the form usually practiced in the new Mass, is a very sad liturgical novelty because it destroys the sense of contemplation and recollection and concentration on Christ immediately before Holy Communion. This new form is distracting and noisy and introduces a worldly atmosphere which is alien to spirit of the liturgy. It gives the liturgy an element of informality and banality. We have to abolish this irreverent form of the sign of peace. It is not necessary for the entire assembly to perform the rite of peace. It is sufficient that the clergy at the altar perform it on behalf of the assembly, and it should be done in a reverent and worthy manner, as it is in the older use of the Roman rite (*usus antiquior*), where the priest and the liturgical assistants embrace each other in an ordered, reserved, and recollected manner. The faithful — seeing this worthy and sacred manner of exchanging peace — can nourish in their souls the attitude of peace and love towards their neighbor. We could imagine, as a possible exterior form of the faithful giving each other the peace of the Lord, that one could turn slightly and discreetly toward one's neighbor and make a slight bow without speaking and without touching him. However, this should not be done at every Mass, but only on special and solemn occasions.

Do you think it is enough to incorporate these elements into the new Mass, or do you believe that the Novus Ordo *should eventually be abolished?*

I do not think it is realistic to abolish the *Novus Ordo*. You cannot accomplish this on such a large scale. We have to restore the constant traditional form of the Mass step by step, in a substantially organic manner. We cannot make another rupture but need to do it organically. Only those things that are absolutely necessary should be imposed in all Catholic churches of the Roman rite by pontifical authority: celebration *ad Deum* and Communion kneeling and on the tongue. The other elements I mentioned should be added as a choice, as a recommendation. In this way they would spread organically and naturally, and after some decades would already be so widespread that they could be made compulsory.

Decades, then. Would you see the Ordinary and Extraordinary Forms of the Mass still coexisting, with elements added to the Novus Ordo?

Yes, I think that both forms of the Mass will coexist for a considerable period of time. The new Mass in time by organic steps will come ever closer and closer to the Old Mass, not completely identical, but very close. So, we will have again one Roman rite with only some slightly different options: the Roman rite of the *usus antiquior*, and the Roman rite in the more recent use. Indeed, before the Council we had several variations of the Roman rite, as for example the uses of the diocese of Lyons, of Braga, of the Orders — the Carmelites, Carthusians, Dominicans. Nothing stands against the coexistence of similar liturgical forms or uses in the same ritual family. It would be an enrichment.

What are your thoughts on the liturgical calendar? Some would like to see the calendar of the Old Rite updated to include new saints and feasts.

On the question of the calendar, we must restore one common calendar. There is no doubt. This also has to be done step by step. But it has to be based on the traditional calendar because the new one is not pedagogical, and too academic. The new calendar does not correspond to the long, continuous, and proven tradition of the Church.

The new lectionary, too, has come under increasing criticism in recent years.

The three-year cycle of readings is too academic and overstraining; with the three-year cycle we have made the liturgy a biblical academy. That is not what liturgy is, and so the three-year cycle is unpedagogical. We have to restore the one-year cycle, the Dominical cycle, because the Church had this tradition of the Sunday Gospels since at least the fifth century. All generations of Catholics of the Roman rite for fifteen hundred years heard the same Gospels on the same Sundays. We cannot simply jettison it. We have to restore this common tradition of Latin Christianity.

Pedagogical experience teaches us: it is better to hear fewer but more essential passages of the Bible. The faithful who assist at Sunday Mass are not scribes or students at a biblical institute. We have to know the essential passages of the Bible, and this is well provided for in the one-year cycle. The Mass is not the liturgy of biblical readings; that is another liturgy, the Liturgy of the Hours, the Breviary, the Divine Office. This is the primary liturgy for praying and reading the Bible: psalms, biblical readings, and commentaries by the Fathers.

The Holy Mass is essentially sacrificial adoration and not in the first place a time for biblical instruction and study. In the traditional liturgy, the first part of the Mass was called the "Mass of the Catechumens"; it had a predominantly catechetical character. However, the essence of the Holy Mass is sacrifice. In order to instruct the faithful in the basic truths of the Word of God and the doctrine of faith, the ancient one-year cycle suffices. A continuous reading of the Bible in the Roman tradition is provided for in the Liturgy of the Hours, particularly Matins or the Office of Readings. The Church as a whole performed this continual reading of the Bible in Matins — not, however, all of the faithful, since the ordinary faithful are usually not able to absorb and mentally digest a great and diversified amount of biblical information in the brief span of the liturgical celebration. It is sufficient for them to hear the essential passages of the Gospel and other books of Scripture.

Priests, and monks and nuns in monasteries, pray the Liturgy of the Hours. Many lay faithful also pray the Breviary. The Liturgy of the Hours is the Liturgy of the Word *par excellence*. The Mass is essentially the liturgy of the Sacrifice. Yes, it contains as an integral part the proclamation of the Word of God, but this proclamation is subordinated to the sacrificial part of the Mass, as the purely spiritual and symbolic presence of God in the written word of Holy Scripture is subordinated to the real and incarnational presence of God in the sacrament of the Eucharist. In a certain sense, we could compare the first part of the Mass, the Mass of the Catechumens, to the Old Testament, and the sacrificial part of the Mass, the Mass of the Faithful, to the New Testament. The entire Mass is ultimately the Liturgy of the Word — the Word of God *made flesh*. The Liturgy of the Word in the sense of the written word of God, Holy Scripture, is realized as such primarily in the Divine Office, in the Breviary. Therefore, the first part of the Mass should not be called the "Liturgy of the Word," as it is now called in the new Mass. In both East and West, the first part of the Mass was always called the "Mass of the Catechumens."

Why was it called that?

Because the aim of the first part of the Mass is not to inculcate biblical literacy as such, but rather, to offer a basic instruction on the creed, on the faith. Therefore, specific suitable chapters of the Bible were chosen, and they were sufficient for instruction and adapted to the mental capacity of the common faithful to absorb the biblical texts.

Originally, when adults were being prepared for baptism, they had to participate in the first part of the Mass, and then they had to leave the church! Then the Mass of the Faithful began, with only those who were baptized. The Holy Mass as a whole is the Liturgy of the Word, of the Word made Flesh, made Eucharist, made Sacrifice. Naming only the first part of the Mass "Liturgy of the Word" is a theological and liturgical reductionism, since it reduces the dimension of the Word of God to the first part of the Mass and moreover reduces the expression "Word of God" to the written form. If they *had* to change the terms, the liturgical reformers should consequently have named the first part of the Mass "liturgy of the written Word" or "liturgy of the Holy Scripture," or "liturgy of the Bible." The liturgy of the WORD, written in capital letters, is the liturgy of the Sacrifice because of the Word-made-flesh. The Word-made-flesh became the universal redeeming sacrifice on the Cross, and His immolated Body and Blood become truly present, incarnate under the veils of the sacramental species on the altar. In this context we have to recall the precise theological expression of St. Thomas Aquinas in his hymn *Pange lingua*: "The Word-made-flesh makes, through the word, the true bread flesh" (*Verbum caro panem verum verbo carnem efficit*).

Therefore, calling the first part of the Mass "Liturgy of the Word" is confusing, because it takes a Protestant approach which sees the true liturgy as the word, i.e., the Scripture. By "word," the Protestant *sola scriptura* theory means the written word, the Bible, and not the Incarnate Word in the Sacrament. For Protestants, there is no Blessed Sacrament, no authentic liturgy; there are only words to be pronounced and to be read. Of course, they believe that the Word was made Flesh, but for them this is a singular past historical event, and the Church with her sacraments has no incarnational dimension. There is a danger in the reformed liturgy that the so-called "Liturgy of the Word" and the "Liturgy of the Eucharist" are put on the same level — they are "two tables," as is frequently said today. There is, indeed, an expression in St. Augustine which says that in the first part of the Mass, God nourishes us with His Word on one table, and that in the second part of the Mass He nourishes us with His Body and Blood on the table of the Eucharist. However, in using this analogy St. Augustine is stressing the aspect of the spiritual nourishment which God provides for the faithful during the Mass. For St. Augustine, nourishment with the Eucharist is fuller and more perfect, as his commentary on the episode of the disciples of Emmaus shows, when he writes: "They know Christ in the breaking of bread. It isn't every loaf of bread, you see, but the one that receives Christ's blessing and becomes the body of Christ. That's where they recognized Him. They were overjoyed and went straight to the others" (*Sermo* 234, 2). And, "Where did the Lord wish to be recognized? In the breaking of bread.... It was for our sake that He didn't want to be recognized anywhere but there, because we weren't going to see Him in the flesh, and yet we were going to eat His flesh" (*Sermo* 235, 3).

The Eucharistic celebration in the strict sense stands above the biblical reading service. Putting both parts of the Mass almost on the same level with the expression "two tables" objectively leads to the perception that the second part of the Mass, the Eucharist, is substantially a table service or has the same liturgical and spiritual value as the first part of the Mass.

The Liturgy of the Eucharist is oftentimes much shorter than the Liturgy of the Word...

Yes, your observation is true. The aforementioned expression is dangerous because it puts the presence of Christ in the written word and His presence in the Eucharistic sacrament at the same level. Furthermore, similar to Protestant theories, it reduces the second part of the Mass to a table service. The moment of receiving Holy Communion is the true "table-moment" in the Mass at the Communion rail, which in some languages is called "the table of the Lord." However, the essence, the central component of the whole Mass, which is the Liturgy of the Word-made-flesh, is the Eucharistic Prayer, the Consecration, the Sacrifice. The first part has to be subordinate to the second part; it has to be lesser in meaning and importance, even in terms of time. The dividing of the Mass into two liturgies, i.e., "the Liturgy of the Word" and "the Liturgy of the Eucharist," or the "two tables" of the Mass, represents a shift toward a different theological understanding and is indeed much closer to the Protestant understanding, rather than to the apostolic and catholic tradition of the ages.

In the traditional order of readings in the Mass, only the season of Lent had special readings for every day. During the rest of the year, there are no daily readings; only for the feasts of saints are there specific readings. Generally, the ordinary people do not go to Mass every day, and the Church is very maternal and says, "We cannot oblige all the faithful to go to daily Mass all year long, so they will not hear the continuous readings." But those faithful who are more zealous can pray the Breviary and there one will find the continuous readings. It is very pedagogical. However, once a year, there is a special school of virtue: Lent. During this liturgical season, the Church invites her children to come every day to Mass. It is a school for virtue. That is why she provides daily readings for Lent. It is so pedagogical. But I would not introduce daily readings during the entire year. It is spiritually so healthy and pedagogically wise to repeat sometimes during the week the beautiful Epistle and Gospel of the previous Sunday. One could also highlight the time of Advent as a special time of spiritual recollection in providing daily liturgical readings. This could be a suggestion for a future reform of a common order of biblical readings for both forms of the Roman rite.

And sometimes one forgets what the Sunday Gospel was. But if one hears it again during the week, one reflects on it again. It is very conducive to a more contemplative life.

After the Council, stress was placed on contemplating the Word and even engaging in *lectio divina*, which means to "chew" on the Word of God. You have to read the same words again and again, and then reflect once more. So, it is a beautiful practice during the week to "chew" on the Word of God again. Therefore, it is not necessary to have different readings every day in "Ordinary Time." In the traditional liturgy, when there is a feast of a saint, even a simple feast (of the third class), one must take the Epistle and Gospel of the saint, usually from one of the Commons — Martyrs, Virgins, Doctors, Bishops, Holy Women, and so forth. Unfortunately, in the new Mass, on the day of an obligatory memorial of a saint, one does not have to take the readings from the Commons of Saints but can instead take the continuous readings of the liturgical season. Often there is no harmony between these readings and the character of the saint who is celebrated in the Mass. In the old calendar, you have at least two or three times a week a saint with his or her appropriate readings, as well as room for votive Masses. And so, in practice, the repetition of the Sunday readings was not excessive.

To conclude regarding the reform of the liturgical calendar: more choices could be offered for biblical readings for the feasts of the saints. In this way the lectionary of the traditional Mass and calendar could be somewhat enriched, which was also the intention of the Liturgical Constitution of the Second Vatican Council, *Sacrosanctum Concilium*. In general, we should strive to have a common calendar for the *Vetus Ordo* and the *Novus Ordo*, based on the old calendar, with some meaningful new feasts which the new calendar offers.

What are your thoughts regarding the place of Latin in the liturgy?

It was always a law, in the Old Testament and in other religions, to have a sacred language. Islam has Classical Arabic in all countries without exception. The Jews until the time of Jesus had a sacred language for the liturgy because they had to use Hebrew in the Psalms and prayers in the synagogue and Temple, not the common Aramaic language, which Our Lord spoke, and which was used during the day. Even Our Lord and the Apostles observed the principle of a sacred language. They had the Targum, the commentaries on the Holy Scriptures, which were read in the synagogues after the Bible, which was read in the Hebrew language. Not everyone understood Hebrew well, and so the rabbis read it, translating into the Aramaic language, the common daily language. This shows us that there has to be a liturgical language. To celebrate the entire liturgy in the vernacular, in the daily language of the street and the newspapers, is contrary to all religious experience and the constant Tradition of the Church.

We have to restore the principle of a sacred language, because this is also expressive of the truth that God is an ineffable mystery. He cannot be expressed in words. The Latin language is a tool for expressing the truth that we cannot totally comprehend God with our intellect, and that He remains a mystery. The lack of a sacred language is a sign of the intellectualization of public worship. In one's private prayer, everyone speaks with God in his mother tongue, but when we speak in public worship and the cult of God, we speak publicly about the truth of God, who is an ineffable mystery — a mystery which is fascinating but cannot be expressed, an awesome and fascinating mystery: *mysterium tremendum et fascinosum*. "God is a consuming fire" (Heb 12:29): this is written not in the Old Testament, but in the New Testament. We therefore have to veil the mystery of God, also with a liturgical and sacred language.

However, after the Council the Latin Rite almost completely lost its sacred language. This is contrary to the entire Christian and Old Testament tradition and that of all religions, and it is contrary to the intention and the letter of Vatican II (see *Sacrosanctum Concilium*, n. 36 and n. 54). The Second Vatican Council had a balanced approach, stating that the vernacular had to be given a space in the liturgy: a wider extension, a wider usage, which can be interpreted in different ways. This "wider usage" led to an almost exclusive use of the vernacular, which goes against the Council. We therefore have to restore this balanced manner of using the vernacular and, as the Council said, the vernacular should be used

only in those parts which are didactical, meaning the first part of the
Mass, the Mass of the Catechumens. It could be used more there. But
when the mystery as such, the sacrifice, is expressed, it is fitting to use
Latin. We have to return to it at least there.

*There was also a multiplication of Eucharistic Prayers after the Second
Vatican Council.*

In the Reform of the Reform, I think we have to make it compulsory for the entire Roman rite Church to pray only one Eucharistic
prayer — that is, the Roman Canon. It is a characteristic feature of the
Roman rite to have only one Eucharistic prayer. When we introduce
several Eucharistic prayers, we destroy the essential character of the
Roman liturgy. The Oriental Rites sometimes have several Eucharistic
prayers (called "anaphoras"), but they are Oriental. We cannot get mixed
up. This is the beauty of the Church: the riches of several rites, which
conserve their original, essential characteristics. A characteristic in the
Roman rite is to have one Eucharistic prayer: the Canon. It is a parallel
of the canon of faith, the Symbol of Faith (*canon fidei*). In the liturgy
of the Mass in the Roman rite we have only one Symbol of Faith; we
do not have, on alternating Sundays, Creed 1, Creed 2, Creed 3, and so
on. We have to return to one Eucharistic prayer in the entire Roman
rite Church, entirely in Latin, and in silence — or at least in a subdued
tone — to express the mystery in a more fitting manner.

*Returning to the question of Latin in the liturgy, what parts of the new
Mass would it be essential to restore to Latin?*

To preserve the unity of the entire Roman Church, in the new Mass
there have to be Latin expressions used in all churches around the world.
The Eucharistic prayer — which begins with the Preface and ends with the
Per ipsum et cum ipso — ought to be in Latin in all Roman rite Catholic
churches of the world, making it common among all different languages
and peoples. At least this has to be always in Latin, along with the short
initial dialogue: *Dominus vobiscum* through *Dignum et justum est*. It is
not too much to expect of all people around the world. Even the simplest
people are able to learn these short responses.

*Often, the laity seem to be treated like little children who can't develop to
their potential because nothing is expected of them. I am reminded of the*

discussion a few years ago over the new English translation of the Mass. One bishop in the United States said we shouldn't use the word "consubstantial" because it's too much to expect the laity to understand it. If you speak to a child as a baby forever, he or she will never develop a rich vocabulary. It completely underestimates his potential and is a huge disservice. In a similar way, in the case of the liturgy, are we also doing a great disservice to young people and adults?

As I said earlier, when I was in Africa the little children responded *in perfect Latin*, even the articulation was beautiful. I was moved when I heard the little boys from the school there say, in perfect Latin, slowly the *Confiteor*, the *Misereatur*, the *Suscipiat Dominus*. These African children can speak better Latin than some priests, better than some bishops today in the Church. Even bishops, I say! Some bishops cannot pronounce liturgical Latin properly. It is not a condemnation of them, because they simply were not taught it in the seminary. So, when people travel, at least when hearing some Latin expressions during Mass, they will feel at home, because these are the same expressions they learned and use at home.

We should also foster the use of Gregorian chant throughout the entire Church in the new Mass, which was also the desire of the Second Vatican Council, but which, unfortunately, for the most part is not observed. It could be made a general law of the Church that cathedrals, basilicas, important shrine churches, and big city parishes must, at least once a month, have a Sunday Mass completely in Latin (with the exception of the lectionary of course), and that the Ordinary be in Gregorian chant. This would already spread the use of Latin throughout the entire Church over time. After two generations, the majority of Catholics in the world would know some minimal responses in Latin and some Gregorian chant.

Your Excellency, why do you think the traditional Latin Mass is drawing an increasing number of young people, young families, and particularly young men? Why is the traditional Mass so attractive to them?

The traditional Latin Mass is truly the Mass of all ages and of all Catholic generations, not in the sense of every little ritual detail, but regarding its essential characteristics. It is the Mass of all ages because of the fact that its rite expresses in a clearer and more beautiful manner the essential truth of the sacrifice of Mass, i.e., the adoration of God the

Father, which Jesus Christ, His Incarnate Son, offered on the Cross in the name of the whole of creation in the power of the Holy Spirit. The Holy Mass with its rite should reflect, as much as humanly possible, the awe and beauty of the worship that is offered to the Most Holy Trinity by the Church Triumphant in heaven.

God has inscribed in the human soul a deep longing for truth and beauty. The purer a human soul is, and the more it is filled with the graces of faith, the more spontaneously is it attracted by supernatural truth and supernatural beauty. Therefore, the pure souls of innocent children, the sincere souls of young people, the souls of simple faithful people, of souls who are not yet contaminated by the clerical ideology of anthropocentrism in the liturgy, are drawn by the magnetism of truth, order, and beauty that radiates from the traditional Latin Mass.

Young people feel in the depths of their souls that they are born for a higher ideal, even for heroism. The style of the Novus Ordo Mass, with its significantly reduced sacredness and ritual beauty, instead transmits mediocrity. Young people who really believe are not attracted by mediocrity. The rite of the traditional Latin Mass also transmits a clear hierarchical order and even in some way the solemnity of a military discipline, characteristics which especially attract young men.

It is an undeniable fact that, at least since the publication of Benedict XVI's epochal motu proprio *Summorum Pontificum*, the traditional Latin Mass has increasingly become the Mass of youth. *Introibo ad altare Dei: ad Deum qui laetificat iuventutem meam,* "I will go unto the altar of God, to God who giveth joy to my youth." These words of Psalm 42, which are recited at the beginning of the traditional Latin Mass, proclaim a fact we can all see and rejoice in: the traditional Latin Mass is drawing an increasing number of young people, young families, and particularly young men.

And yet this groundswell of interest is often met with incomprehension, coolness, or outright hostility.

The pope and bishops of our day should listen to the growing voice of young people who ask for a restoration of the living and venerable world of supernatural truth and sublimity which is the traditional Latin Mass. The call of young people could be paraphrased in the following words: "Now we know and love the liturgical treasure of our Mother the Church, the treasure of which we have been deprived!"

Of Pope Benedict's motu proprio *Summorum Pontificum,* German novelist Martin Mosebach writes: "Against overwhelming opposition he opened a floodgate. Now the water has to flow, and no one who holds the liturgy to be an essential component of the Faith can dispense himself from this task. The liturgy IS the Church — every Mass celebrated in the traditional spirit is immeasurably more important than every word of every pope. It is the red thread that must be drawn through the glory and misery of Church history; where it continues, phases of arbitrary papal rule will become footnotes of history.... The totality of the progressive claims has been broken — that is the work of Pope Benedict XVI."[1]

Today, the revival of the traditional Latin Mass is mostly carried out by younger clergy, by young people, and by young families. This is an encouraging sign of hope in the midst of a general liturgical catastrophe. The traditional liturgy of our Mother the Church is invincible; it has nothing to fear from any catastrophe.

---

[1] Martin Mosebach, *The Heresy of Formlessness: The Roman Liturgy and Its Enemy,* trans. Graham Harrison (Brooklyn: Angelico Press, 2018), 188.

16

Reform of the Clergy

Your Excellency, you have said that renewal will come through a return to Our Eucharistic Lord, and through formation of Catholic families and chaste priests with an ardent zeal for the salvation of souls. This seems to presuppose a large-scale reform of bishops and clergy. How would you advise a pope regarding the appointment of bishops?

The pope has to choose bishops very carefully, for bishops have so much influence. They can form an entire generation, or generations, of a diocese in a good or bad way. This has become abundantly evident over the last fifty or sixty years. An unsuitable bishop can spiritually destroy a diocese for generations. So, a bishop first has to be a man of God. I do not mean that he has to be a candidate for beatification, but he has to be a man of God, in that he must first be a deeply spiritual man. This is for me the basic quality that is required: he must a deeply spiritual man. He has to live a life of prayer. When a candidate does not faithfully live a life of prayer, with a love of the Mass, the Breviary, and personal prayer, he is not suitable for the episcopacy. He may be a good priest, but as a bishop he has to be an example for his priests and his people as a man of God. So, he must be a prayerful man, a spiritual man.

The second quality required is the purity and integrity of orthodox doctrine and morals. This has to be the second quality. I stress this: he must be one hundred percent orthodox, faithful to the entire doctrinal and moral tradition of the Church, without compromise and without ambiguity. He has to be a proven faithful advocate and promoter of the purity and integrity of the Catholic faith and morals. As it is said in the Roman Canon: *una cum famulo tuo Papa nostro et Antistite nostro et omnibus orthodoxis atque catholicæ et apostolicæ fidei cultoribus*, i.e., those who cultivate — that is the bishops — the apostolic and Catholic and orthodox faith.

The third quality a bishop must possess is a good character and freedom from serious character defects — that is, he has to be very balanced on a human level, since *gratia supponit naturam*. Here we have to observe nature. Besides being a man of prayer and doctrinal orthodoxy, he has to be a man of balanced character, without complexes and without psychological problems.

One would hope that bishops would not have psychological problems.

I mean especially in character. For example, there cannot be a tendency to tyranny or careerism. Some are pious and orthodox, but they have tyrannical and despotic characters. We cannot take them as candidates for the episcopacy. It should be out of the question, even when they are orthodox, if there are evident character complexes. On the natural level, there has to be balance in his character, and he has to be humble. So, we have to seek these candidates and they do exist.

What is true humility for a bishop?

St. Thérèse of the Child Jesus said that humility is courage for the truth and courage to serve. Humility means that in all situations you set aside your ego. In what you do, in how you act, you always have to set your ego aside. Of course, humility always begins in the mind. Humility will lead a priest or bishop to put his ego and his ambitions aside and to put Christ at the center, together with the salvation of souls and the service of souls. To serve, really and truly, not to "seek one's own," as St. Paul says (see Phil 2:21), but to seek the good of the others sincerely. Putting your ego to the side in order to give honor to God, to Christ, is for me how you grow in true humility.

We have to seek such candidates for the episcopacy, and they do exist. Pope St. Gregory the Great was very demanding and exacting in his choice of candidates for the episcopacy, so he was reproached sometimes by bishops for his demanding approach. Pope St. Gregory responded, "There are indeed good candidates. Our Lord said in the Gospel, 'Seek and you will find.' The good candidates for the office of bishops are, however, hidden. Those who are not suitable often present themselves for the episcopal office. I, however, will seek the hidden candidates" (see *In primum librum regum* 6, 85). Seek them and you will find them. We have to seek them out even in our days.

One of the main tasks of the pope is to provide the Church with truly good and spiritual men for the episcopacy. The pope should confirm the bishops and the entire Church in the true Catholic faith and seek out true men of God for the episcopacy. These two tasks are indeed the most important ones: confirming the brothers in the faith and providing the universal Church with spiritual and orthodox bishops. In zealously promoting the catholic and apostolic faith, bishops will then reform and renew the faith of their dioceses for decades and ages to come. This is the best strategy for renewing the Church, even from a human point of view. Therefore, the enemies of the Church, well aware of the vital strategic importance of the episcopacy, succeeded in infiltrating — directly or indirectly — the process of episcopal appointments, especially after the Second Vatican Council. It would be dishonest to deny this fact; the poor quality of too many episcopal and cardinalatial appointments over at least the past fifty years is there for all of us to see.

Popes particularly since Pope John Paul II have spent a considerable amount of time travelling on apostolic journeys.

The pope does not have to travel. He should speak very little and give the bishops the opportunity to exercise their magisterium, since they are teachers of the faith in their dioceses. The pope ought to use his precious time to discretely organize committees for the purpose of researching good candidates for the episcopacy, without yielding to any compromise. Once a good candidate has been chosen, he will likely be attacked at first by those inside and outside the Church, who will insist with much noise that this good bishop be removed. The pope has to support this good bishop and call on the other bishops to do the same, saying to the good bishop when he is under attack, "We will not forsake you, we will protect you, and we will not yield to any pressure."

History has shown that the Holy See has sometimes made political compromises in episcopal appointments.

It is regrettable that, even in our own time, the Holy See has often yielded and sacrificed truly good and holy bishops on the "altar" of political expediency. History and experience have proven time and time again that these compromises do not help the Church to promote the Catholic faith and the kingship of Christ.

If we look back at history, we see that an attitude of political compromise began already in the nineteenth century with Pope Pius VII, when, at Napoleon's request, he deposed almost forty diocesan bishops in France, including numerous zealous shepherds and confessors of the faith. Pius VII should have taken a longer view, since Napoleon's political defeat came only ten years later. Pius IX, on the other hand, did not yield to the pressures of Bismarck, the powerful anticlerical Chancellor of the German Reich. Instead, he uncompromisingly supported the heroic German bishops during the Kulturkampf. The German confessor bishops of the Kulturkampf remain a glorious example in history.

Another sad example of undue political compromise by the Holy See that we touched on earlier was the so-called "Ostpolitik" with the governments of the European Communist countries, especially during the pontificate of Paul VI. The removal of Cardinal Mindszenty as archbishop primate of Hungary, which Paul VI carried out at the request of the Communist Hungarian regime, was a great injustice and remains a shameful disgrace that has stained the honor of the Holy See.

In our own day, we are witnessing the Holy See compromising with the Communist regime in China. Heroic bishops, priests, and faithful of the underground Church are being sacrificed for the sake of the acceptance of regime-backed bishops — who include political opportunists. In reflecting on this, I am reminded of the motto of Pope Gregory VII: the Church must be *casta et libera*, "chaste and free." He labors so that "the holy Church, the bride of God, our lady and mother, might return to the beauty which is rightly hers and remain free, chaste, and catholic" (*Ep.* 64). A chaste Church maintains the purity of doctrine and the chaste life of the clergy; a free Church maintains her independence from worldly powers in spiritual matters.

Your Excellency, you have mentioned that bishops frequently don't actually teach their people. Why do you think this is the case?

I think that, since the Council, the bishops' teaching office has been somewhat overshadowed by excessive bureaucratization and the multiplication and inflation of papal pronouncements. This is against the sound tradition of the Church and the affirmations of the Second Vatican Council, which wanted to reevaluate the ministry of the episcopacy. The pope has to choose very good candidates for the episcopacy and the cardinalate, without yielding to any compromise. He has to seek out, for the episcopacy and the cardinalate, only true men of God who are faithful beyond any doubt to the tradition of the Church in purity of doctrine, in liturgy, and in moral integrity. The Apostles and Fathers of the Church would never have appointed a bishop out of secular political considerations. Church history has demonstrated this truth convincingly. Indeed, it is better for the Church's missionary efforts and for the spiritual good of souls to have fewer bishops and cardinals than to have doctrinally and spiritually weak and politically correct bishops...

And cardinals, who should be wise counselors to the pope...

Exactly. The electors of a pope should have a profound and apostolic spirit of holiness and fidelity to the constant doctrine of the Church.

How do you believe a future pope should reform the College of Cardinals?

The first task of the pope is to strengthen the whole Church in the doctrine of the faith. When he speaks, the pope must be very careful, sparing, and precise. He should speak rarely, and when he does, he should speak clearly and give more voice to the bishops in their dioceses. The pope ought to use his time to choose good candidates for the episcopacy and to renew his College of Cardinals with really pious men, who are not worldly and are orthodox with a one hundred percent commitment to the Tradition of the Church.

In the future, once the present crisis in the Church is over, the College of Cardinals has to be reduced in number because it will be far more effective when it is smaller. The first criterion for choosing candidates for the cardinalate should not be geographical representation but quality. The Church and the pope should not feel forced into naming candidates from every geographical region. This is an error. It would of course be desirable to have cardinals from every part of the world, but only under the indispensable condition that they are truly suitable candidates. The College of Cardinals is not essentially about geography but about the spiritual quality of men of God who are capable of being counselors to the pope.

What do you think is the key to seminary formation?

Even if the doctrinal formation in seminaries were to be one hundred percent orthodox and faithful to the Tradition of the Church, this means nothing when the moral and ascetic life of young priests and those preparing for the priesthood are not in accord with the spirit of the Gospel, and with the lives of the Apostles and saints. Priests whose moral, ascetic, and spiritual life is lacking will not bear much fruit, even if they have academic degrees, preach Catholic doctrine, and celebrate the liturgy correctly. If the priests are not living a life really in harmony with the ideal of an apostle, they will not bear much fruit. We have to stress this indispensable aspect of holiness of life in the priestly formation of traditional communities, too, since the concern for a beautiful and correct celebration of Holy Mass sometimes overshadows the continual and essential demand for personal sanctity.

How would this best be achieved?

I think that we simply have to propose to seminarians the example of holy priests and recommend to them the timeless papal documents on the priesthood, especially those documents issued from Popes Pius X to John Paul II — in particular his annual letters to priests on Holy Thursday. In these documents one finds doctrinal, ascetical, and practical norms and proposals which are not only theoretical, but also very concrete. I prefer concreteness, because when we talk to seminarians in a general and theoretical way about the duty of the priest to strive for holiness, it is often ineffective. *Verba docent, exempla trahunt*: words teach, examples attract, human experience says.

We have to give seminarians and priests concrete instruction and practical examples of what they have to do on a daily basis, and of what exactly they have to avoid throughout their entire life. Besides the faithful, attentive, and devout praying of the Breviary, they have to be faithful to daily mental prayer or Eucharistic adoration, custody of the eyes, and some form of corporal mortification. Seminarians and priests — like every true Christian — must avoid absolutely any kind of pornography or voluntary watching of immoral films. Every seminarian and priest must lead an intense spiritual life. For this purpose, he must have a spiritual director. Here, for example, we can be grateful for the Personal Prelature of Opus Dei, as it provides a good help in offering spiritual direction for priests.

For a lasting and effective reform of the Church to take root, we need a renewed love for the purity of doctrine, for the glory of Christ in the liturgy and in human society, and for personal holiness in the episcopacy and the papacy, that is, *reformatio ecclesiae in capite et in membris* — the reform of the Church in her head and in her members.

Your Excellency, you have studied deeply the Fathers of the Church. How important do you think it is for seminarians and priests to rediscover the wisdom of the Desert Fathers on the nature of the human heart and the ascetical and interior life?

The Fathers of the Church, and particularly the Desert Fathers, realistically described the state of the human soul, which bears deep spiritual wounds in both intellect and will, as the consequence of original sin. Man's intellect is darkened and his will is weakened. Only the grace of Christ can heal these wounds through the gifts of supernatural illumination for the intellect and the strengthening of the will, so that man can begin to know and rejoice in the truth, and love and long for the true good that is God. However, God requires man's free cooperation and calls him to engage in spiritual warfare, since, in His inscrutable wisdom, God permits Satan and the evil spirits to tempt men.

The Desert Fathers were both experienced psychologists and sure spiritual directors, who highlighted the interdependence between nature and grace. They have left us with very apt instructions for the spiritual battle. It is significant that prominent priestly and episcopal figures among the Fathers of the Church received their spiritual training either with the Desert Fathers or within a monastic community. This was the case with St. Athanasius, whose spiritual master was St. Anthony the Great in the desert. St. Athanasius's biography of St. Anthony was a kind of "bestseller" on spirituality, before the appearance of the *Imitatio Christi* of Thomas à Kempis in the Middle Ages. St. Basil the Great, St. Gregory Nazianzen, and St. John Chrysostom spent many years in a solitary monastic community, as did St. Augustine, St. Jerome, and St. Gregory the Great.

One could say that their seminary training took place in an eremitical and monastic environment. These Church Fathers left us three classic and in some ways unsurpassable treatises on the priesthood: St. Gregory Nazianzen's writing *Apologia de fuga sua* (*Oratio* 2), St. John Chrysostom's work *De sacerdotio*, and St. Gregory the Great's *Regula pastoralis*. According to these Church Fathers, the priest is the main instrument in God's work of the sanctification of men. The care of souls is the "art of arts." Memorable for seminarians in every age are the following words of St. Gregory Nazianzen: "Before a man has, as far as possible, gained superiority over material things, and sufficiently purified his mind, and far surpassed his fellows in nearness to God, I do not think it safe for him to be entrusted with rule over souls, or the office of mediator between God and man, for such, I take it, a priest is"

(*Or.* 2:91). I would summarize the image of the priest according to the Church Fathers with these three characteristics: a priest is an "athlete" of Christ, a man of prayer, and a wholly apostolic man.

In his 11-page testimony released on August 25, 2018, and in subsequent statements, Archbishop Carlo Maria Viganò spoke about the presence of "homosexual networks" in the Vatican and the Church. He was not alone. One week before the release of Archbishop Viganò's initial testimony, now-deceased Bishop Robert C. Morlino of Madison, Wisconsin, issued a letter in which he said that "it is time to admit that there is a homosexual subculture in the hierarchy of the Church." What would you do regarding the "homosexual networks" that appear to have infested the Church?

I personally do not have much proof of this phenomenon. However, the facts that have already been made public about this are conspicuous and very sad. It seems that there is still much more about the clerical homosexual networks that has not yet been brought to public knowledge. Surely, these networks — or the "gay lobby," as it is also called — were not created yesterday. It had to have been cultivated in the life of the Church over many years. The infiltration of homosexual men, i.e., those actually engaging in homosexual activity or with proven homosexual tendencies, into the priesthood and seminaries has brought so much damage to the Church. One of the greatest injuries to the priesthood was the pedophilia crisis. Even in traditional seminaries there have been cases where homosexual seminarians and priests have entered under the mask of piety and love for the traditional liturgy. Those in positions of responsibility for priestly formation have to be very vigilant against homosexual infiltration in seminaries.

Could you say more about this?

Those who are responsible for priestly formation have to be very watchful and dismiss men with proven homosexual tendencies from seminaries, even when such men present high intellectual qualities or piety. I would suggest the issuance of concrete binding norms on the universal level of the Church, about the categorical unsuitability for the priesthood of men with proven homosexual tendencies. In the case when a seminarian, as an adult man, commits external acts of homosexuality or willingly watches homosexual pornography, he must forever be excluded from receiving priestly ordination. It would be complete naïveté to suggest that such seminarians could be healed through professional therapy. We have to consider that they are not minors, but already adults when they commit homosexual acts and watch homosexual pornography. Thanks be to God there are true healings of men with homosexual tendencies. However, such men, even after being healed, sometimes carry in themselves a trauma in their affections and present a lack of psychological stability. The best and surest way for these men who have been healed of homosexuality would be to love and marry a good Christian woman and have their own children. The love of a good wife and the children will, over time, heal such a man and strengthen his psychological stability and his self-esteem. The psychologically demanding pastoral and celibate lifestyle of a priest, however, would be too great a risk for such a healed man. The priesthood is too great and too sacred to be an experimental field for healing men with proven homosexual tendencies. The Church, especially in our days, has already had too many bitter and financially costly experiences of priests with such tendencies. This has enormously damaged the reputation and the sacred mission of the Catholic priesthood.

Your Excellency, in recent decades there has been an increasing effort to normalize homosexuality. At least a generation of young people have been taught through television, film, and social media, as well as by teachers, and at times even parents, that homosexual relationships are normal and one option among many. As you know, this is completely contrary to the Catholic Church's vision of the human person and human sexuality. What is the remedy?

Let us speak frankly on the spiritual and moral plane. Engaging in homosexual activity is patently against nature (*Catechism*, no. 2357), so much so that in the Old Testament God singled out this act as one of a handful of grave sins that cry out for His vengeance (*Catechism*, no. 1867; Gen 18:20–21, 19:13). God deemed it an "abomination," even punishable by death (Lev 18:22, 20:13; Ez 16:50). St. Paul unambiguously denounces homosexual acts as unnatural and notes their attendant grave spiritual consequences (Rom 1:26–28; 1 Cor 6:9; 1 Tim 1:10). This has been the unbroken tradition and teaching of the Church. Beyond its grave sinfulness, homosexual activity is personally self-destructive and detrimental to the moral health of society.

More generally, in European and Christian societies, and in many other places throughout the world, homosexual acts were historically punished because governments viewed these acts as morally contaminating society and constituting a defilement of human dignity. From a purely legal perspective, in every human society, it is inevitable that when you forbid something, people will do it clandestinely, but this is not the issue. Where homosexual acts are prohibited and subject to sanction, the danger of spreading an intrinsic and contagious evil is already reduced. Also, from the pedagogical point of view, such prohibition of homosexual activity more broadly protects vulnerable youth and the moral health of human society.

What sort of "punishment" do you support and what do you not support?

Ideally, there should be a sanction, if you will, that would have pedagogical and preventative characteristics, so as to help these persons to heal from homosexual activity and overcome it. To be clear, I am against imprisonment and any coercive policies, because such punishments will only worsen the moral and spiritual health of these persons. In any case, those in authority could at the same time provide means to help these persons recover the dignity of a lifestyle of "being a man" and "being a woman" according to common sense, according to biological sexual reality, created by the wise will of God. All such measures should be undertaken with discretion, without shaming or publicly exposing these persons. I will leave it to the expert competencies of others to determine how best to implement a legally constructive and remedially effective framework. This, of course, presupposes the existence of a government inspired by Christianity, or at least a government that recognizes the necessity of maintaining the basic order of natural law. Today, we've obviously lost such foundations and so there's much to be regained culturally before such a framework would be plausible.

Your Excellency, what should happen to disgraced clergymen convicted of sexual abuse crimes, like former cardinal Theodore McCarrick?

The ex-cardinal and ex-bishop Theodore McCarrick and other clergy who were reduced to the lay state are ultimately very poor souls, since they must give a detailed account before the divine Judge of all their life and such an account will be grave indeed. In true Christian love for the salvation of a soul, one should really pray that these men receive the grace of deep conversion and contrition, so that they can use the brief time God still grants them here on earth to make acts of reparation and expiation, and with a truly contrite and humble heart publicly beg pardon for all their misdeeds as clerics. May divine mercy triumph also in the personal life of such disgraced clergy. We have to think as Our Lord did: "There will be more joy in heaven over one sinner who repents than over ninety-nine righteous persons who need no repentance" (Lk 15:7).

The working document (Instrumentum Laboris) *for the upcoming synod of bishops for the Amazonian region suggests a relaxation in the discipline of priestly celibacy for the region. Number 129.2 of the working document says: "Affirming that celibacy is a gift for the Church, it is asked that, for the most remote areas of the region, the possibility be studied of priestly ordination for elders, preferably indigenous ones, who are respected and accepted by their community, even though they may already have an established and stable family, in order to ensure the sacraments that accompany and support Christian life." Cardinal Raymond Burke said that "it is not honest" to suggest that the October meeting is "treating the question of clerical celibacy for that region alone."[1] He said that if the synod takes up the question (something he believes it should not do), "it will be treating a discipline of the universal Church." His Eminence also noted that "already a certain bishop in Germany has announced that, if the Holy Father grants a relaxation of the obligation of perfect continence for the clergy in the Amazon region, the bishops of Germany will ask for the same relaxation."*

Yes, it is quite clear that the Amazonian Synod is being used as a cunning pretext to make priestly celibacy optional and ultimately to abolish it. Because in making celibacy optional for diocesan clergy, you abolish celibacy. The supposed sacramental crisis in the Amazon region is the pretext. I hope that the Holy Spirit will intervene and will not permit this to happen. This is my prayer. Or that the pope will clearly reject such proposals. I pray for this.

Some priests have suggested that changing the discipline of celibacy for the Latin clergy would have much more profound and lasting effects than the doctrinal confusion we are now experiencing in the Church.

---

1 Diane Montagna, "Cdl. Burke: Relaxing priestly celibacy for Amazon region would affect universal Church," *LifeSiteNews*, June 20, 2019.

I don't know, it could be. It would change the entire shape of the priesthood of the Latin Church, were rectories suddenly to be filled with priests and their families. That would substantially change the shape of the Catholic Church of the Latin Rite.

The question of contraception and of admitting those who are divorced and living in a second union to Holy Communion is more of an individual phenomenon because there is no witness — they commit these acts, but it is unseen. In other words, unless one knows the private lives and personal history of the people in the parish, we do not know who among those going to Communion is divorced or not, or who is using contraception or not. Of course, allowing contraception and the admittance of adulterers to Holy Communion is objectively more dangerous. But from the point of view of the visible effects, the introduction of married clergy into the Latin Church would also cause great spiritual damage to the Church.

For this reason, I hope the Holy Spirit will enlighten the pope — and it has to be the pope — not to permit this and to issue a declaration once again that the Latin Church will never and cannot change the tradition of the celibate priesthood which the Apostles handed down to us. Even though priestly celibacy is not a dogma, it is so deeply rooted in Christ's own example and in the apostolic tradition that there is no authority in the Church that can legitimately abolish it. A future pope must issue a declaration, valid for every age, shutting out all attempts to abolish priestly celibacy.

There are a lot of studies that prove that the celibate priesthood is not only a Church law but an apostolic tradition. In 1995, Cardinal Alphons Stickler wrote *The Case for Clerical Celibacy: Its Historical Development and Theological Foundations*. Several other well-known studies have also been done, most recently that of Father Stefan Heid, laying out the apostolic origin of priestly celibacy. So we cannot say that "because it is just the Church's law, the pope can change this." The pope has no authority to change the apostolic tradition of priestly celibacy for the entire Church. Indeed, were a pope to introduce an "optional" priestly celibacy or a new category of married Catholic priests in the Latin Rite through the trick of the so-called *viri probati* (approved men), priestly celibacy would de facto be abolished, and an apostolic tradition would be abolished with it.

What is another example of an apostolic tradition that is not dogma?

Infant baptism. The Church cannot forbid infant baptism, as the Protestant group, the Baptists, forbid it. Even so, it is not a dogma of faith that an infant has to be baptized. Infants *should* be baptized, and the Church recommends that little children be baptized. It is not a dogma of faith, but it is an apostolic tradition.

The celibate priesthood is the most fitting and visible realization of the priesthood of Jesus Christ, even in a bodily way, because Christ our High Priest was corporeally virginal. Priestly celibacy stems from the example of Jesus Christ Himself. He offered the sacrifice of His Body and Blood on the Cross being virginal. Therefore, the entire tradition of the Church requires that a priest who offers the Sacrifice of Christ in the Holy Mass should be virginal as well, meaning living in sexual continence.

Oftentimes in the West, we get very caught up in the "discipline" of celibacy or the "law" of celibacy, without seeing the deeper meaning and gift that it is to a priest and to the Church.

This is the incarnational dimension again — the sign, since the priest is *alter Christus*, another Christ. Our Lord Jesus Christ was visibly, corporeally a man and a virgin. The priest must be as another Christ at this level of signs, and so it is more fitting and demanding and necessary that he be a celibate, and in this sense *a virginal priest*.

That is why in the Orthodox and Greek Catholic Church — which have a married priesthood — the night before they celebrate the Divine Liturgy they cannot have sexual relations with their legitimate wife: they have to be celibate at least the day before celebrating the Holy Mass. We see how illogical a married priesthood is, because the priest has to celebrate Mass every day and he is always a priest, day and night; therefore, he has to live always in celibacy.

I remember a conversation I had with a devout old Muslim man on a train in Kazakhstan. I was wearing priestly attire, so the Muslim man recognized me as a Catholic priest and started a conversation on several religious topics. At one point during the conversation, he said to me, "I heard that Catholic priests are unmarried. How long do they have to remain unmarried?" I answered, "They have to remain unmarried for their entire life." The old Muslim was very astonished at my reply and said, "For their entire lifetime? Oh, how I pity you! You are not allowed to have even one wife, whereas we Muslims can have four wives.

Please, explain to me, how it is possible to be unmarried for an entire lifetime!" I briefly thought about it, and answered him, "A Catholic priest is unmarried for life, because he has to belong entirely to God. With his soul and also with his body, day and night, he belongs exclusively to God." To this the old Muslim man replied, "How beautiful this is, to belong exclusively to God day and night! I have never heard this. How beautiful it is!"

Afterward, I was thinking about these words of the old Muslim man, and I said to myself, "This devout old Muslim man is putting to shame so many Catholic priests and bishops who in our days are advocating the weakening of priestly celibacy or who are working to abolish it." I would say to those participants of the Amazonian Synod who advocate the ordination of *viri probati*, i.e., the ordination of sexually active married men: "If you knew what the Catholic priesthood really is, you would never for any reason whatsoever advocate weakening or abolishing the apostolic tradition of priestly celibacy."

The working document for the Amazonian Synod also states that, in light of certain indigenous cultures, the Church should "reconsider the notion that the exercise of jurisdiction (power of government) must be linked in all areas (sacramental, judicial, administrative) and in a permanent way to the sacrament of Holy Orders" (n. 127). One ultimate effect of such an approach would be that the laity all over the world could use the Church's moral authority and material wealth to support the worst sort of regimes. There are more than a few politicians and ideologues who would like to use the German Church's billions to further global secularism. What should we make of this recommendation?

The Catholic Church, the Church of God on earth, has received its essential constitution from Christ Himself. And the essential constitution of the entire Mystical Body of Christ on earth is hierarchical. Our Savior constituted the Apostles and their successors in the hierarchy of the Church as the only ones who have His divine power to teach, govern, and administer the sacraments (see Mt 28:19–20). Pope Pius X taught that "the Church is essentially an unequal society, that is, a society composed of two types of people: shepherds and sheep" (*Vehementer Vos*, February 11, 1906). The same constant and immutable teaching since the time of the Apostles was again presented at the Second Vatican Council when it stated that bishops, with priests and deacons as helpers, "have taken up the service of the community, presiding in place of God over the flock, whose shepherds they are, as teachers for doctrine, priests for sacred worship, and ministers for governing" (*Lumen Gentium*, n. 20).

If the exercise of jurisdiction (power of government) were to be dissociated from the sacramental and judicial areas, it would no longer be the Church of Christ, but, instead, a human institution according to allegedly democratic categories of secular and political life. Such an essentially altered structure could no longer call itself catholic and apostolic, but perhaps "new catholic church," "reformed catholic church," "catholic democratic church," "popular democratic catholic church," but surely not the one, holy, catholic, apostolic, and Roman Church. It would certainly be a fake Catholic church. And every fake product will collapse sooner rather than later. Such reforms as envisaged by the *Instrumentum Laboris* for the Amazonian Synod, by introducing an essential alteration to the divine constitution of the Church regarding the sacramental and hierarchical order of the Church, will surely collapse, since it will be a purely human work, and moreover, a work which will contradict the revealed will of God. The divinely established hierarchical order of the Church can by no tricks, sophisms, or impressive rhetoric be changed or reversed, not even by a pope or a synod, and also not by the 2019 Amazonian Synod.

In 1997, in response to Protestantizing elements among Catholics, the Church declared, in a document that was approved specifically by the pope and signed by an extraordinary number of cardinals, that the term "ministry" cannot be conferred on the laity as a proper ecclesiastical role — that the laity are always "extraordinary" with respect to liturgical roles.[2] How, then, should we interpret the request of authors of the Instrumentum Laboris *for the Amazonian Synod to consider "official ministries" that can be "conferred" on women in the Church, and to "guarantee to women their leadership" in the Church (n. 129, 3)? What does divine revelation and Catholic tradition have to say?*

The conferral of "official ministries" on women in the Church will only further increase the confusion regarding the Church's divine hierarchical constitution. The word "ministry" is already sanctioned by the

---

2 *Instruction on Certain Questions Regarding the Collaboration of the Non-Ordained Faithful in the Sacred Ministry of the Priest*, August 15, 1997.

constant Tradition of the Church as referring primarily to the ordained ministers in the episcopate, presbyterate, and diaconate. The first time the Church used the word "ministry" as an expression for the episcopate was during the election of St. Matthias, when St. Peter said, "Thou, Lord, who knowest the hearts of all men, show which of these two thou hast chosen, to take the place of this ministry (*ministerium*) and apostleship, from which Judas hath by transgression fallen" (Acts 1:24–25).

God gave to woman her own distinctive and irreplaceable task in the order of creation, and that is motherhood. In a similar way, God gave to woman her own distinctive and irreplaceable task in the order of redemption, i.e., in the Church, and that is spiritual motherhood. Both natural and spiritual motherhood have their authority and their power. God gave to the female person a special power of the heart, which is another power than that of the male person. If we start to reverse this order on the natural and supernatural levels, serious functional disturbances will arise. St. Paul already warned the Church against this danger, saying: "For the body [of the Church] is not one member, but many. If the foot should say, because I am not the hand, I am not of the body; is it therefore not of the body? And if the ear should say, because I am not the eye, I am not of the body; is it therefore not of the body? If the whole body were the eye, where would be the hearing? If the whole were hearing, where would be the smelling? But now God has set the members every one of them in the body as it has pleased Him. And if they all were one member, where would be the body? But now there are many members indeed, yet one body.... But God has tempered the body together ... that there might be no schism in the body" (1 Cor 12:15–20, 25).

What do the female saints have to teach us on this matter?

One of the greatest female saints in the history of the Church is without doubt St. Thérèse of the Child Jesus. She is also a Doctor of the Church. The following words, contained in her autobiography, spiritually remain worth their weight in gold, and should be honestly and supernaturally considered by all the participants of the Amazonian Synod. St. Thérèse wrote: "I knew that the Church has a heart, that this heart burns with love, and that it is love alone which gives life to its members. I knew that if this love were extinguished, the Apostles would no longer preach the Gospel, and the Martyrs would refuse to shed their blood. I understood that love embraces all vocations, that it is all things, and that it reaches out through all the ages, and to the uttermost limits of the earth, because it is eternal. I knew that the Church had a heart and that such a heart appeared to be aflame with love. I have found my place in the Church, and you gave me that very place, my God. In the heart of the Church, my mother, I will be love, and thus I will be all things, as my desire finds its direction."[3] In our days, we urgently need the female "ministry" of a St. Thérèse of the Child Jesus!

An eloquent and moving example of a woman who exercised her positive and efficacious reforming influence at a time when the clergy were predominately morally corrupt was St. Margaret, Queen of Scotland (d. 1093). In Butler's *Lives of the Saints*, we read: "She found Scotland a prey to ignorance and to many grave abuses, both among priests and people. At her instigation synods were held which passed enactments to meet these evils. She herself was present at these meetings, taking part in the discussions. The due observance of Sundays, festivals and fasts was made obligatory, Easter communion was enjoined upon all, and many scandalous practices, such as simony, usury, and incestuous marriages, were strictly prohibited. St. Margaret made it her constant effort to obtain good priests and teachers for all parts of the country and formed a kind of embroidery guild among the ladies of the court to provide vestments and church furniture."[4] In our own day, we urgently need the motherly "ministry" of a St. Margaret of Scotland. The Amazonian Synod should propose female "ministries" like those of St. Thérèse and St. Margaret!

The most urgent "ministry" of women is that of a Catholic mother of a family, who will give birth to future priests and bishops, who will form and educate them in the family, as in their first seminary.[5] And since a "seminary" education by Catholic mothers was carried out in families spanning all times and cultures, the Amazonian Catholic mothers in our own day are not inferior, and are surely also capable of doing this.

3 *The Story of a Soul*, ch. 10, p. 193.

4 *Butler's Lives of the Saints*, ed., rev. and suppl. Herbert J. Thurston, S.J. and Donald Attwater (Westminster, MD: Christian Classics, 1990), 2:516.

5 The Second Vatican Council spoke of the family as the first "seminary": see *Optatem Totius*, 2.

17

Advice for Families and Laity

Your Excellency, earlier in our conversation you said that one of the positive aspects of Vatican II was its teaching on the call of the laity to live fully their baptismal consecration. What advice would you give to the laity today, specifically to mothers and fathers and couples preparing for marriage?

That they should awaken in themselves the gifts they received in baptism and confirmation — the Seven Gifts of the Holy Spirit. The laity should reflect on and study these seven gifts. They have been chosen to be the soldiers and confessors of Christ in the world, wherever they are living. The first task in the family for the father and mother is to be teachers of faith to their children and to form the domestic church — this is such a beautiful mission for them! — to transmit the pure Catholic faith to the children with their mother's milk, and to give an example by their way of life.

The same goes for preparing couples for marriage: we have to say to them, "You have such a beautiful and lofty mission, because you will prepare for and establish a domestic church in your family! That is the task of a Christian father and mother, and therefore you need to awaken in yourselves the gifts of confirmation."

From among the seven gifts of the Holy Spirit, young laypeople, even those who are not yet married, as well as those who are, need in these times to cultivate in a particular way the gift of Courage, or Fortitude. They need to reawaken this gift in order to profess Christ without fear in our neo-pagan society, which as we now observe — especially in Europe — will likely bring about a new wave of persecution. The Islamization will continue, and in decades to come I do not exclude the possibility that there will be a marginalization of Christians and even a persecution of Christians. I don't know if it will take a form similar to the age of the catacombs or the Communist gulags, but there will be concrete measures of persecution and marginalization of Christians in European countries.

We have to nourish in ourselves this gift of Fortitude as well as the gift of Piety. Real piety is a gift of the Holy Spirit. This means that fathers and mothers have to have a deep sense of the supernatural and reverence for God, for His presence and glory. To seek His glory and to love prayer and glorifying God — this is piety. I would therefore stress Fortitude, Piety, and the Fear of the Lord. The Gift of Fear must be understood and lived in the sense of loving God's commandments and fearing to fail in observing His commandments, out of love and respect for Him. This disposition of the soul and spirit has to be transmitted to children by their parents.

I would also tell young people: be proud that you are Christians, that you are soldiers of Christ, and do not forget that our goal is Heaven. Even when we are still young, we should consider temporal affairs and realities as secondary. We must put on "the helmet of salvation" (Eph 6:17) and see our entire life as a holy battle to engage in for the sake of reaching eternity.

Your Excellency, in the midst of the present crisis, how should the Church evangelize all the young people who have been submerged in the sea of secularism for most of their lives, and whose minds have been conformed to the present age?

We have to show them the beauty of the truth. Beauty is attractive; all beauty is attractive. We have to show them the reasonableness of the truth which Christ has revealed to us, and which the Church has unchangingly taught for two thousand years. We find this truth primarily in the catechisms, and in the teachings of the Fathers and the Doctors of the Church. We have to explain this to young people and show them the beauty and the unshakeable solidness of the Catholic faith.

If you could implement only three elements for a new evangelization, what would these be?

Actually, the program is one: Christ Himself. The new evangelization is a way out of the crisis in the Church. We first have to increase and intensify the life of prayer in the Church at all levels. This means restoring the centrality of the adoration of God, of Christ. It means restoring the centrality of the Eucharist and the sacrament of confession. To honor Christ in the Eucharist is the first and best means of evangelization. We cannot evangelize if we do not give Christ due honor, especially in the Eucharist. We have to renew with all seriousness and without any compromises the Eucharistic cult. This is indispensable. This is one of the most efficient and important tools of the new evangelization: to spread the beauty and dignity of the worship of God, i.e., to spread the importance of the first commandment of God and of the lofty end for which man was created, namely, to adore God with love and knowledge and to give Him glory.

Prayer, adoration, and worship have supernatural power...

Exactly. It is supernaturally attractive. Secondly, we have to proclaim once again the truth of the Gospel, the basic truths of the Catholic faith, in a very clear and, at the same time, very simple manner — not in a manner that is too abstract or academic. We must avoid abstract formulations and terminology, which are overflowing today in the Church. Young people are not touched spiritually by verbosity and abstract formulations. We must present the traditional catechism to them in a very clear, unambiguous, and simple way. Afterwards, we can guide them to a more profound theological reflection.

Returning to the Second Vatican Council's universal call to holiness, we have to promote a deep and serious striving for holiness in daily life. For me, these three realities must be inseparably united: the renewal of worship in the liturgy of the Eucharist, Catholic doctrine with sound and sure catechesis, and its implementation in daily life. The *lex orandi*, the law of prayer, has primacy regarding man's ultimate end, because we were created to adore God. The *lex orandi*, however, must faithfully reflect the *lex credendi*, the law of belief, because faith is the basis and rock of our whole life. Then comes the *lex vivendi*: we must carry the faith and experience of the liturgy into daily life. In evangelization, we have to stress practical and concrete means of living morally as Christians, as a new creature, avoiding mortal sins. In order to avoid mortal sins, we have to *name* them. We also need to help young people to overcome their addictions to the internet, to pornography, and to all the other spiritual diseases which are so common today. These three points (*lex orandi, lex credendi, lex vivendi*) are a concrete path to the new evangelization. We have to make the path of the new evangelization less academic and less abstract.

We are living in the age of the internet. Could you offer some advice specifically to Catholic bloggers and websites?

The Catholic blogosphere is an instrument of Divine Providence today to spread the eternally valid truth of Christ and His Church in the midst of an unprecedented crisis of the Church. I consider this a truly providential help to connect those who have the same aims and intentions, to feel in some way that they belong to a family of faith. May God bless the good Catholic bloggers! Of course, one has to avoid sterile polemics. We can provide information on what is happening — and sometimes we have no choice but to give negative information and facts; otherwise we would be living on another planet. However, it must be done in a balanced manner, not continuously providing negative news, but also providing positive information on good things that are happening in the Church across the world, things that promote the purity of doctrine, of prayer, and of the beauty of the liturgy. Also, it is very useful to present examples of beautiful Christian lives that were lived in the history of the Church and in our own time as well. Catholic bloggers will work well if they observe these guidelines.

They should also ask the intercession of the holy angels...

Exactly. The angels can help, by illuminating them to write the truth always and to have ever before them the glory of God, as the angels do.

And to elevate minds rather than leading them into despair...

In providing news and information, Catholic agencies and bloggers should help to elevate the minds of the people and seek to promote the beauty of truth and the glory of God. This should be the aim of a Catholic blogger: to help renew Holy Mother Church in our time.

I'm sure in your travels, mothers and fathers ask you for advice. What counsel would you offer to married couples?

In order to live a godly married life, one has to strive, with the help of God's grace and with personal efforts, to observe the following:

1. Put Christ in the center of the mutual love of husband and wife. Marriage cannot be just between two; it has to include a third one, and this is Our Lord Jesus Christ.
2. Banish egoism, using more the word "you," and rarely the word "I."
3. Be considerate of the other; one must exercise oneself in stepping back and look at the whole.
4. Make little spiritual sacrifices in renouncing one's will, for love of one another and the children.

5. Seek mutual forgiveness always, and never go to bed without a reconciliation, even in little matters.
6. Husband and wife should never speak negatively of one another, and categorically never in the presence of their children.
7. Spouses have to pray intensely for one another.
8. Common prayer should have a central place in the life of the family.
9. Practice Christian charity towards needy and poor people and be very hospitable.
10. Spouses and all members of the family have to learn and practice patience with one another, avoiding insults and offensive or dirty words. Such words should never be spoken in a Catholic family.
11. Ask God for the grace to accept the crosses of this earthly life out of love for Him and as a means of intercession and expiation for the eternal salvation of all the members of the family.
12. Above all is the daily exercise of Christian mutual love.

And what points would you offer to parents?
1. See persecution as a grace from God for being purified and strengthened, not simply as something negative.
2. Root yourself in the Catholic faith through the study of the catechism.
3. Protect your family's integrity above all else.
4. Catechize your children as your first duty.
5. Pray with your children daily, such as litanies and the Rosary.
6. Turn your home into a domestic church.
7. In the absence of a priest and Sunday Mass, make a Spiritual Communion.
8. Withdraw your family from a parish spreading error and attend a faithful parish, even if you have to travel far.
9. Withdraw your children from school if they are encountering moral danger in "sex education."
10. If you cannot withdraw your children, establish a coalition of parents to fight for that right.
11. Fight for parental rights using available democratic tools.
12. Build up a wide-reaching crusade of prayers among Catholic families and lay faithful, priests and bishops under the protection of the Immaculate Heart of Mary and the holy angels. This will defeat all attacks of the unbelieving world. *Christus vincit!*

And how can lay people help the Church in this time of confusion?

1. Through intense, persevering, and confident personal prayers, and united in a wide-reaching prayer crusade, imploring the end of the crisis in the Church and a divine intervention.

2. Through a diligent and zealous study of Catholic truths according to proven Catholic catechisms, especially the *Catechism of the Council of Trent* and the *Baltimore Catechism*, which are surer and clearer in their content.

3. Through a personal witness in professing and spreading those truths which, in our days, are mostly denied or distorted. Here the internet provides very helpful technical means.

4. Through theological, pastoral, and liturgical conferences and symposiums in which the clear and perennial truths of the Catholic Church are stated, explained, and defended.

5. Through public manifestations, such as marches, processions, and pilgrimages, in order to manifest and proclaim the integrity and the beauty of the Catholic faith.

6. Through acts of reparation and expiation for sins against the Catholic faith and for sins against the divine commandments, especially the following sins:

   a. Against the first Commandment ("Thou shalt not have strange gods before me"), because of relativism and indifferentism regarding the uniqueness of the faith in Jesus Christ.

   b. Against the fifth Commandment ("Thou shalt not kill"), because of the horrendous machinery of the mass murder of unborn children and even of newly born children, and the killing of sick or elderly people through so-called euthanasia.

   c. Against the sixth Commandment ("Thou shalt not commit adultery"), because of the epidemic of divorce, of the social and governmental propaganda on behalf of degrading sexual immorality such as homosexual acts and pornography, and the moral corruption of innocent children through a cruel sexual education and indoctrination with anti-natural gender theory.

7. Through acts of reparation for the most grievous sin and evil of our time, that is, the horrendous sacrileges, desecrations, and trivializations of Our Lord in the Most Blessed Sacrament.

18

The Holy Angels

We talked about the loss of the supernatural as one of the root causes of the crisis in the Church. The angels, those incorporeal, purely intellectual creatures of which St. Thomas Aquinas eloquently speaks, still arouse interest among many people, but few know much about their nature and mission. Your religious congregation, the Canons Regular of the Holy Cross of Coimbra, has a particular devotion to the holy angels. Can you tell us a little about this?

Even in the ancient historical Order of the Holy Cross, in the time of St. Anthony of Padua at the end of the twelfth and the beginning of the thirteenth centuries, there was engraved in stone on the façade of the conventual church of the Order in the city of Coimbra the Order's coat of arms, with the Cross and two angels adoring the Cross. This was the original coat of arms of my Order. The Order was suppressed in 1834 by the Masonic government of Portugal, and the last member died in 1903.

In the 1970s, upon the request of several Portuguese bishops, and with the approval of the Holy See, the Order was revived by priests who belonged to the Work of the Holy Angels (*Opus Angelorum*). This movement was begun in 1949 by a very pious mother of a family in Innsbruck, Austria, who had six children. Her name was Gabriele Bitterlich. She had deep mystical experiences of the world of the angels, but also a very deep mystical life with Christ, centered on the Passion of the Lord and on the Eucharist. Mother Gabriele Bitterlich had her spiritual director assigned to her by the bishop of Innsbruck. In this way, the bishop accompanied closely this new movement and in 1961 he erected the Confraternity of the Guardian Angels in Innsbruck.

The *Opus Angelorum* chose for itself the same coat of arms as the historical Order of the Holy Cross, without knowing at the time of the coat of arms of the older Order. This coincidence was really a demonstration of Divine Providence. In the old constitutions of the Order, the canons were called "the brothers of the Cross" because the Cross is on the coat of arms and the first Church of the Order was dedicated to the Holy Cross. Also, in the *Opus Angelorum*, the central spiritual characteristic has to be the veneration and love for the Cross. It is not the angels who are at the center of the *Opus Angelorum*, but the Cross which the angels adore. The revived Order only added to the coat of arms the Holy Eucharist in the place where the two beams of the Cross meet. It is a beautiful addition, because it is the Eucharist which the angels adore. And so, this coat of arms is the synthesis of the entire spirituality of the Order of the Canons Regular of the Holy Cross.

What is the role of the angels in our regard?

The holy angels are our companions and our examples in adoring the Lord, in giving Him honor, in adoring the Eucharist. They are our best companions on our path to heaven. They will be our companions for all eternity in loving and worshipping God, as the Book of Revelation shows us (Rev 5:11–13).

The angels are a very expressive work of God's creativity. As St. Thomas Aquinas says, each angel is a different species. As you rightly note, they are incorporeal and purely intellectual creatures. They belong to the invisible world. The angels by their very existence present a very powerful appeal to the Church to turn towards eternity, towards the invisible world that awaits us. Here on earth, we already anticipate eternal life in the New Jerusalem. There we will be one community composed of men and angels — one family of God, made up of all those who belong to Christ and to His Mystical Body, as St. Thomas Aquinas says: "It is manifest that both men and angels are ordained to one end, which is the glory of the divine fruition. Hence the Mystical Body of the Church consists not only of men but also of angels" (*Summa theologiae* III, q. 8, a. 4). So, we ought to begin now to practice and live this reality here on earth, by consciously praying, working, and fighting for Christ together with our heavenly brothers and companions, the holy angels.

In ancient times, and before the Second Vatican Council, the reality of the guardian angels was stressed more. After the Council, there was a diminished veneration of the holy angels; a kind of obliviousness to the supernatural and invisible world of the angels rolled in across the ecclesial landscape. Over the past fifty years, the Church has tended toward naturalism, toward what is natural, to secularism, and away from the supernatural. Devotion to the holy angels is therefore a very powerful means of turning again toward the supernatural, of leaving behind this naturalistic tendency for the sake of the life of grace, and of becoming aware that God has given every man a personal brother, his guardian angel. Each of the baptized has a unique guardian angel, who has never served as guardian to anyone else. God is so lavish with His gifts that He chose an angel from all eternity to be, only once, the guardian angel for a specific person, even if this person lives for only one instant here on earth. And he will not be the guardian angel of another.

Does every child who is conceived have a guardian angel?

Already at conception, God creates the soul, and thus, a human person comes into being. This human person has a guardian angel who protects him in the mother's womb and prays for him.

This could be very consoling for a mother who has had a miscarriage. We do not know what happens to the souls of unbaptized babies, but for a mother to know that there was an angel praying for the child in her womb could be very consoling.

Yes.

Do non-Christians have guardian angels, too?

Yes. But the guardian angel enters into a special relationship with a human soul through baptism, because in Christ, angels and men are all more closely united, as St. Paul says (see Col 1:20).

Let us remember and keep firmly in mind: my guardian angel was given only for me, and he is a very powerful spiritual being who is always in the presence of God, and who remained faithful to God during the trial of the angels, when some of his brother angels apostatized with Lucifer.

To clarify, then, God does not create an angel every time He creates the soul of a new baby?

No, the entire angelic world was created in one instant in the beginning of Creation. Then there came the trial. The angels had to accept God freely with profound humility. The sin of the first among the angels, who in the tradition is called Lucifer, consisted in his will to be like God but without God, as St. Thomas Aquinas explained: "The devil desired resemblance with God by desiring, as his last end of beatitude, something which he could attain by virtue of his own nature, turning his appetite away from supernatural beatitude, which is attained by God's grace. Or, if he desired as his last end that likeness of God which is bestowed by grace, he sought to have it by the power of his own nature; and not from divine assistance according to God's ordering" (*Summa theologiae*, I, q. 63, a. 3). With this act of pride, Lucifer influenced and drew with him a part of the angelic world. According to St. Thomas Aquinas, the greater part of the angelic world remained faithful to God: "More angels stood firm than sinned, because sin is contrary to the natural inclination; while that which is against the natural order happens with less frequency; for nature procures its effects either always, or more often than not" (*Summa theologiae* I, q. 63, a. 9). An image of this may be given to us in the Apocalypse, when we read that the tail of the dragon swept away a third of the stars (Rev 12:4). In some traditions, the word "stars" is also an indication of the angels. So, one can suppose that probably one third of the angelic world apostatized.

Some have proposed that the angels were shown the Incarnation in advance, and that their refusal to accept and adore the God-Man precipitated their fall.

Many theologians have conjectured that the mystery of the Divine Incarnation was revealed to the angels, that they saw that a nature lower than their own was to be hypostatically united to the Person of God the Son, and that all the hierarchy of heaven must bow in adoration before the majesty of the Incarnate Word; and this, it is supposed, occasioned the pride of Lucifer (cf. Suárez, *De Angelis*, lib. VII, xiii). However, it remains a mystery. It is very probable that God revealed to them the mystery of the Incarnation in order that they might bow down and serve the Incarnate God. They had to accept serving God not only in His majesty, but in veiled and hidden form as a future Incarnate God-Man. To this the first angel said, "No, I will not do this. I will not serve. *Non serviam!* I will not serve and bow down beneath my dignity to serve a man. I want to be like God." The famous German Neo-Scholastic theologian Matthias Scheeben (d. 1888) said that the connection between the mystery of the Incarnation and the fall of the angels gives a plausible and probable explanation for the intensity with which the devil hates Christ, the Blessed Virgin Mary, and the human race. In this sense we can also understand the words of Our Lord: "The devil was a murderer from the beginning, and he stood not in the truth; because truth is not in him" (Jn 8:44).

In the weakness of our intellect and will, we do not see all the consequences and ramifications of our actions. It is not so with the angels, is it?

When the angels expressed their will, it was forever. With their intellects they saw all the consequences and accepted this. Tradition holds that pride was so powerful in Lucifer and his followers that they preferred the ego — "I am I," said Lucifer — and then, in the midst of this trial, one of the lowest angels, St. Michael, who belonged to the penultimate choir, said, "*Quis ut Deus?*" ("Who is like God?"). And with this humble word, St. Michael threw down Lucifer and all his followers from heaven into the abyss.

My guardian angel and every guardian angel remained faithful to God in this trial and accepted Christ in the spirit of humility and of service. Therefore, since then, the most fervent desire of every angel is one day to become a humble servant guardian angel of a human being. Every angel ardently desires this. The career ambition of every angel is to bow down. His "dream career" is to be little, to descend, and not to ascend like men in their career ambition.

We human beings, with the wounds of original sin, including pride, desire to pursue a career and to be in high positions. (Unfortunately, in some way, this could be called the original sin of the clergy: to attain higher positions.) The opposite is true with the holy angels. They desire in their career to move down. So, for example, when a Cherub becomes a guardian angel for a limited time, during the life of a person, he descends from the second choir down to the ninth. He is stripped and reduced to the dignity of the lowest choir, and this is his deepest desire, to be low, to imitate Christ his Lord, to be a servant. Therefore, the ambition of every angel is to be one day a guardian angel, to experience the lowliness of the last angelic choir and of humble and patient service to a concrete human person. Then when he finishes his service of guardian angel, he returns to his original choir.

Is the guardian angel's mission temporary then?

Well, in some way it is not temporary. Once the person entrusted to him reaches heaven, they will be together for all eternity. They will praise God together as brothers. In heaven we will know the name and see the personality of our own guardian angel. But many saints already saw the personality of their guardian angel and even gave a name to him. If friends give nicknames to each other, when I love my guardian angel, why can't I give him a name? To be clear: only for my private spiritual life, and not to spread it publicly. According to some theological authors, including scholastics such as St. Bonaventure, the guardian angel will accompany the soul into Purgatory as well, to help the soul through this difficult purification. This is also depicted in Dante's *Divine Comedy*.

Didn't the Vatican prohibit the naming of angels some years ago?

Yes, and this was the problem faced by the *Opus Angelorum*. Mother Gabriele Bitterlich wrote down some angels with names which she saw and experienced. Some names were similar to Michael, Raphael, and Gabriel, ending of "el," in the biblical manner. The use of angelic names beyond the three biblical names was prohibited by the Holy See. This was the central issue in the examination of the writings of Mother Gabriele Bitterlich, which the Congregation for the Doctrine of the Faith carried out in 1984 and in 1992. I understand the concern, because it was a very detailed presentation of the angelic world. Such a description is not wrong in itself, because the Bible gives us names of angels. And we know that the Byzantine Orthodox Church and the Greek Catholic Church celebrate on November 8 the "Synaxis of the Chief of the Heavenly Hosts Archangel Michael and the Other Heavenly Bodiless Powers," venerating thereby the seven archangels with their names, and not only three archangels, because in the Bible St. Raphael says to Tobit, "I am one of the seven holy angels who present the prayers of the saints and enter into the presence of the glory of the Holy One" (Tob 12:15). From Holy Scripture we know only the names of Michael, Gabriel, and Raphael, but seven are mentioned, so there must logically be four other names. The Eastern Orthodox Church and Eastern Catholic Churches of the Byzantine tradition venerate seven archangels and sometimes an eighth: Michael, Gabriel, Raphael, Uriel, Selaphiel (Salathiel), Jegudiel (Jehudiel), Barachiel, and the eighth, Jerahmeel (Jeremiel). In the Coptic Orthodox tradition, the seven archangels are named as Michael, Gabriel, Raphael, Suriel, Zadkiel, Sarathiel, and Ananiel. The Holy See always recognized the liturgical feast of the Seven Archangels with the explicit seven names, which are mentioned during the liturgy.

In Manila, there is a shrine in honor of the Seven Archangels, with the seven angelic names written under the statues surrounding the main altar. This shrine has an old tradition and received approval from the Holy See. There are also old churches in Mexico with the representation of the Seven Archangels with their seven names.

Should one ask one's guardian angel for his name? Or could opening oneself in this way to the spiritual world be dangerous?

It is dangerous to ask for the name. You can give your guardian angel a name if you choose. This is your personal affair; you should not publish this in the newspaper and preach it. In themselves, the names of angels do not constitute a doctrinal problem. It is a prudential problem. The angelic names in the writings of Mother Gabriele Bitterlich were too extensive, and therefore the Holy See forbade the use of them. And I understand this.

The main intention of the *Opus Angelorum* is surely not centered on the names of angels, which pertained more to a personal mystical experience of Mother Gabriele Bitterlich. The main intention is to make people more aware of the existence and presence of the guardian angels and of the other angels, as our brothers, our co-worshipers, our co-fighters, in adoring God, in fighting for Christ in this spiritual battle which is increasing in our days. God gives particular charisms needed for each age. In the present age, when demonic and satanic powers have so increased — we are in a spiritual battle of a magnitude rarely seen before in history! — God sends us the assistance of the holy angels to combat the evil spirits. This is the essence of the *Opus Angelorum*, the Work of the Angels, only this and nothing more.

St. Thomas Aquinas — the Angelic Doctor — says that no one can directly move the will except for God, but the good angels can illuminate the mind.

This is very important. When I venerate my guardian angel or the other angels, I am asking them to bring me the light of God so that I may better understand the mystery of faith, that I may better adore Christ, that I may better fight in the spiritual life.

How can one incorporate this practice into daily life?

To give just one example, many of the saints sent their guardian angel to another person when it was difficult for them to speak to that person.

Some might look upon that as superstition.

No, St. Padre Pio did this on numerous occasions and so did many other saints. Why could it not be so? The angels are living persons. When I say to someone, "Please go to my friend and convey to him my greetings," why can I not say this to my guardian angel? This has nothing to do with superstition. This is theologically and spiritually sound.

Another great means of fostering union with our brothers the guardian angels is a kind of consecration to the holy angels. There are consecrations to the Sacred Heart of Jesus, to the Immaculate Heart of Mary, to St. Joseph. Why not to the holy guardian angels? This is very logical. So, it is a very good tool for fostering one's spiritual union with one's angel.

How is this consecration made?

There is a formula that was approved by the Congregation for the Doctrine of the Faith in 2000 specifically for the *Opus Angelorum*. Therefore, I think we need to spread devotion to the holy angels, to be spiritually united in a common and holy battle for Christ.

How do the angels help us in temptation?

When I love my guardian angel and am consecrated to him, I will be more conscious of his presence and, in his presence, I will not dare to offend God. It is a help for me to meditate on this and to ask him, saying: "Oh my guardian angel, when I am in danger of offending the Lord, please give me a very strong reminder." Sometimes the saints did this and then the guardian angel reminded them by hitting them over the head when they wanted to do something wrong. The angels also protect us in our physical needs and in our travels, and from accidents and so on. But especially from accidents of the soul.

Pope John Paul II made a beautiful contribution to spreading devotion to the holy angels. In 1987, he dedicated his Wednesday general audiences to catechesis on the holy angels. These catecheses are beautiful.

Do you have favorite prayers to the holy angels?

The common prayer that we know from childhood, of course. But do you know which prayer is the most beloved to the holy angels?

Which one?

The Sanctus of the Holy Mass: "*Sanctus, Sanctus, Sanctus . . .*" This prayer was heard by Isaiah from the mouth of the Seraphim. It is the prayer of the angels *par excellence*. So, oftentimes when I am traveling, in my soul I pray the *Sanctus*. When I enter a Church, I kneel down and pray first the *Sanctus* with my guardian angel, and with the angels that surround the Tabernacle; they are there. So, I recommend the use of the *Sanctus*.

Devotion to the holy angels should not be a devotion consisting only in beautiful prayers. We have to be aware that we are the one family of God: we are the children of the Church and the holy angels are also members of the Church, of the Church Triumphant. Christ united men and angels, heaven and earth through His Cross, through His blood, as St. Paul writes (cf. Col 1:20). We must therefore renew our awareness that the holy angels are members of the Church and they are our brothers and our helpers. In some way, they are our true elder brothers. They were created before us, and before us they passed through the trial and remained faithful to Christ. After the trial in the beginning, the angels received this new "indelible imprint" in their spirit, meaning their deep desire to be servants like Christ. Therefore, they want to serve us in the Church, especially our guardian angels. God entrusted the entire creation and every detail of creation to the protection and care of the holy angels, as Catholic tradition has always said.

Does each country have a protecting angel?

Yes, it is a traditional Christian belief in East and West that each country has a protecting angel. It is written in the Scriptures, in the Old Testament, that St. Michael is the Angel of the people of God, of Israel (cf. Dan 10:21 and Dan 12:1). Some of the Church Fathers even said that not only every nation, but even every town has its own protecting angel. A feast of the Guardian Angel of Brazil, *Angelus Custos Brasiliae*, with a Mass formula, a feast day, and a Divine Office formula are still contained in the old missal of Brazil — I have a copy from the nineteenth century.

Our Lady of Fatima speaks of the Angel of Portugal.

Portugal — in the past it formed one kingdom together with Brazil — still has in the new missal the feast of the Angel of Portugal. It is celebrated on June 10 and predated the Fatima apparitions. Therefore, when the Angel of Portugal appeared to the children, it was not strange for them because the feast of the Angel of Portugal had already been known in their country for generations and centuries. It would be spiritually and pastorally helpful for each country to have and to celebrate a feast of their protecting guardian angel.

Are there guardian or protecting angels for other entities, or for special persons?

The entire creation is protected by the angels. Therefore, one might hold as a pious opinion that even every state of life has a protecting angel or an intercessor; in other words, that there is a special angel that prays before God for priests, or for families, or for workers. Through several popes, the Church has proclaimed and assigned patron saints to various professions. Why then could there not be a special angelic patron for each state of life or for a profession? This is only a pious opinion, but it could encourage people of specific states of life or professions to cooperate more consciously with the holy angels.

Do you experience the working of your own guardian angel?

The angels are very modest; they do not impose themselves on us. They are eager to come to help us, but we have to ask. The more we ask them, the more they help us. By growing in our awareness of their action in our lives, we come to see in a new light the striking events of our life that very likely happened through the action of the holy angels. This is their work. But one can find examples of their assistance in the little events of daily life. Even in simple, daily things: at times, my guardian angel has awakened me at the exact minute that I had to wake up — when the alarm clock was not working. These are little signs, but I am convinced it is the work of the guardian angel.

Returning to the theme of the supernatural, it seems that living this way requires a certain disposition in the soul and a belief in the supernatural world.

When I was young, maybe sixteen years old, I consecrated myself to my guardian angel. Oftentimes, I have asked him to accompany me in all my prayers and I especially ask him to bring me the necessary illumination to understand the Catholic faith in the right manner. In the forty years since I first made this consecration, I have experienced this help in my mind to penetrate more deeply the truths and beauty of the Catholic faith. And in these forty years, in my prayers that my guardian angel bring me the light of God and help me to remain faithful to Christ, I have had the sensation and experience that one acquires a sort of instinct of what is Catholic, of what is true. I gratefully attribute this to my guardian angel and to the consecration I made to him. I have been living my consecration to my guardian angel now for more than forty years, and I can feel his silent presence, and the light he brings during prayer. So

I think we have to be more conscientious in invoking the holy angels, that they might strengthen us in faithfulness to Christ and especially in the deep sense and instinct for the holiness of God.

Their beloved prayer is the *Sanctus*. The essence of every angel says: "God is holy, and God alone is holy, and God is great." We have to magnify Him as Our Lady did in her Magnificat: "My soul magnifies the Lord" (Lk 1:46). The holy angels burn to magnify God and to glorify Him. We need to ask them to give us a little of their burning fire, this holy zeal for the glory of God, and then we will be sanctified and saved. Our most efficacious sanctification here on earth is to glorify God. He does not need our praise, as the Church says in her liturgy, but *we* need to do it. The more we glorify God and put Him at the center — especially Christ in the Eucharist — the more we sanctify ourselves, the more we open our heart to the light of God, to the true mercy of God, to receive His graces.

Especially in this time of crisis, I think that we greatly need a new awareness of the holy angels in the Church and of their work in the kingdom of God. We need to invoke them, to engage them, in order to glorify God in Christ and to spread the reign of Christ over creation and in society — Christ is King — and also to have the spiritual weapons to fight against the fallen angels. We cannot do this effectively without the presence of the holy angels, especially of St. Michael the Archangel.

The holy angels are also very grateful and attentive to us, so I think it could be good for a bishop to consecrate his diocese to the guardian angels.

Also in family life: if a family gathers for daily prayer, whether it is the Rosary or another prayer, perhaps a first step would be for the parents and children to remember that they are not alone, that each of their angels is present in the room praying with them.

This is very beautiful and practical. Parents need to tell children that they have a guardian angel whom they can invoke. Children are very open and sensitive to this. Children can ask their guardian angel to adore the Lord on their behalf while they are sleeping. Children love the guardian angels. When the family prays, it would be good to say, "We are gathered here with our guardian angels, and we are all one family." If both parents are present, and five or six or seven children, they can say: "There are actually 14, or 16, or nearly 20 here." It would be good for families to learn the prayer to St. Michael the Archangel. Or a family could entrust themselves to the holy angels.

Perhaps one day a pope could entrust the entire Church Militant to the protection of the holy angels, and to St. Michael specifically. It would be very helpful, since we are in a time of spiritual battle that has rarely been seen in the Church—a battle between truth and heresy, between naturalism and the supernatural perspective. A battle, ultimately, between the holy angels and the evil spirits of deceit, of pride, and of hatred against Christ, the Incarnate God.

Could you explain what you mean by that?

I mean that a situation of battle is under way, in which there is no clear vision of the truth that was always handed on by the Church. Inside the Church we need the presence of the holy angels to bring us the true vision of God which the Church has always had. Today, there is tremendous and widespread doctrinal, moral, and liturgical confusion, and even good people begin to have doubts about fundamental, evident truths that have been taught by the Church for two thousand years. The good ones have begun to doubt, through seductive theories and words, even the fundamental truths about contraception, divorce, and living in adultery. In some way, these words have a magical and demagogical effect. They often conceal the truth with seemingly beautiful and suggestive and impressive formulations, like "primacy of mercy," "surprises of the Holy Spirit," "paradigm shift," "individual conscience," "pastoral accompaniment," and "process of discernment." These all may conceal and invert the divine truth which the Church has always taught on moral issues.

It sounds like a kind of spell has been cast inside the Church, immersing many minds in spiritual slumber.

Even some good priests and some of the faithful are already so deceived and confused that they consider a clear affirmation or a public declaration of Catholic truths unnecessary. Instead they maintain that one has to dedicate one's forces to a new evangelization and to pastoral questions, as if proclaiming truths were not pastoral! They forget that a clear enunciation of revealed divine truths, in the definitive formulations of the Magisterium of the Church, is one of the highest expressions of pastoral care and love of neighbor. This truth was aptly recalled by Pope Benedict XVI, when he said: "To defend the truth, to articulate it with humility and conviction, and to bear witness to it in life are therefore exacting and indispensable forms of charity. Charity, in fact, 'rejoices in the truth' (1 Cor 13:6)" (*Caritas in Veritate*, n. 1).

We need the light of the holy angels who clearly see the truth. Only the clarity of the truth will bring us peace in our lives and allow us to experience true mercy.

We are being attacked from both sides: on the one side, from the liberal Freemasonic world powers which more or less are reigning in each country of the Western world, and from the new power of radical Islam. Both have the same aim: to destroy Christianity, to eliminate Christ. Here also, with the visible exterior enemies of Christ, we need the assistance of the holy angels who are the angels of Christ. And so, I think in this situation it would be meaningful and fitting for a pope one day to consecrate the Church to St. Joseph and to St. Michael and all the angels. In my opinion, it would be very meaningful and a very efficacious spiritual help in our time. We have the examples of Pope Leo XIII who entrusted the world to the Sacred Heart in 1899, and then Pope Pius XII who entrusted the Church and the world to the Immaculate Heart of Mary in 1942, a consecration which was repeated by other popes — for example, by Pope John Paul II (for the first time) in 1984.

In one of his last speeches before his death, Pope Pius XII left us the following luminous exhortation: "Revive your sense of the invisible world which is all around us — because we look not to the things that are seen but to the things that are unseen (2 Cor 4:18) — and have a certain familiarly with the angels, who are forever solicitous for your salvation and your sanctification. If God wishes, you will spend a happy eternity with the angels: get to know them here, from now on" (Address to American pilgrims, 3 October 1958).

19

Fatima and the "Third Secret"

We have considered the role of the angels in the life of the Church as a whole, and for each individual. This reminds me of the angel at Fatima, who appeared to the children Francisco, Jacinta, and Lucia. The message of Fatima surely remains relevant in our day. Your Excellency, do you believe that the consecration of Russia to Our Lady has been made, and do you think what is commonly known as the "Third Secret" has been fully revealed?

As we know, on March 24, 1984, Pope John Paul II consecrated all mankind to the Immaculate Heart in the presence of the real, original statue of Fatima, in St. Peter's Square. In that consecration, he especially mentioned those people whose consecration Our Lady desires to be made. Therefore, it was an implicit consecration of Russia.

In the Cathedral of Our Lady of Fatima in Karaganda, the centenary of the first apparition of Our Lady in Fatima, May 13, 2017, was celebrated in the context of a Mariological Congress. Pope Francis sent for this occasion a Papal Legate, Cardinal Paul Josef Cordes, and in the homily Cardinal Cordes mentioned the so-called consecration of Russia to the Immaculate Heart, which Pope John Paul II did in 1984. He said that sometime after the 1984 consecration, he was invited by the pope to his apartment for dinner, and during this meeting he asked the Holy Father: "Why did you not explicitly consecrate Russia?" John Paul II answered him, saying, "It was my intention to do so." The pope then added that, due to concerns of the Vatican diplomats, he could not make the consecration as he had initially intended, consecrating Russia in an explicit manner. We can therefore see that, because of political consequences presented by Vatican diplomacy, Pope John Paul II made the consecration in this implicit way. These are the facts.

Sister Lucia was asked about this act. She said: "Heaven accepted it." But this phrase of Sister Lucia, or other similar phrases, do not mean for me that this act was the most perfect. Of course, when a pope makes such a beautiful prayer and consecration, heaven accepts this. Heaven accepts every sincere and beautiful prayer. But it does not mean, in my opinion, that in the future a more perfect act of consecration could not be made, which heaven will also receive and accept.

So, do you believe that the consecration, as Our Lady asked for it at Fatima, has been made or not?

It has not yet been made in the manner Our Lady requested. In my opinion, the consecration has to be made more perfectly, and this means with the explicit mention of Russia along with the other conditions, as Our Lady specified. I hope and believe that one day, by a perfect act of consecration of Russia to the Immaculate Heart by a future pope, heaven will pour out many abundant graces for the Church and mankind, and for the full conversion of Russia.

And the "third secret"...

There is also the so-called "third secret." It was the text of the third part of the secret that was read in Fatima by Cardinal Ratzinger in the presence of Pope John Paul II. On that occasion, the Holy See said: "This is everything." Hence, I cannot imagine that a person with such a high moral standard as Cardinal Ratzinger, later Pope Benedict XVI, in the presence of a pope, would deceive the entire world. This is for me impossible. I believe what the Holy See said, that this is the entire text. Therefore, we don't need to seek a kind of "fourth" secret of Fatima. Some people say: "I know the Third Secret of Fatima." However, no one knew it, because it was secret. Some say they saw the comments of a cardinal who saw it, but it is very weak to base a theory, or more than a theory—a conviction—on such things. For me this is not serious.

But there may be a reason that explains the misunderstanding. Sister Lucia's biography contains an expression which says that Our Lady told her that she had to write down the text of the secret, but not what she explained to her about the secret. These are two different things. The text itself was revealed completely, but there could still be some explanations Our Lady gave to her that have not been revealed. I don't know. It could be. But the explanations Our Lady gave to Sister Lucia are not the text of the secret itself. We have to distinguish this.

Would the explanations be housed in the Vatican?

I don't know. What I am proposing is only a hypothesis that there might exist an explanation of what the secret means more concretely, a kind of exegesis. It could be that this explanation has been written down and that it was very uncomfortable in view of the current crisis of the Church. But, I repeat, this is a hypothesis and I have no means of proving it. Maybe this is a plausible hypothesis. This is the only way I can answer those who are still expecting an alleged unrevealed part of the text of the secret itself.

I think it is not sane to wait for a text which, in fact, might not exist. Some people claim that Our Lady must have spoken about the entire interior crisis in the Church. But we do not need a text from Our Lady to demonstrate that this is happening. The crisis is so clearly before our eyes that we don't need a secret. It is surely not a secret that we are living in a crisis. We need no further confirmation from heaven. The enormity of the crisis in the Church that we are now witnessing is evident.

In light of the current crisis, I think we have to maintain a somewhat sober attitude and concentrate on the essence of the message of Fatima, which is penance; to stop sinning because God is already too offended; to make reparation and expiation for the sins against God, against the Most Holy Eucharist, and against the Immaculate Heart of Mary. The part of the Fatima message concerning the Eucharist, in the apparitions of the angels, is so important and timely. And then to pray the Rosary for the conversion of sinners, to make the Five First Saturdays, to consecrate ourselves and our families, our countries, Russia and the world to the Immaculate Heart. It's so beautiful, so rich.

How do you believe we should interpret the third part of the secret of Fatima?

The third part of the secret is very timely. It shows that we are moving towards an era of martyrdom inside the Church. It shows us the scene of the divine wrath against sin. There is no trivialization of sin, unlike what we see to be fashionable today in the Church with the new so-called pastoral approach of "mercy," which ultimately says: "You may continue to sin without offending God." This is the wrong pastoral approach. Unfortunately, it is used by many priests and bishops and, to some extent, is also supported by the Holy See. But this is contrary to the message of Fatima — of the third part of the secret — in which God shows the Angel with the sword, calling for "Penance, Penance, Penance,"

penance for sins committed. Then comes the consolation, because Our Lady extends her hands. As the Angel announces the coming wrath of God, fire from his sword reaches Our Lady's hands and is transformed into rays of mercy and conversion. Our Lady is the refuge of all sinners. This is very consoling. The third part of the secret is so rich and serious. For me, this is a message regarding the seriousness of sin. We need to preach again about the seriousness and the peril of sin.

The text then speaks about martyrdom: we need to prepare ourselves to be attacked by the world. Our Lord said clearly, "The world cannot hate you; but it hates me because I testify of it that its works are evil" (Jn 7:7). These words of the Lord shaped the spiritual physiognomy of the Church of all times.

The content of the third part of the secret contradicts the mentality that we have been living since the Second Vatican Council, even since the pontificate of Pope John XXIII. Such a mentality claims that the world is not attacking us, and that we have to make friends with the world and in some way to cede to the demands of the world. To think and to speak in this way is quite ingenuous and unrealistic. Since the time of Pope John XXIII, a continual adaptation and yielding to the world—to the desires and the mentality of the world—has characterized so many representatives of the Church. Fyódor Dostoyevsky said: "If one distorts faith in Christ by uniting it with the goals of this world, the whole meaning of Christianity will at once also be destroyed and the mind will necessarily fall prey to unbelief."[1]

The representatives of the Church have demonstrated and still continue to demonstrate in our own day a clear inferiority complex towards the unbelieving and un-Christian world. However, the fact is this: from the beginning, the Church was always being persecuted by the world and will be persecuted until the end of time; this is a significant part of the message of Fatima.

How do you interpret the part of the text that speaks of the city half in ruins?

In the Bible, the city—specifically the city of Jerusalem—is the symbol of the Church, and the heavenly Church is described as a city, the New Jerusalem.

---

1   Opening address at the "Literary Morning Meeting" for students at the University of Saint Petersburg, December 30, 1879, before the reading of the chapter "The Grand Inquisitor."

Yes, and particularly in the Old Testament, cities are often described in the feminine and they are laid desolate when they have been unfaithful to God.

The Church is described in the Holy Scripture, and especially in the patristic tradition, as a city. In the text of the secret of Fatima we discover the city half-destroyed. This means that the spiritual situation of the Church is in ruins — the consequence of a process of spiritual demolition in doctrine, liturgy, and the moral life. From the spiritual point of view, the Church in our days is half-destroyed by heresies and doctrinal confusion, by chaos in the liturgy, by the chaos of immorality. It is such an obvious reality. It is plain for all to see; no one can reasonably deny it.

And the corpses the pope met along his way through the city half in ruins?

The text of the secret speaks about the pope passing by the corpses of priests. The image of the corpses has a deeper meaning. There are not only physical, but first and foremost spiritual priestly corpses strewn across the Church. Today we are witnessing a tremendous crisis among the clergy. This crisis has not only affected the lower clergy but has torn through the higher clergy, i.e., the episcopacy and the cardinalate and has been going on for half a century. To a great extent, this crisis has been caused by the frequent irresponsible and extremely superficial selection of candidates for the episcopacy and the cardinalate. Such morally deplorable episcopal and cardinalatial candidates, who oftentimes lost the faith and betrayed their Master, Jesus Christ, owed their promotion to favoritism, to membership in the same ideological clerical club. I would also not exclude membership in a sort of Masonic clerical old-boy network.

Today the spiritual corpses of pedophile, sodomite, and plainly heretical bishops and cardinals have been exposed for the whole world to see. One of the messages one can find in Dostoyevsky's famous passage "The Grand Inquisitor," in his novel *The Brothers Karamazov*, is that even a high-ranking prelate can become an atheist. As in the past decades, so also in our day, one can have the impression that a particular bishop or cardinal is not so far away from being an atheist. The demanding and crystal-clear truths of Christ disturb these bishops and cardinals in their work of abolishing the divine commandments. They say to the world, "Sin does not exist. The first and sixth Commandments are not feasible for people today. In our day, the merciful Christ positively allows the living out of a diversity of sexual orientations because of the dignity of 'LGBT' people, and He allows also the living out of the diversity of religions for the sake of global human fraternity." Like the Grand Inquisitor in Dostoyevsky's novel, bishops and cardinals who speak and behave in this way say to Christ, who is the Truth, "Go, and never come again!" These liberal and worldly bishops and cardinals have imprisoned the constant und unchanging Catholic truth. Yet the truth is Christ, and so they have imprisoned Christ as did the Grand Inquisitor in Dostoyevsky's story. By this very fact, these bishops and cardinals in our days have proven to be spiritual corpses. We can therefore see how timely and relevant the third part of the Secret of Fatima is today.

From these obvious facts we can conclude that there is no need for a "fourth" secret of Fatima. Perhaps Our Lady gave an explanation to Sister Lucia; and if it does indeed exist, perhaps it will be revealed in the future. But I believe that there could not be a worse situation in the life of the Church than the one we are now witnessing.

Christus Vincit

Your Excellency, you have spoken about the current crisis in the Church as the worst she has ever experienced. As Christians, how are we to understand this crisis with a contemplative gaze, that is, from a supernatural perspective? Would it be accurate to say that the current crisis is the Church's participation in the Lord's Sacred Passion?

The Church is the Mystical Body of Christ. In that sense, the Church is Christ Himself living through history until the end of the time. This truth can be perceived from the very beginning of the existence of the Church, when she had to endure suffering and persecution at the hands of the leadership of the Synagogue, particularly at the hands of the Pharisee named Saul. In the moment of his conversion before the gates of Damascus, Saul heard the words of Christ, in which He identified Himself with His persecuted Church: "Saul, Saul, why do you persecute Me?" (Acts 9:4).

In an age when the Church was persecuted from within, as was the case with the Arian crisis in the fourth century, St. Hilary — the Athanasius of the West — made the following encouraging statement: "In this consists the particular nature of the Church, that she triumphs when she is defeated, that she is better understood when she is attacked, that she rises up, when her unfaithful members desert her" (*De Trin.* 7,4).

How do you see the mysteries of the Lord's Sacred Passion manifest in the Church today?

As Christ's Mystical Body and His Bride, the Church must pass through the mysteries of her Divine Spouse. The current crisis is without any doubt the moment of the deepest suffering for the Church, of her most intense participation in the Sacred Passion of Christ. The greatest Passion of the Church is not persecution by her enemies from outside, but persecution by her enemies from within: ruthless people without faith who have managed to reach high and influential ecclesiastical offices. When Christ suffered in Gethsemane, He didn't receive support from

His Apostles, since even the three whom He took with Him into the garden slept while He prayed and suffered the deepest spiritual anguish, His agony. When Christ was arrested and interrogated, the Apostle Peter, whom He constituted the visible rock of His Church, in a cowardly way thrice denied Him. When Christ was crucified, there remained only one faithful Apostle at His side, St. John, together with Our Lady and the other holy women. From the circumstances of Christ's Passion, we can better understand the spiritual and even mystical sense of the suffering of Christ's Bride, the Church. The current crisis within the Church represents the deepest form of suffering, since the Church is now persecuted, scourged, stripped, and derided not by her enemies but to a large extent by her Shepherds, by many of those who are successors of the Apostles, by many traitors in the clerical ranks who are the new Judases.

Here I cannot fail to quote the following words of Archbishop Fulton Sheen, which he wrote in 1948 and which are strikingly relevant and significant for the current situation: "[Satan] will set up a Counter-church, which will be the ape of the Church. It will have all the notes and characteristics of the Church, but in reverse and emptied of its divine content.... The False Prophet will have a religion without a cross. A religion without a world to come. A religion to destroy religions. There will be a counterfeit Church. Christ's Church will be one, and the False Prophet will create the other. The false Church will be worldly, ecumenical, and global. It will be a loose federation of churches and religions, forming some type of global association, a world parliament of Churches. It will be emptied of all divine content; it will be the mystical body of the Antichrist. The Mystical Body on earth today will have its Judas Iscariot, and he will be the False Prophet. Satan will recruit him from our bishops."[1]

This is a fearsome thought, that Satan will corrupt the hierarchy of the Church in order to establish a false Church. How should the faithful respond?

When Christ suffered in Gethsemane, He was strengthened by an angel. This is a deep mystery: God in His human nature wanted to be consoled and strengthened by a creature. In this enormous spiritual crisis we are witnessing inside the Church, Christ is being consoled and strengthened by the souls who remain faithful to the purity of the Catholic faith, by souls who live a chaste Christian life, by souls who are

---

1 *Communism and the Conscience of the West* (Indianapolis: Bobbs-Merrill, 1948), 24–25.

committed to a life of intense prayer, by souls who do not run away from the suffering Christ, from the suffering Mother Church. The consolation and strength which Christ received from the angel in Gethsemane already contained the acts of expiation and reparation of all the faithful souls throughout the history of the Church. So many souls are suffering in our day, especially over the past fifty years, because of the tremendous crisis of the Church. The most precious are hidden sufferings of the little ones, of the persons who were put out to the periphery of Church by the liberal, worldly, and unbelieving ecclesiastical establishment. Their sufferings are precious, since they are consoling and strengthening Christ who is mystically suffering in our current crisis within the Church.

We also know the famous expression of Blaise Pascal in his *Pensées*: "Jesus will be in agony even to the end of the world. We must not sleep during that time" (n. 533). The current crisis of the Church, which is a mystical suffering of Christ in and for His Church, should call us to avoid spiritual sleep and be watchful, so that we may not be deceived by the spirit of the world which has so penetrated the Church.

When the Church was passing through the great tempest of spiritual crisis in the sixteenth century — a crisis caused mainly by the infidelity, spiritual laziness, and scandalous lifestyle of the clergy — St. Peter Canisius, the second apostle of Germany, formulated this shocking phrase: "Peter sleeps, but Judas is awake." We can fully apply this statement to the current crisis in the Church. The highest ecclesiastical authorities were to a great extent sleeping during the past five decades, by not preventing the promotion of unworthy persons to influential ecclesiastic positions. Unbelieving and oftentimes morally corrupt bishops and cardinals were the new Judases, who were very much awake and ready to betray Christ in various ways. Memorable are the words of St. Vincent de Paul, who said that priests who live like the vast majority are the greatest enemies of the Church, and that the depravity of the clerical state is the principal cause of the ruin of the Church.[2] These words are fully applicable to the current situation of the crisis within the Church.

Cardinal Robert Sarah, in his recent book *Le soir approche et déjà le jour baisse* [*The Day is Now Far Spent*], speaks about the shattering reality and mystery of Judas in the ranks of the clergy. The first chapter of his book is entitled, "Alas, Judas Iscariot," where we read

---

2 See *Conferences, Discourse, Exhortation*, 55.

the following words: "The mystery of betrayal oozes from the walls of the Church.... We experience the mystery of iniquity, the mystery of betrayal, the mystery of Judas.... The evil of an efficacious activism has infiltrated everywhere.... We seek to imitate the organization of large companies. We forget that only prayer is the blood that can irrigate the heart of the Church.... The one who does not pray anymore has already betrayed. Already he is ready for all the compromises with the world. He is walking on the path of Judas."

However, even in midst of so many clerical Judases inside the Church today, we have to maintain always a supernatural vision of the victory of Christ, who will triumph through the suffering of His Bride, who will triumph through the suffering of the pure and little ones in all ranks of the members of the Church: children, youth, families, religious, priests, bishops, and cardinals. When they remain faithful to Christ, when they keep unblemished the Catholic faith, when they live in chastity and humility, they are the pure and little ones in the Church. The following words of St. Paul, which aptly apply to individual souls, apply in much the same way to the Church, and to the Church of our days in particular: "If we suffer with him, we shall also be glorified with him" (Rom 8:17).

St. Alexander of Alexandria, the immediate predecessor of St. Athanasius, left us the following precious statement on the invincibility of the Church: "The only one catholic and apostolic Church will remain always indestructible, even if the entire world wages war against her. Because her Lord strengthened her, saying: 'Take heart! I have overcome the world' (Jn 16:33)."[3] On the obelisk in St. Peter's Square are inscribed the words *Christus vincit*, and the tip of that obelisk contains a relic of the true Cross. The Roman Church, the Apostolic See of St. Peter, is crowned, so to speak, with these luminous words *Christus vincit*, and with the power of the Holy Cross of Christ. Even if during the present crisis and spiritual obfuscation one might have the impression that the enemies of Christ and His Cross have to a certain extent occupied the Holy See, Christ will defeat them. *Christus vincit!*

Your Excellency, what is the path out of the current crisis towards victory in Christ?

The path is the ever-valid way which Christ Himself, His Apostles,

---

3   *Ep. ad Alexandrum Thessalonicensem*, in Theodoret, *Church History* 1, 4.

and the Church over two millennia have shown us: the path of the inseparability of truth and love. It is the path which puts Christ—the Incarnate Word, Incarnate Truth, the Incarnate Son of God—unmistakably in the center of the doctrinal teaching, the celebration of the liturgy, the moral life, and especially at the center of the missionary zeal and activity of the entire Church. This path could be summarized in the brilliant and succinct phrase, which I once read on the tomb of Warren H. Carroll, the founder of Christendom College in Front Royal, Virginia, USA: "Truth exists. The Incarnation happened."

The path to victory for the Catholic Church has to begin with a thorough renewal of the Eucharistic liturgy and the Eucharistic life of the Church, since the Church has been suffering for many decades from the spiritual disease of "Eucharistic cardiac insufficiency." This renewal has to be driven by a supernatural and awe-inspiring Christocentrism, since the sacrament of the Eucharist is the heart of the Church, from which her entire life is built up and vitally sustained.

For some time now, Divine Providence has been preparing the ground for the true springtime of the Church, since the alleged springtime of the Church announced by Pope John XXIII failed indeed, as we have witnessed in the decades since the end of the Second Vatican Council. Up to now we have been living in a phantom ecclesiastical springtime.

Where do you see signs of hope?

By the grace of Divine Providence, which never fails, we can already observe the signs of a true springtime. We can see many little spiritual snowdrops: these are the little ones in the Church, those who do not belong to the administrative and power structure of ecclesiastical "*nomenklatura*." These spiritual snowdrops are little children, innocent boys and girls, young chaste men and virgins, true Catholic spouses, fathers and mothers of families, single persons, widows, monks, cloistered nuns, who are the spiritual "gems" of the Church—and also simple priests who, because of their fidelity to the faith, are oftentimes marginalized and humiliated. There are also lay people and members of the clergy who courageously defend Christ the Truth in the middle of the battlefield at the cost of personal and temporal advantage. I would call them the spiritual "salmon" of our day, since they are swimming against the tide and jumping over obstacles towards the pure waters of their origin. The very pure source and origin of the Church is precisely the Person of Jesus

Christ, and concretely the Most Holy Eucharist. The increasing number of the spiritual "snowdrops" and "salmons" will definitely contribute to the benefit of the whole Church Militant and to the happy estate of the holy Roman Church, *pro felici statu sanctae Romanae ecclesiae.*

Amid the darkness of the current crisis of the Church, we can draw light and encouragement from the words Pope St. Leo the Great (†461) used to describe the invincible faith of the little ones in the Church. He said: "The faith established by the gift of the Holy Ghost was not terrified by chains, imprisonments, banishments, hunger, fire, attacks by wild beasts, refined torments of cruel persecutors. For this faith throughout the world, not only men, but even women, not only beardless boys, but even tender maids, fought to the shedding of their blood" (*Sermo* 74, 3).

Christ will overcome the current crisis of His Church in and through the Eucharist. One of my favorite saints, St. Peter Julian Eymard (1811–1868), a modern saint with an ardent veneration of the Most Blessed Sacrament and deep insights into its sacred mystery, left us the following words about the triumph of Christ through the Eucharist, the Eucharistic *Christus vincit*, which I now quote at length and with which I would like to conclude our conversation.

* * *

THE TRIUMPH OF CHRIST THROUGH THE EUCHARIST

Christus vincit, regnat, imperat; ab omni malo plebem suam defendat.

Christ conquers, He reigns, He commands. May He defend His people from all evil.

Pope Sixtus V had these words engraved on the obelisk which stands in the center of St. Peter's Square at Rome. These magnificent words are in the present tense, and not in the past, to indicate that Christ's triumph is always actual, and that it is brought about in the Eucharist and by the Eucharist.

CHRISTUS *vincit. Christ conquers.*

Our Lord has fought; He has won control of the field of battle, on which He has planted His flag and pitched His tent: the Sacred Host and the Eucharistic tabernacle. He conquered the Jew and his temple, and He has a tabernacle on Calvary where all the nations come to adore Him beneath the sacramental species. He conquered paganism and has chosen Rome, the city of the Caesars, for His capital.

He conquered the false wisdom of the sages; the divine Eucharist rose on the world and shed its rays over the whole earth, darkness withdrew like the shades of night at the coming of day. The idols have been knocked down and the sacrifices abolished. The Eucharistic Jesus is a conqueror who never halts but ever marches onward; He wants to subject the universe to His gentle sway.

Every time He takes possession of a country, He pitches His Eucharistic royal tent therein. The erection of a tabernacle is His official occupation of a country. In our own day He still goes out to uncivilized nations; and wherever the Eucharist is brought, the people are converted to Christianity. That is the secret of the triumph of our Catholic missionaries and of the failure of the Protestant preachers. For them, man is battling alone; for us, Jesus is battling, and He is sure to triumph.

CHRISTUS regnat. Christ reigns.

Jesus does not rule over earthly territories, but over souls, and He does so through the Eucharist. A king must rule through his laws and through the love of his subjects for him. The Eucharist is the law of the Christian: a law of charity and of love, which was promulgated in the Cenacle in the admirable discourse after the Supper: "This is My commandment, that you love one another as I have loved you. If you love Me, keep My commandments."

This law is revealed in Communion; the eyes of the Christian are opened in Holy Communion as were those of the disciples of Emmaus, and he understands the fullness of the law. The "breaking of bread" is what made the first Christians so brave in the face of persecution and so faithful in practicing the law of Jesus Christ.

Christ's law is one, holy, universal, and eternal. It will never change or be impaired in any way; Jesus Christ Himself, its divine Author, is defending it. He engraves it on our hearts through His love; the Legislator Himself promulgates His divine law to each of our souls. His is a law of love. How many kings rule by love? Jesus is about the only one whose yoke is not imposed by force; His rule is gentleness itself. His true subjects are devoted to Him in life and death; they would rather die than be disloyal to Him.

CHRISTUS imperat. Christ commands.

No king has command over the whole universe; one earthly king has another equal to him in power. But God the Father has said to Jesus Christ: "I will give Thee all the nations for Thy inheritance." And Our Lord told His lieutenants when He sent them throughout the world: "All power is given to Me in heaven and on earth. Go and teach ye all nations, teaching them to keep all that I have commanded you."

He issued His commands from the Cenacle. The Eucharistic tabernacle, which is a prolongation or replica of the Cenacle, is the headquarters of the King of kings. All those who fight the good fight receive their orders from there. In the presence of the Eucharistic Jesus all men are subjects, all must obey, from the pope, the Vicar of Jesus Christ, down to the least of the faithful.

CHRISTUS ab omni malo plebem suam defendat. May Christ defend His people from all evil.

The Eucharist is the divine lightning-rod that wards off the thunderbolts of divine justice. As a tender and devoted mother presses her child to her bosom, puts her arms around it, and shields it with her body to save it from the wrath of an angry father, so Jesus multiplies His presence everywhere, covers the world and envelops it with His merciful presence. Divine Justice does not know then where to strike; it dares not.

And what a protection against the devil! The blood of Jesus which purples our lips makes us a terror to Satan; we are sprinkled with the blood of the true Lamb, and the exterminating angel will not enter. The Eucharist protects the sinner until time for repentance is given him. Ah! Were it not for the Eucharist, for this perpetual Calvary, how often would not the wrath of God have come down upon us!

And how unhappy are the nations that no longer possess the Eucharist! What darkness! What a confusion in the minds! What a chill in the hearts! Satan alone rules supreme, and with him all the evil passions. As for us, the Eucharist delivers us from all evil. *Christus vincit, Christus regnat, Christus imperat; ab omni malo plebem suam defendat!*

—St. Peter Julian Eymard

"The Church of the Living God— The Pillar and Bulwark of Truth"

(1 Tim 3:15)

DECLARATION OF TRUTHS

Relating to Some of the Most Common Errors in the Life of the Church of Our Time[1]

THE FUNDAMENTALS OF FAITH

1. The right meaning of the expressions "living tradition," "living Magisterium," "hermeneutic of continuity," and "development of doctrine" includes the truth that whatever new insights may be expressed regarding the deposit of faith cannot be contrary to what the Church has always proposed in the same dogma, in the same sense, and in the same meaning (see First Vatican Council, *Dei Filius*, sess. 3, c. 4: *"in eodem dogmate, eodem sensu, eademque sententia"*).

2. "The *meaning* of dogmatic formulas remains ever true and constant in the Church, even when it is expressed with greater clarity or more developed. The faithful therefore must shun the opinion, first, that dogmatic formulas (or some category of them) cannot signify truth in a determinate way, but can only offer changeable approximations to it, which to a certain extent distort or alter it; secondly, that these formulas signify the truth only in an indeterminate way, this truth being like a goal that is constantly being sought by means of such approximations. Those who hold such an opinion do not avoid dogmatic relativism and they corrupt the concept of the Church's infallibility relative to the truth to be taught or held in a determinate way" (Sacred Congregation for the Doctrine of the Faith, *Declaration* Mysterium Ecclesiae *in defense of the Catholic doctrine on the Church against certain errors of the present day*, 5).

---

1 Bishop Athanasius Schneider initiated and was one of the main contributors in the editing process of this Declaration.

THE CREED

3. "The Kingdom of God begun here below in the Church of Christ is not of this world whose form is passing, and its proper growth cannot be confounded with the progress of civilization, of science, or of human technology, but it consists in an ever more profound knowledge of the unfathomable riches of Christ, an ever stronger hope in eternal blessings, an ever more ardent response to the love of God, and an ever more generous bestowal of grace and holiness among men. The deep solicitude of the Church, the Spouse of Christ, for the needs of men, for their joys and hopes, their griefs and efforts, is therefore nothing other than her great desire to be present to them, in order to illuminate them with the light of Christ and to gather them all in Him, their only Savior. This solicitude can never mean that the Church conforms herself to the things of this world, or that she lessens the ardor of her expectation of her Lord and of the eternal Kingdom" (Paul VI, Apostolic Letter *Solemni Hac Liturgia [Credo of the People of God]*, 27). The opinion is, therefore, erroneous that says that God is glorified principally by the very fact of progress in the temporal and earthly condition of the human race.

4. After the institution of the new and everlasting covenant in Jesus Christ, no one may be saved by obedience to the law of Moses alone without faith in Christ as true God and the only Savior of humankind (see Rom 3:28; Gal 2:16).

5. Muslims and others who lack faith in Jesus Christ, God and man, even monotheists, cannot give to God the same adoration as Christians do, that is to say, the supernatural worship in Spirit and in truth (see Jn 4:24; Eph 2:8) of those who have received the Spirit of filial adoption (see Rom 8:15).

6. Spiritualities and religions that promote any kind of idolatry or pantheism cannot be considered either as "seeds" or as "fruits" of the divine Word, since they are deceptions that preclude the evangelization and eternal salvation of their adherents, as it is taught by Holy Scripture: "the god of this world has made blind the minds of those who have not faith, so that the light of the good news of the glory of Christ, who is the image of God, might not be shining on them" (2 Cor 4:4).

7. True ecumenism intends that non-Catholics should enter that unity which the Catholic Church already indestructibly possesses in virtue of the prayer of Christ, always heard by His Father, "that they may

be one" (Jn 17:11), and which she professes in the Symbol of Faith, "I believe in one Church." Ecumenism, therefore, may not legitimately have for its goal the establishment of a Church that does not yet exist.

8. Hell exists, and those who are condemned to hell for any unrepented mortal sin are eternally punished there by divine justice (see Mt 25:46). Not only fallen angels but also human souls are damned eternally (see 2 Thess 1:9; 2 Pet 3:7). Eternally damned human beings will not be annihilated, since their souls are immortal, according to the infallible teaching of the Church (see Fifth Lateran Council, sess. 8).

9. The religion born of faith in Jesus Christ, the Incarnate Son of God and the only Savior of humankind, is the only religion positively willed by God. The opinion is, therefore, wrong that says that just as God positively wills the diversity of the male and female sexes and the diversity of nations, so in the same way He also wills the diversity of religions.

10. "Our [Christian] religion effectively establishes with God an authentic and living relationship which the other religions do not succeed in doing, even though they have, as it were, their arms stretched out towards heaven" (Paul VI, Apostolic Exhortation *Evangelii Nuntiandi*, 53).

11. The gift of free will with which God the Creator endowed the human person grants man the natural right to choose only the good and the true. No human person has, therefore, a natural right to offend God in choosing the moral evil of sin, the religious error of idolatry, blasphemy, or a false religion.

THE LAW OF GOD

12. A justified person has sufficient strength with God's grace to carry out the objective demands of the divine law, since all of the commandments of God are possible for the justified. God's grace, when it justifies the sinner, does of its nature produce conversion from all serious sin (see Council of Trent, sess. 6, *Decree on Justification*, c. 11; c. 13).

13. "The faithful are obliged to acknowledge and respect the specific moral precepts declared and taught by the Church in the name of God, the Creator and Lord. Love of God and of one's neighbor cannot be separated from the observance of the commandments of the covenant renewed in the blood of Jesus Christ and in the gift of the Spirit" (John Paul II, Encyclical *Veritatis Splendor*, 76). According to the teaching of the same

encyclical, the opinion of those is wrong who "believe they can justify, as morally good, deliberate choices of kinds of behavior contrary to the commandments of the divine and natural law." Thus, "these theories cannot claim to be grounded in the Catholic moral tradition" (*ibid*.).

14. All of the commandments of God are equally just and merciful. The opinion is, therefore, wrong that says that a person is able, by obeying a divine prohibition — for example, the sixth commandment, not to commit adultery — to sin against God by this act of obedience, or to morally harm himself, or to sin against another.

15. "No circumstance, no purpose, no law whatsoever can ever make licit an act which is intrinsically illicit, since it is contrary to the Law of God, which is written in every human heart, knowable by reason itself, and proclaimed by the Church" (John Paul II, Encyclical *Evangelium Vitae*, 62). There are moral principles and moral truths contained in divine revelation and in the natural law which include negative prohibitions that absolutely forbid certain kinds of action, inasmuch as these kinds of action are always gravely unlawful on account of their object. Hence, the opinion is wrong that says that a good intention or a good consequence is or can ever be sufficient to justify the commission of such kinds of action (see Council of Trent, sess. 6, *Decree on Justification*, c. 15; John Paul II, Apostolic Exhortation *Reconciliatio et Paenitentia*, 17; Encyclical *Veritatis Splendor*, 80).

16. A woman who has conceived a child within her womb is forbidden by natural and divine law to kill this human life within her, by herself or by others, whether directly or indirectly (see John Paul II, Encyclical *Evangelium Vitae*, 62).

17. Procedures which cause conception to happen outside of the womb "are morally unacceptable, since they separate procreation from the fully human context of the conjugal act" (John Paul II, Encyclical *Evangelium Vitae*, 14).

18. No human being may ever be morally justified in killing himself or causing himself to be put to death by others, even if the intention is to escape suffering. "Euthanasia is a grave violation of the law of God, since it is the deliberate and morally unacceptable killing of a human person. This doctrine is based upon the natural law and upon the written word of God, is transmitted by the Church's Tradition, and taught by the ordinary and universal Magisterium" (John Paul II, Encyclical *Evangelium Vitae*, 65).

19. Marriage is by divine ordinance and natural law an indissoluble union of one man and one woman (see Gen 2:24; Mk 10:7–9; Eph 5:31–32). "By their very nature, the institution of matrimony itself and conjugal love are ordained for the procreation and education of children, and find in them their ultimate crown" (Second Vatican Council, *Gaudium et Spes*, 48).

20. By natural and divine law no human being may voluntarily and without sin exercise his sexual powers outside of a valid marriage. It is, therefore, contrary to Holy Scripture and Tradition to affirm that conscience can truly and rightly judge that sexual acts between persons who have contracted a civil marriage with each other can sometimes be morally right or requested or even commanded by God, although one or both persons is sacramentally married to another person (see 1 Cor 7:11; John Paul II, Apostolic Exhortation *Familiaris Consortio*, 84).

21. Natural and divine law prohibits "any action which either before, at the moment of, or after sexual intercourse, is specifically intended to prevent procreation — whether as an end or as a means" (Paul VI, Encyclical *Humanae Vitae*, 14).

22. Anyone, husband or wife, who has obtained a civil divorce from the spouse to whom he or she is validly married, and has contracted a civil marriage with some other person during the lifetime of his legitimate spouse, and who lives in a marital way with the civil partner, and who chooses to remain in this state with full knowledge of the nature of the act and with full consent of the will to that act, is in a state of mortal sin and therefore cannot receive sanctifying grace and grow in charity. Therefore, these Christians, unless they are living as "brother and sister," cannot receive Holy Communion (see John Paul II, Apostolic Exhortation *Familiaris Consortio*, 84).

23. Two persons of the same sex sin gravely when they seek venereal pleasure from each other (see Lev 18:22; Lev 20:13; Rom 1:24–28; 1 Cor 6:9–10; 1 Tim 1:10; Jude 7). Homosexual acts "under no circumstances can be approved" (*Catechism of the Catholic Church*, 2357). Hence, the opinion is contrary to natural law and divine revelation that says that, as God the Creator has given to some humans a natural disposition to feel sexual desire for persons of the opposite sex, so also He has given to others a natural disposition to feel sexual desire for persons of the same sex, and that God intends that the latter disposition be acted on in some circumstances.

24. Human law, or any human power whatsoever, cannot give to two persons of the same sex the right to marry one another or declare two such persons to be married, since this is contrary to natural and divine law. "In the Creator's plan, sexual complementarity and fruitfulness belong to the very nature of marriage" (Congregation for the Doctrine of the Faith, *Considerations regarding proposals to give legal recognition to unions between homosexual persons*, June 3, 2003, 3).

25. Unions that have the name of marriage without the reality of it, being contrary to natural and divine law, are not capable of receiving the blessing of the Church.

26. The civil power may not establish civil or legal unions between two persons of the same sex that plainly imitate the union of marriage, even if such unions do not receive the name of marriage, since such unions would encourage grave sin for the individuals who are in them and would be a cause of grave scandal for others (see Congregation for the Doctrine of the Faith, *Considerations regarding proposals to give legal recognition to unions between homosexual persons*, June 3, 2003, 11).

27. The male and female sexes, man and woman, are biological realities created by the wise will of God (see Gen. 1:27; *Catechism of the Catholic Church*, 369). It is, therefore, a rebellion against natural and divine law and a grave sin that a man attempt to become a woman by mutilating himself, or even by simply declaring himself to be such, or that a woman may in like manner attempt to become a man, or to hold that the civil authority has the duty or the right to act as if such things were or may be possible and legitimate (see *Catechism of the Catholic Church*, 2297).

28. In accordance with Holy Scripture and the constant tradition of the ordinary and universal Magisterium, the Church did not err in teaching that the civil power may lawfully exercise capital punishment on malefactors where this is truly necessary to preserve the existence or just order of societies (see Gen 9:6; Jn 19:11; Rom 13:1–7; Innocent III, *Professio fidei Waldensibus praescripta*; *Roman Catechism of the Council of Trent*, p. III, 5, n. 4; Pius XII, *Address to Catholic Jurists*, December 5, 1954).

29. All authority on earth as well as in heaven belongs to Jesus Christ; therefore, civil societies and all other associations of men are subject to His kingship so that "the duty of offering God genuine worship concerns man both individually and socially" (*Catechism of the Catholic Church*, 2105; see Pius XI, Encyclical *Quas Primas*, 18–19; 32).

THE SACRAMENTS

30. In the most holy sacrament of the Eucharist, a wonderful change takes place, namely of the whole substance of bread into the body of Christ and the whole substance of wine into His blood, a change which the Catholic Church very fittingly calls transubstantiation (see Fourth Lateran Council, c. 1; Council of Trent, sess. 13, c. 4). "Every theological explanation which seeks some understanding of this mystery must, in order to be in accord with Catholic faith, maintain that in the reality itself, independently of our mind, the bread and wine have ceased to exist after the Consecration, so that it is the adorable Body and Blood of the Lord Jesus that from then on are really before us under the sacramental species of bread and wine" (Paul VI, Apostolic Letter *Solemni Hac Liturgia [Credo of the People of God]*, 25).

31. The formulations by which the Council of Trent expressed the Church's faith in the Holy Eucharist are suitable for men of all times and places, since they are a "perennially valid teaching of the Church" (John Paul II, Encyclical *Ecclesia de Eucharistia*, 15).

32. In the Holy Mass, a true and proper sacrifice is offered to the Blessed Trinity, and this sacrifice is propitiatory both for men living on earth and for the souls in Purgatory. The opinion is, therefore, wrong that says that the sacrifice of the Mass consists simply in the fact that the people make a spiritual sacrifice of prayers and praises, as well as the opinion that the Mass may or should be defined only as Christ giving Himself to the faithful as their spiritual food (see Council of Trent, sess. 22, c. 2).

33. "The Mass, celebrated by the priest representing the person of Christ by virtue of the power received through the sacrament of Orders and offered by him in the name of Christ and the members of His Mystical Body, is the sacrifice of Calvary rendered sacramentally present on our altars. We believe that as the bread and wine consecrated by the Lord at the Last Supper were changed into His body and His blood which were to be offered for us on the Cross, likewise the bread and wine consecrated by the priest are changed into the body and blood of Christ enthroned gloriously in heaven, and we believe that the mysterious presence of the Lord, under what continues to appear to our senses as before, is a true, real, and substantial presence" (Paul VI, Apostolic Letter *Solemni Hac Liturgia [Credo of the People of God]*, 24).

34. "The unbloody immolation at the words of consecration, when Christ is made present upon the altar in the state of a victim, is performed by the priest and by him alone, as the representative of Christ and not as the representative of the faithful. (. . .) The faithful offer the sacrifice by the hands of the priest from the fact that the minister at the altar, in offering a sacrifice in the name of all His members, represents Christ, the Head of the Mystical Body. The conclusion, however, that the people offer the sacrifice with the priest himself is not based on the fact that, being members of the Church no less than the priest himself, they perform a visible liturgical rite; for this is the privilege only of the minister who has been divinely appointed to this office. Rather it is based on the fact that the people unite their hearts in praise, impetration, expiation, and thanksgiving with the prayers or intention of the priest, even of the High Priest Himself, so that in the one and same offering of the victim and according to a visible sacerdotal rite, they may be presented to God the Father" (Pius XII, Encyclical *Mediator Dei*, 92).

35. The sacrament of Penance is the only ordinary means by which grave sins committed after baptism may be remitted, and by divine law all such sins must be confessed by number and by species (see Council of Trent, sess. 14, can. 7).

36. By divine law the confessor may not violate the seal of the sacrament of Penance for any reason whatsoever; no ecclesiastical authority has the power to dispense him from the seal of the sacrament and the civil power is wholly incompetent to oblige him to do so (see *Code of Canon Law 1983*, can. 1388 § 1; *Catechism of the Catholic Church*, 1467).

37. By virtue of the will of Christ and the unchangeable Tradition of the Church, the sacrament of the Holy Eucharist may not be given to those who are in a public state of objectively grave sin, and sacramental absolution may not be given to those who express their unwillingness to conform to divine law, even if their unwillingness pertains only to a single grave matter (see Council of Trent, sess. 14, c. 4; Pope John Paul II, Message to the Major Penitentiary Cardinal William W. Baum, on March 22, 1996).

38. According to the constant Tradition of the Church, the sacrament of the Holy Eucharist may not be given to those who deny any truth of the Catholic faith by formally professing their adherence to a heretical or to an officially schismatic Christian community (see *Code of Canon Law 1983*, can. 915; 1364).

39. The law by which priests are bound to observe perfect continence in celibacy stems from the example of Jesus Christ and belongs to immemorial and apostolic tradition according to the constant witness of the Fathers of the Church and of the Roman Pontiffs. For this reason, this law should not be abolished in the Roman Church through the innovation of an optional priestly celibacy, either at the regional or the universal level. The perennial valid witness of the Church states that the law of priestly continence "does not command new precepts; these precepts should be observed, because they have been neglected on the part of some through ignorance and sloth. These precepts, nevertheless, go back to the Apostles and were established by the Fathers, as it is written, 'Stand firm, then, brothers and keep the traditions that we taught you, whether by word of mouth or by letter' (2 Thess 2:15). There are in fact many who, ignoring the statutes of our forefathers, have violated the chastity of the Church by their presumption and have followed the will of the people, not fearing the judgment of God" (Pope Siricius, Decretal *Cum in unum* in the year 386).

40. By the will of Christ and the divine constitution of the Church, only baptized men (*viri*) may receive the sacrament of Orders, whether in the episcopacy, the priesthood, or the diaconate (see John Paul II, Apostolic Letter *Ordinatio Sacerdotalis*, 4). Furthermore, the assertion is wrong that says that only an Ecumenical Council can define this matter, because the teaching authority of an Ecumenical Council is not more extensive than that of the Roman Pontiff (see Fifth Lateran Council, sess. 11; First Vatican Council, sess. 4, c. 3, n. 8).

   May 31, 2019

   ✠ *Cardinal Raymond Leo Burke*
   Patron of the Sovereign Military Order of Malta

   ✠ *Cardinal Janis Pujats*
   Archbishop emeritus of Riga

   ✠ *Tomash Peta*
   Archbishop of the archdiocese of Saint Mary in Astana

   ✠ *Jan Pawel Lenga*
   Archbishop-Bishop emeritus of Karaganda

   ✠ *Athanasius Schneider*
   Auxiliary Bishop of the archdiocese of Saint Mary in Astana

ABOUT THE AUTHORS

ATHANASIUS SCHNEIDER was born in 1961 in Kyrgyzstan to a German family and baptized with the name Antonius. In 1973 the family emigrated to Germany. He joined the Order of Canons Regular of the Holy Cross in Austria in 1982 and received the religious name Athanasius; he was ordained a priest in Brazil in 1990. Having earned a doctorate in Patrology at the Augustinianum in Rome, he has taught since 1999 at the seminary in Karaganda,  Kazakhstan. In 2006 he was ordained bishop in the Basilica of St. Peter in Rome and appointed titular bishop of Celerina and auxiliary bishop of Karaganda. From 2011 to the present he has been auxiliary bishop of the Archdiocese of Saint Mary in Astana, Chairman of the Liturgical Commission, and Secretary General of the Conference of the Catholic Bishops of Kazakhstan. Bishop Schneider is the author of two books on the Holy Eucharist: *Dominus Est — It Is the Lord* and *Corpus Christi: Holy Communion and the Renewal of the Church.*

DIANE MONTAGNA is an American journalist based in Rome.